Psychoanalysis and the New Rhetoric

Psychoanalysis and the New Rhetoric: Freud, Burke, Lacan, and Philosophy's Other Scenes is an innovative work that places the fields of psychoanalysis and rhetoric in dynamic resonance with one another. The book operates according to a compelling interdisciplinary conceit: Adleman provocatively explores the psychoanalytic aspects of rhetoric and Vanderwees probes the rhetorical dimensions of psychoanalytic practice.

This thoroughly researched text takes a closer look at the "missed encounter" between rhetoric and psychoanalysis. The first section of the book explores the massive, but underappreciated, influence of Freudian psychoanalysis on Kenneth Burke's "new rhetoric." The book's second section undertakes sustained investigations into the rhetorical dimensions of psychoanalytic concepts such as transference, free association, and listening. *Psychoanalysis and the New Rhetoric* then culminates in a more comprehensive discussion of Lacanian psychoanalysis in the context of Kenneth Burke's new rhetoric. The book therefore serves as an invaluable aperture to the fields of psychoanalysis and rhetoric, including their much overlooked disciplinary entanglement.

Psychoanalysis and the New Rhetoric will be of great interest to scholars of psychoanalytic studies, rhetoric, language studies, semiotics, media studies, and communication studies.

Daniel Adleman, PhD, is an Assistant Professor of Writing and Rhetoric at the University of Toronto.

Chris Vanderwees, PhD, RP, is a psychoanalyst, registered psychotherapist, and clinical supervisor at St. John the Compassionate Mission in Toronto, Canada.

The Lines of the Symbolic in Psychoanalysis Series

Series Editor

Ian Parker, Manchester Psychoanalytic Matrix

Psychoanalytic clinical and theoretical work is always embedded in specific linguistic and cultural contexts and carries their traces, traces which this series attends to in its focus on multiple contradictory and antagonistic "lines of the Symbolic." This series takes its cue from Lacan's psychoanalytic work on three registers of human experience, the Symbolic, the Imaginary and the Real, and employs this distinctive understanding of cultural, communication, and embodiment to link with other traditions of cultural, clinical, and theoretical practice beyond the Lacanian symbolic universe. The Lines of the Symbolic in Psychoanalysis Series provides a reflexive reworking of theoretical and practical issues, translating psychoanalytic writing from different contexts, grounding that work in the specific histories and politics that provide the conditions of possibility for its descriptions and interventions to function. The series makes connections between different cultural and disciplinary sites in which psychoanalysis operates, questioning the idea that there could be one single correct reading and application of Lacan. Its authors trace their own path, their own line through the Symbolic, situating psychoanalysis in relation to debates which intersect with Lacanian work, explicating it, extending it, and challenging it.

Psychoanalysis, Politics, Oppression and Resistance
Lacanian Perspectives
Chris Vanderwees and Kristen Hennessy

Lacanian Fantasy
The Image, Language and Uncertainty
Kirk Turner

Psychoanalysis and the New Rhetoric
Freud, Burke, Lacan, and Philosophy's Other Scenes
Daniel Adleman and Chris Vanderwees

For more information about the series, please visit: https://www.routledge.com/The-Lines-of-the-Symbolic-in-Psychoanalysis-Series/book-series/KARNLOS

"Daniel Adleman and Chris Vanderwees have performed a miracle. In *Psychoanalysis and the New Rhetoric* they lay out the manifold connections between psychoanalytic theory and rhetorical analysis that now seem clear and self-evident, but only because they have written this path-breaking work. Picking up some clues left by Kenneth Burke, Adleman and Vanderwees take both psychoanalytic thinking and rhetoric where neither has gone before, uncovering how their shared territory is replete with new theoretical insights. For anyone who wants to consider either psychoanalysis or rhetoric, this book is impossible to miss."

– **Todd McGowan,** *Professor of Film Studies at the University of Vermont; author of* Emancipation after Hegel and Capitalism and Desire.

"In one of his last seminars, Lacan declared that the psychoanalyst is above all a 'rhetor,' both an orator intent upon convincing an audience and a specialist of rhetoric. *Psychoanalysis and the New Rhetoric* argues cogently that Lacan's return to Freud entailed the elaboration of a 'new rhetoric' identical to what Kenneth Burke was teaching at the same time. Burke, like Lacan, a close reader of Freud, is shown to provide an innovative way of understanding the language of psychoanalysis. By detailing the multiple aspects of such a rhetoric, Adleman and Vanderwees offer an original thesis that radically modifies our conception of psychoanalysis."

– **Jean-Michel Rabaté,** *Professor of English at the University of Pennsylvania, member of the American Academy of Arts and Sciences.*

"Particularly for those engaging with Freudianism from Lacanian angles, it has long been appreciated that the unconscious of the 'talking cure' is 'structured like a language.' However, in *Psychoanalysis and the New Rhetoric*, Daniel Adleman and Chris Vanderwees, instead of relying solely on Saussurian linguistics and its offshoots, deftly utilize Burke's rhetorical theory to renew and enrich our appreciation of the language-related dimensions of the theory, practice, and teaching of psychoanalysis. In so doing, Adleman and Vanderwees admirably demonstrate that only a multi-dimensional approach to language can do justice to psychoanalysis as an inherently interdisciplinary field."

– **Adrian Johnston,** *Distinguished Professor of Philosophy at the University of New Mexico*

"This is a brave and brilliant book by Daniel Adleman and Chris Vanderwees which reads Burke's revival of rhetoric as similar to many principles taken from Freud such as identification and free association. Rhetoric is a function of language for Burke and Lacan, offering psychoanalytic vitality. Lacan's Seminars are portrayed as modes of listening to speech action and take rhetoric as their model. While Burke's speaking symbol is not Lacan's Symbolic, Lacan's rhetoric displays thoughts in action. Lacan performed rhetoric in his Seminars with an attitude intended for an audience's unconscious. Like Burke, Lacan aimed to persuade. The Other for both was fragmented and disunified. Lacan, like Burke, listened for metonymy, periphrastic, gaps, and so on. The Seminars were spontaneous speech, body and voice, an act of persuasion. Rhetoric and psychoanalysis are kindred disciplines that probe the unknowable limits of connection and eloquence."

– **Ellie Ragland,** *Professor Emerita of English at the University of Missouri; author of* Jacques Lacan and the Logic of Structure.

"This volume stages an eloquent encounter between psychoanalysis and the rhetorical arts of persuasion, where the psychoanalytic relation is both an ethical and socio-symbolic address that takes place in and as language. Grounded in accessible and compelling contemporary examples, psychoanalysis and rhetoric emerge here as parallel histories, the symbolic/symptomatic action of each as the unconscious of the other. *Psychoanalysis and the New Rhetoric* brings to light an interdependence that was always there but is seldom theorised. In addressing this oversight, it makes a substantive interdisciplinary contribution to rhetorical studies, to psychoanalysis, and to the understanding of an increasingly anxious and polarizing political scene."

– **Stuart J. Murray,** *Professor of Rhetoric and Ethics at Carleton University; author of* The Living from the Dead: Disaffirming Biopolitics.

Psychoanalysis and the New Rhetoric

Freud, Burke, Lacan, and Philosophy's Other Scenes

Daniel Adleman and Chris Vanderwees

Routledge
Taylor & Francis Group

LONDON AND NEW YORK

Cover image: Dan Starling

First published 2023
by Routledge
4 Park Square, Milton Park, Abingdon, Oxon OX14 4RN

and by Routledge
605 Third Avenue, New York, NY 10158

Routledge is an imprint of the Taylor & Francis Group, an informa business

British Library Cataloguing-in-Publication Data
A catalogue record for this book is available from the British Library

Library of Congress Cataloging-in-Publication Data
Names: Adleman, Daniel, author. | Vanderwees, Chris, author.
Title: Psychoanalysis and the new rhetoric : Freud, Burke, Lacan,
and philosophy's other scenes / Daniel Adleman, Chris Vanderwees.
Description: Abingdon, Oxon ; New York, NY : Routledge,
2023. | Includes bibliographical references and index. |
Summary: "Psychoanalysis and the New Rhetoric: Freud, Burke,
Lacan, and Philosophy's Other Scenes is an innovative work that
posits the fields of psychoanalysis and rhetoric into reciprocal
dialogue. It explores the rhetoric of psychoanalysis and the
psychoanalytic aspects of rhetoric, and discusses what could be
termed as the "missed encounter""-- Provided by publisher.
Identifiers: LCCN 2022027289 (print) | LCCN 2022027290
(ebook) | ISBN 9781032101811 (hardback) | ISBN 9781032101835
(paperback) | ISBN 9781003214069 (ebook)
Subjects: LCSH: Psychoanalysis. | Rhetoric.
Classification: LCC BF173 .A557 2023 (print) | LCC BF173 (ebook) |
DDC 150.19/5--dc23/eng/20220909
LC record available at https://lccn.loc.gov/2022027289
LC ebook record available at https://lccn.loc.gov/2022027290

ISBN: 978-1-032-10181-1 (hbk)
ISBN: 978-1-032-10183-5 (pbk)
ISBN: 978-1-003-21406-9 (ebk)

DOI: 10.4324/9781003214069

Typeset in Bembo
by KnowledgeWorks Global Ltd.

Contents

Preface

Sigmund Freud was a master of rhetoric, formulating his extrapolations from case studies in such a way as to persuade the reader not only that what he described was the case but also that the consequences of each particular case should be borne in mind by a psychoanalyst listening to their own analysands. That gorgeous rhetorical trickery bore fruit in the production of a host of concepts that then became reified, in the course of the history of psychoanalysis, as ostensibly real things under the surface of language.

The task fell to another master rhetorician, Jacques Lacan, to desubstantialize that paraphernalia and dissolve the mechanisms Freud pointed to into language itself. Lacan showed us that the language of psychoanalysis had constructed what it spoke of in symbolic conditions that were not of its own making. That is, psychoanalysis both pointed to and was embedded in something beyond itself; it was embedded in the symbolic and was a symbolic achievement. Something of that symbolic achievement is revisited in the work of every singular analysis, by every analysand.

While we engage in that symbolic work, we also often become bewitched by it, which is why we need theory to disentangle what we speak of from the temptation to reduce it to what we easily "understand" and what we can, it seems, transparently communicate to others. That is, our rhetorical work, which we do not entirely control, is always also a lure into the imaginary, and then we imagine not only that we control meaning but that we also access and describe things below the surface of language that we have actually constructed as if we can directly access the real and make it visible, tangible, understandable.

Others have followed this path to a rhetorical engagement with subjectivity outside psychoanalysis and, this book shows, then have had to connect with what is unconscious to us as we speak. And so, while it was Lacan that turned psychoanalysis into many different contradictory forms of rhetoric, it was Kenneth Burke who journeyed into psychoanalytic territory with his compass points furnished from rhetoric itself.

Is this "osmosis," as Daniel Adleman and Chris Vanderwees claim? If it is to be so, if we are to be guided along the paths to theoretical and clinical inquiry opened up by that particular rhetorical figure – for "osmosis" should be conceived of here as a rhetorical device – then we need to attend to the moments where psychoanalysis, which here is Lacanian, intersects with, touches upon, rhetoric, which here is Burkean. Osmosis, of course, is a characteristic of living matter. It is of the real, and sometimes idealized as such, taken to be a model for how human beings may coexist with each other and with nature; its opposite, predation, and parasitism, is often feared, a more dangerous model of bloody strife that makes peaceful coexistence impossible.

This book fashions an argument from a debate, a position from counterposing conceptual disciplinary standpoints, that psychoanalysis and rhetoric must live together in order to authentically be what they are, for what each claim for themselves. The singularity of each of the two standpoints is made possible by the combination of the two. This is an encounter with philosophy, with Burke's "new rhetoric" that renews psychoanalysis.

Psychoanalytic clinical and theoretical work circulates through multiple intersecting antagonistic symbolic universes. This series opens connections between different cultural sites in which Lacanian work has developed in distinctive ways, in forms of work that question the idea that there could be single correct reading and application. The Lines of the Symbolic in Psychoanalysis series provides a reflexive reworking of psychoanalysis that transmits Lacanian writing from around the world, steering a course between the temptations of a metalanguage and imaginary reduction, between the claim to provide a god's eye view of psychoanalysis and the idea that psychoanalysis must everywhere be the same. And the elaboration of psychoanalysis in the symbolic here grounds its theory and practice in the history and politics of the work in a variety of interventions that touch the real.

Ian Parker
Manchester Psychoanalytic Matrix

Acknowledgements

The authors are especially grateful for Ian Parker's support of this book. Many thanks to Todd McGowan, Jean-Michel Rabaté, Adrian Johnston, Ellie Ragland, and Stuart Murray for reviewing our work. We would like to thank Ellie Duncan and Susannah Frearson at Routledge for their help during the publishing process. We are also thankful to the Lacan Toronto working group for a place to present some of the earlier drafts of these chapters for discussion and feedback. Chapter Seven was originally published in a special issue of *English Studies in Canada* and has been revised and reprinted here with permissions. Thanks to Concetta Principe for her editing and comments on an earlier version of this chapter.

Chris Vanderwees is also thankful to MCL for all of her support. He is especially grateful to JH for her kindness and encouragement.

Daniel Adleman thanks Kana Yamada and his parents, Sladen and Susan, for their continued patience and support.

About the Authors

Daniel Adleman, PhD is an Assistant Professor of Writing and Rhetoric at the University of Toronto. He teaches and writes primarily about the intricate interrelationships between rhetoric, psychoanalysis, media, and social change. He has recently published articles in *Cultural Politics, Cultural Studies, Canadian Review of American Studies, communication +1, English Studies in Canada,* and *Canadian Literature.* He has also published book chapters in *Crossing Borders* (ARP, 2020), *Utopia and Dystopia in the Age of Trump* (Rowman & Littlefield, 2019), and *Performing Utopias in the Contemporary Americas* (Palgrave Macmillan, 2017). In 2012, he co-founded the Vancouver Institute for Social Research, an ongoing critical theory free school held at downtown Vancouver's Or Gallery.

Chris Vanderwees, PhD, RP is a psychoanalyst, registered psychotherapist, and clinical supervisor at St. John the Compassionate Mission in Toronto, Canada. He is the co-editor of an essay collection (with Kristen Hennessy), *Psychoanalysis, Politics, Oppression and Resistance: Lacanian Perspectives* (Routledge, 2022). He is also an affiliate and research guest of the Toronto Psychoanalytic Society and a member of the Lacanian School of Psychoanalysis.

Abbreviations

AH   Attitudes Toward History
ARM A Rhetoric of Motives
CS   Counter-Statement
GM   A Grammar of Motives
LSA   Language as Symbolic Action: Essays on Life, Literature, and
       Method
PC   Permanence and Change: An Anatomy of Purpose
PLF   The Philosophy of Literary Form

Introduction

Missed Encounters

The extraordinary development of the concept of rhetoric belongs to the specific differences between the ancients and moderns: in recent times, this art stands in some disrepute, and even when it is used, the best application to which it is put by our moderns is nothing short of dilettantism and crude empiricism.

                    – Friedrich Nietzsche, "Lecture Notes on Rhetoric"

Perspective by Congruity

This book began, appropriately, with a number of far-reaching dialogues between a practising psychoanalyst and an assistant professor of writing and rhetoric. The topic that we stumbled into, quite organically, came acutely into relief over the course of several years of free-associative discussions is the innumerable parallels and osmoses between psychoanalysis and rhetoric. The premise of this book is that psychoanalysis and rhetoric, when closely scrutinized, often appear, uncannily, as each other's doppelgangers and disciplinary siblings by virtue of their shared interest in human motivation and their perennial struggles with legitimacy (especially vis-à-vis institutional philosophy). In terms of their content, form, and histories, the two disciplines seem to echo each other, as well as philosophy, in a myriad of fascinating ways that call for closer examination.

With these echoes in mind, we decided to stage an extended encounter between these two would-be disciplinary bedfellows. Over the course of our conversations about the influence of psychoanalysis on Kenneth Burke's approach to the "new rhetoric," we also realized that the study of rhetoric itself can and ought to inform psychoanalytic theory and practice. The format of the book is therefore structured chiastically. Daniel Adleman composed the first four chapters, which explore Burke's pioneering integration of Freudian psychoanalytic ideas into rhetorical conversations. Chris Vanderwees wrote the second half of the book, which highlights the underappreciated rhetorical dimensions of psychoanalysis. Before launching into these lines of investigation, however,

DOI: 10.4324/9781003214069-1

we will begin with an account of the parallel histories of rhetoric and psychoanalysis.

In many ways, the undersung hero of this tale is Kenneth Burke. One of the most groundbreaking figures in the entire rhetorical tradition, Burke almost singlehandedly revived rhetoric and made a vociferous case for its continued relevance to a contemporary world saturated with advertising, propaganda, and narrative. Like Jacques Lacan, he continually underscores the work of his master (for Burke it was Aristotle, just as for Lacan it was Freud) by way of an idiosyncratic admixture of close-reading strategies and byzantine detours through more recent innovations in economics, literature, anthropology, and philosophy. But arguably, his least appreciated encounter was with psychoanalysis. As an agile reader of Freud, Burke wove Freudian conceptual frameworks into his own new-rhetorical formulations in a fashion that speaks to an untapped wellspring of shared substance between psychoanalysis and the rhetorical tradition.

Of course, one of the impediments to broad uptake of Burke's cross-pollination of rhetoric and psychoanalysis resides in the density of his analyses and the seemingly insuperable mountain of homework required to render his connections intelligible. His books and articles draw on the entire history of rhetoric, philosophy, economics, historiography, psychology, and literature. Even his most colloquial letters to the editor condense a heady brew of cross-disciplinary intertextuality. This is a lot to ask any readership to take on.

A relentlessly reflexive theorist, Burke describes such uncircumscribable academic and journalistic undertakings as something like an interminable conversation at a party:

> Imagine that you enter a parlor. You come late. When you arrive, others have long preceded you, and they are engaged in a heated discussion, a discussion too heated for them to pause and tell you exactly what it is about. In fact, the discussion had already begun long before any of them got there, so that no one present is qualified to retrace for you all the steps that had gone before. You listen for a while, until you decide that you have caught the tenor of the argument; then you put in your oar. Someone answers; you answer him; another comes to your defense; another aligns himself against you, to either the embarrassment or gratification of your opponent, depending upon the quality of your ally's assistance. However, the discussion is interminable. The hour grows late, you must depart. And you do depart, with the discussion still vigorously in progress.
>
> (*PLF* 110–111)

Adopting Freud's expression, Burke refers to the unending parlour parable as the imaginary "primal scene" of rhetoric ("Postscript" 165). With this primal scene in mind, we have decided to throw in our oar by attending to Burke's discussions of, with, and against psychoanalysis in this book, which we hope will be simultaneously edifying and galvanizing.

At the outset, we must acknowledge that our lines of analysis barely scratch the surface of the Burkean and Freudo-Lacanian icebergs. Still, if our account of the texts and insertion of relevant contexts engenders new pathways for a readership interested in connecting rhetorical concerns and lexicons with psychoanalytic ones, we will consider our mission accomplished. Nevertheless, even this modest task necessitates a vertiginous archaeological dig. In the service of elucidating the import of Burke's innovations, we will return to the primal scene of rhetoric's fraught relationship with philosophy, an issue that might resonate as uncannily familiar to psychoanalytic scholars and practitioners. Once we have laid this foundation, we will examine the history of psychoanalysis and its own travails in relation to institutional psychology and philosophy.

Philosophy's Scapegoats

Philosopher Simon Critchley observes that the Platonic art of philosophy was founded on a campaign of systematic exclusion. In *Tragedy, the Greeks, and Us*, Critchley examines the tangle of excommunications built into "Plato's Pharmacy." According to Critchley, Plato's Socrates mobilizes philosophy as a form of "affect regulation" meant to shepherd the Athenian polity in a rational direction by staving off uncontainable feelings and pernicious influences. In Plato's dialogues, Socrates expels the new media technology of alphabetic writing, the relatively new form of political organization known as democracy, excessively irrational music, theatre, and myth to the margins of philosophy. These noxious activities, arts, and media technologies imperilled the rational scaffolding of Plato's imagined republic by unleashing the unbridled circulation of affect (*pathos*) over reason (*logos*) and pandering to the tyrannical whims of the masses, most of whom are naively oblivious to the immutable Good. From the standpoint of Socratic philosophy, these dangerous influences threatened to transform Athens into "a society of the spectacle that legitimates itself through the production of theatrical or mediatic illusion that gives the impression of legitimacy without any genuine substance" (Critchley and Webster 15).

In *The Phaedrus*, Socrates vigorously opposes the wholesale adoption of the new media technology of alphabetic script, which he characterizes as a *pharmakon*, a drug that impedes students' ability to philosophize. When you dose them with this intoxicating mnemonic supplement, they will be seduced into delusional experiences of grandeur: "You give your disciples not truth but only the semblance of truth; they will be heroes of many things and will have learned nothing; they will appear to be omniscient and will generally know nothing" (Plato 274–275). In the 1950s and 1960s rhetorician Marshall McLuhan foreshadowed future currents in post-structuralism and media studies by drawing attention to Plato's prejudice against the media technology of alphabetic script as inaugurating the Western philosophical tradition's technophobic orientation: "Plato regarded the advent of writing as pernicious. In the *Phaedrus* he tells us it would cause men to rely on their memories rather than their wits" (McLuhan 162).

Years later, Jacques Derrida famously seized on Plato's derogation of writing as a synecdoche for Platonic philosophy's general scapegoating strategy. In "Plato's Pharmacy," he writes, "The incompatibility between the written and the true is clearly announced at the moment Socrates starts to recount the way in which men are carried out of themselves by pleasure, become absent from themselves, forget themselves, and die to the thrill of song" (Derrida 429).[1] An opponent of theatre and poetry, Plato reinvented theatricality as philosophical dialogue and replaced the smooth-talking Odyssean epic hero with a shrewd Socratic philosopher who resists the siren call of irrational affect by tying himself to the stern of his well-crafted philosophical ship.[2] It bears mentioning that the only way Plato was able to choreograph this scene for philosophizing was by authoring written texts that preserved his master's admonitions against writing.

But another target, an insidious nemesis of philosophy, was also clearly in the Platonic crosshairs. Although "sophistry" now connotes deceit and hucksterism under the guise of sophistication, the sophists were a group of wise men whose prestige and influence Socrates sought to subvert. Their art of rhetoric (which is cognate with the word "oratory") was, as far as Socrates was concerned, was false imitation of philosophy, just as writing was a false imitation of speech and narrative fiction (be it in epic poetry or tragic theatre) was a false imitation of fact (especially if the false imitation was enmeshed in an intoxicating musical arrangement). Sophism and philosophy share the root *sophia*, which means something like critical intelligence. But whereas the Socratic philosopher attunes his conversation to the immutable but evasive ideals of Truth, the sophist, according to Socrates, directs his discursive antennae to the irrational elements of his audience's character in order to seduce them, thereby posturing at intellectual acuity without any ethical or scholarly compass.

The most famous sophist was arguably Gorgias, who brought sophism to Athens from Sicily. Gorgias was a dazzling orator who could improvise a speech on most any topic. While the more ascetic wise-man Socrates shunned the employment of his discipline for crude financial gain or personal advancement, Gorgias delivered topical speeches for money and seduced audiences with his ability to argue any issue from any position. Gorgias not only embraced narrative myths and writing but also valorized what Socrates could perceive only as nihilism and irrationality. One of the countless ironies about the historical record is the sad fact that little of

Gorgias' work has survived the millennia in spite of the fact that he harboured none of Socrates' prejudices against the written word.

In his "Encomium of Helen," Gorgias delights in the practice of tackling the more unpopular and difficult side of a popular issue. Against the grain of popular opinion, he contends that the much-maligned fictional Helen of Troy should be exculpated for her role in the Trojan War, as described by Homer. In the speech, which is both an exercise in persuasion and a theoretical examination of the nature of persuasive speech itself, a boisterous Gorgias claims that

> The effect of speech upon the condition of the soul is comparable to the power of drugs over the nature of bodies. For just as different drugs dispel different secretions from the body, and some bring an end to disease and others to life, so also in the case of speeches, some distress, others delight, some cause fear, others make the hearers bold, and some drug and bewitch the soul with a kind of evil persuasion.
>
> ("Encomium" 27)

It is not clear whether Gorgias' valorization of the rhetorical *pharmakon* preceded Socrates' deployment of it as an epithet to describe writing. It just so happens that tropes pertaining to medicine, exercise, and wellness abound in Socratic dialogues. In *the Gorgias,* in which Socrates is depicted as debating with the master orator and his coterie, the master philosopher describes philosophy as akin to medicine, which heals the sick, while rhetoric is more like mere "cookery," which may taste good going down but has negligible tonic qualities. It goes without saying that this was millennia before the invention of chemotherapy or vaccines, so the distinction was far from rigorous. Nevertheless, for Socrates, this disparity spoke to rhetoric's illegitimacy as a *techne,* what present-day scholars would call an art or discipline.

In his much-overlooked lecture notes on rhetoric, Friedrich Nietzsche insists that Plato's exclusion of writing and narrative is inextricably wedded to the exclusion of rhetoric. "The [Platonic] truth," he writes, "can be articulated neither in a written nor in a rhetorical form. The mythical and the rhetorical are employed [only] when the brevity of time allows for no scientific instruction" (Nietzsche 99). It should come as no surprise that Socrates would seize on Gorgias' double-edged characterization of rhetoric as an intoxicating drug. Driven to purify philosophy and insulate the dialectic against the toxic bewitchments of rhetoric, he insists that Gorgias' particular brand of oratory, like writing and theatre, seduces the soul with unwieldy feelings that detract from its ability to attune itself to the ideal Truth. Without such an eidetic sounding, sophism is merely a hollow but deceptive pantomime of dialectical philosophical reasoning.

The most obvious instance of this hollow sophistry is "On Not-Being or On Nature," in which Gorgias anticipates both some of the heavier-handed late twentieth-century exercises in deconstruction and the title syntax of every third liberal humanities paper produced since 1991. In this speech, Gorgias famously makes a mockery of philosophical reasoning by turning it against empirical experience and the pretence of fidelity to objective truth. The crux of the argument is as follows:

1 Nothing exists.
2 Even if something exists, nothing can be known about it.
3 Even if something can be known about it, knowledge about it cannot be communicated to others.
4 Even if it can be communicated, it cannot be understood.

Socrates clearly took umbrage at this kind of parody of earnest philosophical methods and the philosopher's Apollonian efforts to distinguish truth from fiction. In *The Gorgias*, he therefore dedicates himself to putting rhetoric in its place, a project that resurfaces in various interactions across the Platonic dialogues.

Socrates insists that it is, in fact, rhetoric that does not exist, at least not as a *techne* or discipline. Whereas the dialectical system of techniques that constitute philosophy can be cultivated and transmitted, rhetoric is a mere "knack," a talent for getting one's way. The persuasive orator, claims Socrates, is simply a savvy and charismatic snake-oil salesman, a charlatan who is especially adept at identifying and pandering to his audience's prejudices. But charisma cannot be taught, and the immutable Truth has nothing to do with indulging audiences' arbitrary predilections and irrational desires.

Slavoj Žižek points out that many of the Platonic dialogues are more like scripted stage plays designed to highlight Socrates' superior erudition. "There is thus always a basic asymmetry in a dialogue," writes Žižek. "[And] does this asymmetry not break out openly in late Plato's dialogues, where we are no longer dealing with Socratic irony, but with one person talking all the time, with his partner merely interrupting him from time to time with 'So it is, by Zeus!', 'How cannot it be so?'" (*Disparities* 992–993). By the end, his rivals concede to his arguments and Socratic philosophy wins the day. But *The Gorgias* is arguably one of the "problem plays" in that Socrates' arguments largely miss their mark. This is especially the case in his engagement with Gorgias' disciple Callicles, who seems to get the better of his philosophical interlocutor. Anticipating Friedrich Nietzsche's fin-de-siècle anti-Platonism, Callicles accuses Socrates of fabricating a convenient monastic value system that has no real traction in the affairs of the polis. Disparaging philosophy as a moribund children's game, he insists that philosophers are risibly "ignorant in the affairs of the city." Critchley observes that when Callicles refuses to play the philosopher's dialogical game, Socrates seems to betray his inability to adjust to the changing coordinates of the conversation "and simply starts to speak to himself and answer his own questions." In the end, writes Critchley, Socrates is content to turn the dialogue into a monologue and ends up "talk[ing] to himself like a crazy person in the street" while an indifferent Callicles scoffs at his unpersuasive self-justifying theatrics (Critchley 130).

Aristotle's Defence of Rhetoric

In spite of his forebears' reservations about rhetoric, Plato's student Aristotle somehow, improbably, became invested in the popular art of persuasion and insisted on teaching it right alongside philosophy at his academy. His *Rhetoric* is the first known systematic treatise on the discipline. But it is so much more than that. Part psychology treatise, part political strategy manual, and part oratorical handbook, *Rhetoric* responds to Socrates' critiques and advocates for rhetoric's legitimacy and importance as an equal partner to the art of wisdom. If for Socrates, rhetoric is a counterfeit *techne*, Aristotle widens the scope of technicity to account for this worthy "counterpart" to philosophy. He begins with both a new definition of *rhetoric* and a new understanding of disciplinary artistry. "Rhetoric," writes Aristotle, "is the power of observing the means of persuasion on almost any subject presented to us" (Aristotle 7). Its legitimacy does not reside in its monopoly over a proper (even if imaginary) object but in its sophisticated arsenal of techniques and concepts.

While Socrates' assertion that rhetoric is not a proper *techne* hinges on its lack of a distinct disciplinary object (such as Truth for philosophy and the human body for medicine), Aristotle responds by seizing on the rhetorical *topos* of definition. In this especially reflexive moment, he brandishes rhetoric to interrogate Socrates' convenient philosophical presuppositions: rhetoric is not only a *proper* system of techniques; it is a totally different category of practice from philosophy in that it involves the application of persuasion to a wide variety of practical paraphilosophical situations. He then proceeds to explore the application of this discipline to situations like legal disputes, senatorial deliberations, and public ceremonies. Where there is ambiguity about the correct line of interpretation, rhetoric swoops in to participate in the conversation, even occasionally trespassing on what had hitherto been deemed proper philosophical territory.

The Rome Discourse

Both Athenian philosophy and rhetoric fell into disrepute in the Roman empire on account of their association with Rome's putatively effete and inferior Athenian predecessor. The Roman rhetorician Cicero exhumed and popularized the work of Aristotle and Plato and brought Athenian thought back into the conversation, but this time with rhetoric assuming the dominant station. Cicero called for a revised intellectual cartography and, like the sophists, ridiculed Plato for "depict[ing] in his pages an unknown sort of republic, so completely in contrast with everyday life and the customs of human communities" (Cicero 159). Against Plato's hermetic model of wisdom, he advocated for a rhetorical–philosophical "man of sharpness" who, rather than attuning himself to immutable truths, "ought to feel the pulses of every class, time of life, and degree, and to taste the thoughts and feelings of those before whom he is pleading or intending to plead any cause; but his philosophical books he should keep back for a restful holiday" (Cicero 159).

Arguably the second most influential Roman rhetorician was Quintilian, who picked up the mantle from Cicero and dedicated himself to the task of humanistic education. For Quintilian, rhetoric is not so much an amoral art of persuasion as a systematic coupling of virtue (as underscored by the Socratic tradition) and eloquence (as exemplified by Aristotle and Cicero). But he, too, reserved a certain amount of hostility for the Platonic view of philosophical supremacy. Quintilian's "Roman wise man," like Cicero's, derives his wisdom from a rigorous interdisciplinary education and immersion in the affairs of the polity. Quintilian meticulously engineered this form of training to prevent rhetoric from degenerating into a pantomime of wisdom. Some laughable philosophical posturers, observes Quintilian,

> assume a stern air and let their beards grow, and, as though despising the precepts of oratory, sit for a while in the schools of the philosophers, that, by an assumption of a severe mien before the public gaze and by an affected contempt of others they may assert their moral superiority, while leading a life of debauchery at home. For philosophy may be counterfeited, but eloquence never.
>
> (Quintilian 408)

At the end of the day, Quintilian proleptically combats the association of rhetoric with sophistic amorality by insisting that rhetorical "eloquence has its fountain-head in the most secret springs of wisdom, [which is why] for a considerable time the instructors of morals and of eloquence were identical" (Quintilian 385). With this coupling in mind, he integrated rhetoric into a rigorous humanistic system of learning organized around the premise of cultivating *humanitas* in civilized, ethical, eloquent young men.

What Goes by the Name of Enlightenment

While classical sophist rhetoric had been stigmatized for its association with writing and its associated cluster of toxic technics, rhetoric's expulsion from Renaissance and Enlightenment thought was, in no small part, due to its affiliation with orality at the time of print culture's ascendency.

In *The Ends of Rhetoric*, John Bender and David Wellbery track the discipline's fortunes with the advent of Enlightenment scientism, typified by the ideas of Francis Bacon:

> [Bacon's] polemic mirrors central features of Plato's (or Socrates') attack on the Sophists, those purveyors of rhetorical tricks and marketeers of semblance, power, and prestige. But whereas Plato establishes dialectical ascent to the realm of suprasensible ideas as the alternative to rhetoric, Bacon envisions an arhetorical discourse that would ground itself in the empirical givens of nature.
>
> (Bender and Wellbery 6)

At the hands of written philosophy, which valorized science and mathematics as its ultimate touchstones to legitimacy, rhetoric was expelled from the fold yet again. This time it was on account of its investments in superficial ornamentation over scientific truth (which had surmounted its Platonic precursor). By the time John Locke and Immanuel Kant were done "drown[ing it] in a sea of ink" (Bender and Wellbery 15), the immoral, unscientific art of rhetoric had seen its disciplinary purview relegated to inconsequential decorative matters. The residue of this demotion persists to this day, laments Timothy Morton: "When we say nowadays that someone is being rhetorical, we mean that she has style but no substance" (Morton 78). This stigma against "mere rhetoric" still circulates amongst philosophers, in particular, in spite of the fact that, since the dawn of the humanities, rhetoricians have gone to great length to demonstrate that style and substance, like form and matter, are as Burke would say, indivisibly consubstantial.

Bender and Wellbery make the euphemistic claim that "rhetoric survives today in strangely contracted form as a subject taught in universities" (Bender and Wellbery 6). Even though they attribute this drift to the expropriation of rhetoric's traditional concerns by more ascendant disciplines (literary studies, communications, media studies, etc.), part of the fault also lands squarely on the shoulders of contemporary rhetoricians, whose relationship with the modern-day university complex is a moribund one. The pathological blandness of academic and technical writing pedagogy has served what Ian Angus calls the absolute "subordination of communication to the commercial impulse" (Angus 90). Excommunicated from the inner sanctum of the humanities to parochial writing centres and communications programs, many rhetoricians have colluded in sentencing the discipline to instrumentalization by a university system that fails to recognize its refulgent potentials. A disproportionate amount of rhetorical attention is now dedicated to pragmatic compositional concerns, while almost none is allocated to bringing rhetorical theory to bear on a world that is permeated with persuasion, influence, identifications, and propaganda.

The Burkean Watershed

Born in Pittsburgh, Pennsylvania, in 1897, Burke published prolifically over much of the twentieth century until his death in 1993. This book is testament to the fact that contemporary scholarship is only beginning to catch up with his voluminous body of work. In groundbreaking texts like *A Grammar of Motives*, *A Rhetoric of Motives*, and *Language as Symbolic Action*, Burke brought far-reaching insights to bear on cultural currents whose rhetoricity was far from clear to many of his contemporaries. His accomplishments as an author and professor are all the more remarkable since he never so much as completed an undergraduate degree. Burke was a prodigious autodidact. As an undergraduate student of languages, he dropped out of Ohio State University to move to Greenwich Village, where he befriended the likes Eugene O'Neill and William Carlos Williams and got involved with periodicals like *The Dial* (for which he translated Thomas Mann's "Death in Venice" in 1924) and *The Nation*. His work as a rhetorical theorist and public intellectual allowed him to lecture at several colleges, including Vermont's Bennington College, without even an undergraduate degree under his belt.

Burke's role in rehabilitating rhetoric in the early twentieth century cannot be overstated. Lee Thayer characterizes Burke's revolutionary rhetorical approach to theory as anti-tribalist and emancipatory:

> Any way of seeing, of course, is a way of not seeing, as Kenneth Burke has insisted. Thus any theory of communication, any dominant paradigm, any pervasively informing metaphilosophy, will have its limits, and its limitations. No alternative to a dominant paradigm would be perfectly limitless, perfectly unlimiting. Yet the dominant contemporary perspective is especially limiting of specifically *human* possibilities and criteria.
>
> (Thayer 12)

A voracious polymath, Burke was what Wayne Booth has termed a theoretical "pluralist." Refusing to resign himself to any traditional disciplinary cul-de-sacs or respect territorial boundaries, he ceaselessly adopted and invented new frameworks for appreciating the operation of persuasion in a bewilderingly complex world. He applied his insights far and wide, integrating a great many disciplinary and technological *pharmakons* into his version of the new rhetoric. To this end, he brought a panorama of art forms, cultural practices, and philosophical systems into the new-rhetorical fold. When viewed through the Burkean looking glass, no cultural phenomena were deemed arhetorical.

In contrast to Plato's imposition of philosophy as Sovereign of the republic of knowledge, Burke suggests that one of countless other ways to reassess the matter is to view philosophy as a branch of rhetoric: "Bring several rhetoricians together, let their speeches contribute to the maturing of one another by the give and take of question and answer, and you have the dialectic of a Platonic dialogue" (*ARM* 53). Such provocations, for Burke, do not preclude philosophy from participating in the disciplinary parlour. Rather, he sought to open up the theoretical field for hitherto unthinkable modalities of interdisciplinary cooperation and cross-pollination.

And yet, Burke's watershed never fully took root in the twenty-first century critical-theoretical imagination. Even when present-day rhetoricians refer to Burke, it is usually in the form of a perfunctory nod to his concept of "identification" or passing mention of his "dramatistic pentad" rather than employing his ideas as apertures into contemporary cultural phenomena. Wayne Booth refers to this variety of lip service as *eclecticism*, a perfunctory approach to criticism that entails "deliberately hack[ing] other critics' works into fragments, salvaging whatever proves useful" (*Modern Dogma* 21). The tendency of even rhetoricians to draw on Burke "eclectically," if at all, motivates Fredric Jameson to question why so few humanistic thinkers seriously engage with Burke's work:

> The question as to why this immense critical corpus, to which lip service is customarily extended in passing, has—read by virtually everybody—been utterly without influence in its fundamental lessons, has had no following, save perhaps among the social scientists, and is customarily saluted as a monument of personal inventiveness and ingenuity ... rather than as an interpretive model to be studied and a method to be emulated.
>
> (Jameson 508–509)

At this pivotal juncture, Jameson's query strikes a compelling chord. It is as though, even within a post-humanistic scene that is, however sluggishly, beginning to open up to meaningful interdisciplinary collaborations, Burke's *oeuvre* is still forced to occupy rhetoric's perennial ignominious position as a "third class citizen of the republic of knowledge" (Morton 78).

In 1978, René Girard, who organized an entire philosophical-hermeneutic system around Burke's concept of "the scapegoat mechanism," expressed incredulity that Burke's work has faded into obscurity and is frequently overlooked in favour of more fashionable French theory. "I am all for French influence," he insists. "[B]ut I would like to see it sprout vigorous and truly independent offshoots on American soil. The day this happens, Kenneth Burke will be acknowledged as the great man he really is" (Girard 48). Nonetheless, even as French theory has continued to lay deep tracks in North America, Burke has largely been left by the wayside. It is a shame that so much contemporary theory turns a blind eye to Burke. He wrote prolifically on a wide variety of matters that overlap with contemporary theoretical concerns, and his ingenious conceptual repertoire and eclectic methods could inform so many other lines of inquiry.

The New Rhetoric

Burke's ingenious revivification of rhetoric stems from a combination of his rare sensitivity to the nuances of its genesis and evolution throughout Greco-Roman antiquity, on the one hand, with a prodigious level of attunement to its untapped potentials in the twentieth century, on the other. Riffing on Aristotelian characterizations of the human being as "the political animal," "speaking animal," or "rational animal," Burke redefines so-called man as "the symbol-using, symbol-misusing, symbol-inventing animal." Accordingly, he redefines rhetoric as an operation "rooted in an essential function of language, a function that is wholly realistic and continually born anew: the use of language as a symbolic means of inducing cooperation in beings that by nature respond to symbols" (*ARM* 53). His remediation of Aristotle's definitions recalibrates them for modernity by, apropos of Freud and Lacan, removing the human being from the centre of the symbolic cosmos and drawing attention to extrarational symbolic operations: "Words are like planets," avers Burke, "each with their own gravitational pull" (*LSA* 468).

For Burke, rhetoric's lack of clearly defined borders is not so much a disciplinary shortcoming, as Socrates would have it, as a source of analytic vitality. The new rhetoric involves so much more than mesmerizing audiences with charismatic flattery, claims Burke. Rhetoricians wield and orchestrate a mobile army of strategies, for both persuasive and analytic purposes, in a manner that must be calibrated to the intricacies of rhetorical situations. On this matter, writes Burke, Aristotle should serve as a useful Virgilian tour guide:

> Aristotle, who looks upon rhetoric as a medium that "proves opposites," gives what amounts to a handbook on the … art of self-defense. He describes the holds and the counter-holds, the blows and the ways of blocking them, for every means of persuasion the corresponding means of dissuasion, for every proof the disproof, for every praise the vituperation that matches it. While in general the truer and better cause has the advantage, he observes, no cause can be adequately defended without skill in the tricks of the trade. So he studies the tricks from the purely technical point of view, without reference to any one fixed position.
>
> (*ARM* 53)

From Burke's "technical point of view," we are always grappling with the socio-symbolic order, a milieu from which there can be no bird's eye view or metalanguage. A rhetorician therefore brandishes their deracinated "tricks of the trade" to speak to the maelstrom of orientations, fantasies, tropes, attitudes, and actions that constitute the experience of a rhetorically saturated technomodernity. Bender and Wellbery refer to this atmospheric state of affairs as *rhetoricality*, "the groundless, infinitely ramifying character of discourse in the modern world" (Bender and Wellbery 6).

One of Burke's most important theoretical interlocutors was Freud, from whom he borrowed psychoanalytic terms like identification, motivation, and symbolic action. Although he was deeply invested in the ramifications of Freud's work, Burke was wary of the perils of institutional dogmatism. When asked if he considered himself a Freudian or Marxist, he replied, "Marxoid and Freudoid" (qtd. in Selzer 16). Operating at arm's length from the world of Freudian scholarship, he nonetheless explicitly or implicitly mentions Freud and psychoanalysis in every one of his books. Even at his most critical, his attitude towards psychoanalysis is one of utter fascination. We contend that Freudian psychoanalysis is so influential on Burke that it must be understood as elementally constitutive of the new rhetoric.

The Displaced Disciplinarity of Psychoanalysis

Like rhetoric, psychoanalysis has weathered accusations of illegitimacy and has fallen into disrepute amongst its disciplinary neighbours. Psychoanalysis emerged in Vienna at the turn of the twentieth century and spread quickly throughout Europe and the West. This story of psychoanalysis can be understood as a struggle for legitimacy followed by a popular ascent, an era of acceptance in dynamic psychiatry, then a gradual decline as psychiatry surrendered to demands, from inside and outside of the medical field, that it provide objective evidentiary foundations for its theories. Although traces of psychoanalytic terminology remain embedded in everyday speech, North American medicine and psychology have long since purged psychoanalysis from their clinical curricula and training, supplanting its language and ideas with a diagnostic, cognitive-behavioural, and biopsychosocial lexicon. Freud, like Burke, has been relegated to the footnotes of a disciplinary world that he played a significant role in creating.

Regardless of psychoanalysis' reputational travails, even its sternest critics have to admit that it is a singular transdisciplinary field, one that encompasses a clinical mental health practice, a complex metapsychological theory, and an approach to cultural and literary criticism. Its protean vibrancy may partially explain why generations of scholars have returned to this bottomless well for reassessment and inspiration. According to James Daley, "Psychoanalysis is not, like other sciences, a field of inquiry which has a limited area of investigation and a fairly well-defined method and domain of application. Its broad and general character makes it speculative and philosophical" (Daley 26). With the advent of psychoanalysis, John Forrester writes, "all hell breaks loose with the boundaries of disciplinarity" (Forrester 784).

There is something undeniably *unheimlich*, or unsettling, about psycho-analysis that has unnerved observers since the outset. According to Lacan, Freud, upon arriving in view of New York Harbor for the first time, told Carl Jung, "They don't realize we're bringing them the plague" ("The Freudian Thing" 336).[3] In spite of its detractors' interminable efforts to contain it, psychoanalysis has continually bubbled to the surface since it landed on America's shore. While it no longer finds a comfortable home in psychology and psychiatry departments, Freud's language of the "the unconscious," "repression," and "projection" has seeped into the linea-ments of our culture. Even when it appears to have been relegated to the dustbin of history, psychoanalysis continues to haunt the epistemologies of its more reputable successors and adjacent disciplines.

There are innumerable readings of Freud's ideas and biographical stud-ies that approach his life from every interpretive angle. Psychoanalysis his-torian Élisabeth Roudinesco writes that every psychoanalytic school has developed its own reading of Freud. Interpretations vary widely between Freudians, post-Freudians, Kleinians, Jungians, Bionians, Lacanians, cul-turalists, independents, ego-psychologists, self-psychologists, Freudo-Marxists, and relational analysts. Different nationalities and languages have also cultivated their own respective inflections of Freudian thought. There is, it turns out, little consensus amongst either critics or psychoana-lysts themselves about the correct interpretation of Freud and his theories, which remain unsettling and unsettled.

In a nod to Foucault's concept of the illusory author function, Roudinesco suggests that there is actually no single Freud. Instead, we must speak of a plurality of Freuds, each with its own characteristic theoretical and nar-rative agendas:

> Every moment of Freud's life has been discussed and every line of his work interpreted in multiple ways, to such an extent that one can draw up a Georges Perec-style list: Freud and Judaism, Freud and religion, Freud and women, Freud the clinician, Freud the fam-ily man, Freud with his cigars, Freud and neurons, Freud and dogs, Freud and Freemasons, and so on. Turning to the many practitioners of radical anti-Freudianism (or Freud-bashing), still more Freuds can be found: Freud the rapacious, Freud the organizer of a clinical gulag, the demoniacal, incestuous, lying, counterfeiting, fascist Freud. Views of Freud appear in every form of expression and narrative: caricatures, comic books, art books, portraits, drawings, photographs, classical novels, pornographic novels, detective stories, fictionalized narratives in films, documentary films, television series.
>
> (Roudinesco 2)

Roudinesco suggests that in the wake of the hagiographies, revisionist clarifications, cruel rejections, and sympathetic returns throughout the latter half of the twentieth century, we cannot ever really discern a clear picture of Freud. The elucidations, accusations, speculations, and fables constitute an impenetrable haze that renders "the real Freud" opaque beyond reckoning. He has become a blank screen for the projections of adherents and detractors alike. But, by and large, psychoanalysis has been displaced to the margins as an illegitimate, unscientific discipline.[4]

Sciences and Letters

Freud's disciplinary ambivalence towards his future career prospects appears in a letter dated "July 17," 1873, when he was only seventeen years old. He wrote to one of his closest friends, Eduard Silberstein (1856–1925), regarding his upcoming university studies in the humanities and medicine later that fall: "If anyone asks me, or you on my behalf, what I intend to be, refrain from giving a definite answer, and simply say: a scientist, a professor, or something like that" (24). The letter foreshadows his hesitancy to identify with any one existing métier as he went on to immerse himself in a variety of disciplines throughout his extensive career.

Freud understood himself to be a pioneering scientist but sometimes presented his ideas as a speculative synthesis of diverse fields. Shortly after the publication of *The Interpretation of Dreams*, Freud wrote to Wilhelm Fliess, in a letter dated "February 1, 1900,"

> I am actually not at all a man of science, not an observer, not an experimenter, not a thinker. I am by temperament nothing but a conquistador – an adventurer, if you want it translated – with all the curiosity, daring, and tenacity characteristic of a man of this sort. (398)

Split between his investment in science and his fascination with the humanities, he adventurously brought both sensibilities into reverberation with each other. Freudian psychoanalysis became an amalgam of quasi-philosophical conceptual innovations, close-reading strategies, narrative textures, and scientific discoveries.

Freud's early ambivalence about psychoanalysis' relationship with science can also be glimpsed in his neurological studies on language loss and communication impairment in cases of brain damage. Although the significance of his 1895 writing of the *Project for a Scientific Psychology* to Fliess has been studied extensively as the preeminent proto-psychoanalytic text, Freud's 1891 book *On Aphasia*, which was excluded from *The Standard Edition*, reveals some early published germs of psychoanalytic thinking. In it, he pays close attention to speech. Freud was especially preoccupied with patients who had lost the capacity to speak, write, or recognize language, often as a result of a stroke, head injury, or brain tumour. The book marks Freud's efforts to express the idea that the brain and mind are reciprocally constitutive.[5] *On Aphasia* hypothesized that physiological and psychic phenomena exist in dynamic tension with word association, language acquisition, and language retention. Freud's earliest work conveys ideas about the relationship between neurology and oratorial prowess.

Arriving at his conclusions before the advent of structural linguistics, Freud introduced the notions of "word concept" and "object concept" (more commonly known as word-presentations and thing-presentations), closely anticipating Ferdinand de Saussure's notion of the sign as being composed of signifier (sound-image) and signified (concept):

> In the light of observations in speech disorders we have formed the view that the word concept (the idea of the word) is linked with its sensory part, in particular through it sound impressions, to the object concept. In consequence, we have arrived at the division of speech disorders into two classes: 1) verbal aphasia, in which only the associations between the single elements of the word concept are disturbed; and 2) asymbolic aphasia, in which the association between word and concept are disturbed. (78)

He explored the relationship between speech, its referents, and bodily sensation. Aphasia frequently manifests in symptoms that interrupt communicative associations. Research in this area ultimately informed Freud's ideas about free association, memory, parapraxis, repression, and repetition compulsion (Miller 373–374). *On Aphasia* provides an early glimpse of the division throughout Freud's *oeuvre* between his disciplinary commitments to science and his immersion in a humanistic world of speech and writing.

Freud began his career as a medical doctor who studied neurology, and throughout his life, he always understood his work to be in conversation with scientific research. His station as a scientist figures prominently in Frank J. Sulloway's *Freud, Biologist of the Mind*, a biography first published in 1979. Sulloway understands the "father of psychoanalysis" as a scientific thinker engaged in the tireless endeavour to reconcile biological determinism with his patients' psychic lives. He suggests that Freud was much more engrossed in biology than psychology and always contextualized psychoanalysis as a quasi-biological science of the unconscious mind.

Scholars have long noted that Freud's major influences stem from a variety of scientific sources, many of which are now understood as unscientific or protoscientific hypotheses. For instance, he was drawn to French physicians Jean-Martin Charcot's (1825–1893) and Pierre Janet's (1859–1947) respective studies on hysteria, hypnosis, dissociation, and traumatic memory. He was also influenced by German scientific thought, including psychologist and physicist Gustav Theodor

Fechner's (1801–1887) ideas on biophysics and experimental psychology, zoologist August Pauly's (1850–1914) psychological Lamarckism, and physician and biologist Ernst Haeckel's (1834–1919) historical hypothesis of recapitulation. Of course, Freud was also profoundly influenced by British naturalist Charles Darwin's (1809–1882) theories of evolution and behaviour in *Origin of Species*, *The Descent of Man*, and *The Expression of the Emotions in Man and Animals*. Drawing on these manifold influences, he sought to invent a new scientific discourse that would evolve in conversation with leading biological and physiological research of his time.

There is an underrecognized humanistic side to Freud, who, in addition to writing more than twenty volumes of research and several hundred articles, maintained epistolary relationships throughout his life with many thinkers of the psychoanalytic movement and beyond. This included correspondence with Wilhelm Fleiss, Otto Rank, Karl Abraham, Lou Andreas-Salomé, Sándor Ferenczi, Carl Jung, James and Alix Strachey, Ernest Jones, and Albert Einstein.[6] This Freud was inspired by ancient Greek thought (including the works of Empedocles, Sophocles, and Plato) as well as Shakespeare's plays. Despite disavowing the influence of his philosophical antecedents, Freud was also undoubtedly inspired by German philosophers such as Arthur Schopenhauer (1788–1860) and Friedrich Nietzsche (1844–1900) in spite of the fact that he claimed not to have read them.

In his study of 1910 on *Leonardo da Vinci, A Memory of His Childhood*, Freud innovated the literary genre of psychobiography, wherein the life and motivations of an historical figure are diffracted through the lens of psychological interpretations. Throughout his works, Freud also refers many times to Johann Wolfgang von Goethe (1749–1832), the German Romantic poet, novelist, playwright, and naturalist philosopher. According to Matthew von Unwerth, Freud looked to Goethe as a model, "admir[ing] not only Goethe's creativity and his prolific achievements, but also his personality, which like his own, was that of a bourgeois gentleman – learned, generous, humble, honest, and perhaps above all, forbearing in the face of adversity" (von Unwerth 93). In 1930, in the last decade of his life, Freud received the prestigious Goethe Prize for contributions to psychology and letters, an award subsequently bequeathed to diverse thinkers such as novelist Thomas Mann and psychiatrist-philosopher Karl Jaspers (both of whom owed a debt to Freud).

Freud was not the only interdisciplinary intellect amongst the early practitioners of psychoanalysis. The polymathic tendencies of the first generation of psychoanalysts contributed to, amongst other things, the fragmented disciplinary identity of psychoanalysis and its disjunction with other fields. As a self-styled conquistador, Freud grew increasingly afraid that other fields might undermine, subordinate, or absorb psychoanalysis. He vocally lamented the possibility that analysis could be "swallowed up by medicine" or that it might become "a mere house-maid of psychiatry" (Freud, "The Question" 248; qtd. in Jones 323).

Freud and the Question of Style

Freud was keenly aware that his writing did not conform to the rhetorical conventions of scientific rationalist discourse. Following *On Aphasia*, Freud and Breuer published *Studies on Hysteria* (1893), wherein they seem to recognize that Freud's case presentations possess the enjoyable rhetorical qualities of entertaining stories. He was troubled that his psychotherapeutic research (especially the presentation of cases) would not be read or understood as scientific. "I have not always been a psychotherapist," writes Freud in the discussion of the "Frälein Elisabeth von R." case. "Like other neuropathologists," he continues,

> I was trained to employ local diagnoses and electro-prognosis, and it still strikes me myself as strange that the case histories I write should read like short stories and that, as one might say, they lack the serious stamp of science. I must console myself with the reflection that the nature of the subject is evidently responsible for this, rather than any preference of my own.
>
> (Freud, "Frälein" 160)

With an incredible flair for narrative, Freud pushed the boundaries of both what was commonly considered an acceptable rhetorical style for presenting scientific case material and what was understood to be appropriate subject matter for scientific discourse.

Despite his most persuasive efforts, Freud found that the medical establishment was reluctant to entertain his ideas during the early years of the psychoanalytic movement's formation. For instance, it took thirteen years to sell the first-run of 626 copies of *Studies on Hysteria* and eight years to sell all 600 copies of the first edition of *The Interpretation of Dreams*, which was published in 1899 (Makari 147). Not only was he publishing books and essays on topics that could easily be deemed unfit for scientific study (including hypnosis, dreams, myths, fantasies, jokes, parapraxes, personal anecdotes, cocaine, and telepathy), but his work exhibited unusual candour when it came to matters of human sexuality, particularly as it pertained to childhood development. On the whole, the medical establishment and Viennese society were not impressed.

In the first decade of the twentieth century, his ideas captured the attention of a small group of physicians. These included Alfred Adler, Carl Jung, Sandor Ferenczi, Karl Abraham, Otto Rank, and Ernest Jones. Freud and his fellow physician Wilhelm Stekel (1868–1940) gradually brought together a larger Viennese intellectual community comprised of psychiatrists, neurologists, social activists, and cultural theorists.

Members of this early community (then known as the Wednesday Psychological Society, now the Vienna Psychoanalytic Society) clashed on account of their differing suppositions, ambitions, and methodologies. The early years were rife with intellectual debate over psychoanalysis' aims, bounds, and objects of study as the discipline slowly took root and made waves in distant lands.

Freud and Sexual Discourse

At the outset, hostility towards psychoanalysis was not so much oriented towards questioning its status as a science as interrogating Freud's frank manner of speaking and writing about sexuality. Freud's attitude towards sex paved his path to notoriety within a largely parochial Victorian Catholic milieu. In a paper published posthumously in 1939, British physician and sexologist Havelock Ellis claimed that a portion of Freud's struggle for legitimacy was a complication arising from his lucid manner of expression concerning matters of sexuality. Ellis elaborated on what he called Freud's "completely revolutionary" attitude:

> In this way [Freud] shocked alike those who viewed sex as very sacred and those who viewed it as very indecent. In a simple, precise, and detailed manner he described the sex phenomena presented by his patients, without attenuation or apology, but as a matter of course. This had never been done before in medical literature. Even in the outspoken days of the seventeenth century anatomists would ask to be excused if they referred to the sexual organs. Freud never seemed to be aware that even the professional public he was addressing still expected some ... similar apology from those who thus ventured to offend its modesty.
>
> (Ellis 310)

Like a modern-day Martin Luther, Freud did not resort to Latin terminology when discussing his subject. Instead, he wrote mellifluously but matter-of-factly about controversial topics like perversion, incest, and infantile sexuality. After all, if the operations of the censorious superego were largely arbitrary and irrational, this kind of frank talk was an appropriate antidote.

"Until Freud at least," writes Michel Foucault, "the discourse on sex – the discourse of scholars and theoreticians – never ceased to hide the thing it was speaking about" (53). Freud's publication of the *Three Essays on the Theory of Sexuality* in 1905 attracted specialists in sexual pathologies as well as feminists and social reformers. "The publication of the *Three Essays*," claims psychoanalyst and historian George Makari, "made Freud a hero of the Viennese coffeehouse scene." Makari continues, "It placed him at the center of a network of artists, writers, journalists, feminists, and reformers

who believed the decay of Habsburg Vienna was not due to degener-
ative heredity, but rather centuries of unhealthy rules and regulations"
(Makari 151). Freud's unapologetic attitude and refusal to self-censor
when writing or speaking about sexuality may have gained him recognition in the public sphere, but the reception of Freud in academia was
polarized (Makari 150; Sulloway 457). As Foucault notes, Freud and his
contemporaries wove together and popularized a new rhetorical discourse
underscoring the interplay between truth and sex: "The essential point,"
writes Foucault, "is that sex was not only a matter of sensation and pleasure, of law and taboo, but also of truth and falsehood, that the truth of sex
became something fundamental, useful, or dangerous, precious or formidable: in short, that sex was constituted as a problem of truth" (Foucault 56).
Psychoanalysis, like sophist rhetoric before it, was positioning itself as one
of philosophy's unsettling other scenes.

Analysis Medical and Non-Medical

Freud maintained that "the theories of psychoanalysis cannot be
restricted to the medical field, but are capable of application to a variety
of other mental sciences" (Freud, "On the History" 26). In *The Question
of Lay Analysis* of 1926, he expresses his own ambivalence about situating psychoanalysis in relation to medicine and science. Beginning in
the 1920s, the psychoanalytic movement became split over disagree-
ments between medical and non-medical or lay analysts. The disagree-
ments circled around whether or not an analyst should be required to
possess a medical degree to practice psychoanalysis. The debate raised
questions about whether psychoanalysts should be subjected to the reg-
ulatory institutions governing medicine. *The Question of Lay Analysis*
is Freud's response to the American Psychoanalytic Association's resolution to prevent lay psychoanalysts from conducting treatment. He
defended non-medically trained clinicians and their right to practice
psychoanalysis:

> Nothing takes place between [analyst and analysand] except that they
> talk to each other. The analyst makes use of no instruments – not even
> for examining the patient – nor does he prescribe any medicines....
> The analyst agrees upon a fixed regular hour with the patient, gets
> him to talk, listens to him, talks to him in his turn and gets him to
> listen. (187)

In spite of his own medical background, Freud makes it clear that medical
training "is more or less the opposite of what [the clinician] would need as
a preparation for psycho-analysis" (*The Question* 230). In fact, psychoanalytic instruction ought to include disciplines that are alien to medicine,
such as "the history of civilization, mythology, the psychology of religion

and the science of literature .... The great mass of what is taught in medical schools is of no use to him for his purposes" (*The Question* 246).

Freud situated his psychoanalysis as divergent from conventional psychology. It was "not of medical psychology in the old sense, not of the psychology of morbid processes, but simply of psychology. It is certainly not the whole of psychology, but its substructure and perhaps even its entire foundation" (252). He viewed his ideas as potentially foundational for psychology but highlighted the potential limitations of each scientific perspective: "In itself every science is one-sided. It must be so, since it restricts itself to particular subjects, points of view and methods" (231). For Freud, every discipline, including psychoanalysis, harbours its own unconscious blind spots. Despite characterizing analysis as akin to psychology, he proposed that the analyst could best be understood as a "secular pastoral worker" (255). Such an atheistic lay priest would study psychoanalysis as a distinct science (in terms of its theory, methods, and practice) but would also remain attentive to developments in neurology, psychology, and psychiatry. This way, they would be able to maintain the discipline's permeability to vital scientific discoveries and paradigm shifts.

Interrogations of psychoanalysis from scientific fields have been multifaceted throughout its troubled history. Freud's notion of the unconscious was as subversive for philosophy as his discourse on sexuality was for the social. The notion of the unconscious unsettled the Cartesian conception of the self-conscious ego and undermined the philosophical tradition of the knowing subject. James Daley reminds us how easily the humanistic study of the unconscious can lead to misreading and misinterpretation:

> Whether it is a therapy, philosophy, psychology, a natural or a social science, psychoanalysis leads to misunderstanding, because it deals with the character of human beings. Its theory purports to explain why they do what they ought not to do, why they fail to do what they ought to do, why they ever accomplish anything, why they wish to accomplish anything, in short why human beings are not what they think they are and why they are what they think they are not.
>
> (Daley 32)

Freud's theories conjure a dimension of psychic life that is inaccessible to conscious awareness. The unconscious includes memories, interests, affects, and motivations. It is a *topos* of conflict and contradiction that both defies and lurks beneath mundane common-sense perspectives. As such, the unconscious could be discovered but never fully grasped.

In "The Reception of Psychoanalysis in Germany," Hanna S. Decker suggests that psychoanalysis was not especially ignored or maligned in Vienna despite Freud's own dismissive appraisal of his readership. Decker writes that the adverse responses towards psychoanalysis can be seen as multiply determined,

> being affected by the mid-and-late-nineteenth-century rebellion against romanticism and the philosophy of nature; the defining of science so that it could concern only tangible phenomena; the desire of psychiatrists to make their field a part of modern, organically oriented medicine; the wish of psychologists that they cease to be philosophers and become scientists; the desire of both psychiatrists and psychologists for professional status; the continued epistemological influence of idealistic philosophy; the belief that nature was more important than nurture; the warring schools in German psychiatry; ... the psychoanalytic emphasis of the unconscious; ... sexual repressions and suppressions ... the fact that Freud was Jewish; and, finally, the neurotic resistances of some critics.
>
> (Decker 601–602)

Although Freud's work encountered a great deal of resistance for a variety of reasons, it also sent persuasive ripples across the world. Surviving the disorder and destruction caused by World War I, his work was taken up by Dadaists, Surrealists, and existentialists across the early and mid-twentieth century. His theories also gained acceptance in pockets scattered throughout Europe and the Americas, and, against formidable odds, psychoanalysis was ultimately adopted by institutional psychiatry as a legitimate form of psychotherapeutic treatment in the mid-twentieth century.

Fearful Semitry

The psychoanalytic movement then suffered significant attacks from Hitler's Nazis and the Third Reich, whose final solution program included the annihilation of psychoanalysis as a "Jewish science." Hitler's vendetta against psychoanalysis included its ideas, books, activities, organizations, and practitioners.[7] Stephen Frosh reflects on the historical role of anti-semitism in suppressing psychoanalysis, many of whose early practitioners were, like Freud, born Jewish. Although many of the early psychoanalysts may have been atheists, many critics seemed to believe that psychoanalysts could not help but think from a "Jewish perspective":

> [P]sychoanalysis has become broader in its appeal and its personnel, yet there is still an irresistible pull towards associating it with Jews and Jewish culture, due partly to an inward-lookingness and fascination with psychological 'depths' that is often thought of as characteristically Jewish. In some ways this has been to psychoanalysis' advantage, giving it energy and a ready-made sense of collective and cultural

identity; in other ways, the association between psychoanalysis and Jewishness has been costly. In particular, anti-Semitism has infiltrated attitudes towards psychoanalysis, and there have been times when the denigration of psychoanalysis as 'Jewish science' has been murderously dangerous.

(Frosh 1–2)

The "Jewish science" came to signify the inheritance of not just a corrupt Judaic worldview but a deceitful ideology that would contaminate "Aryan science" and culture. As we will discuss in Chapter Three, Kenneth Burke analyzes this constellation of anti-semitic tropes in his close-reading of Hitler's *Mein Kampf.* Writing in 1939, Burke framed Hitler as a modern-day sophist, a charlatan who wielded his sinister powers of persuasion to rally the German public around the shared mission of "scapegoating" the common enemy of the Jews for Germany's deeply ingrained social, economic, and political problems.

When the Nazis expunged psychoanalysis, many European analysts were exiled to North and South America, where psychoanalysis would flourish for decades (and, in some milieus, continues to flourish). Frosh writes that during the post-WWII period,

considerable effort went into maintaining the independence and non-ideological nature of psychoanalysis, based both on opposition to any "racialized" claims in the wake of Nazism, and a liberal antagonism to the idea that any "race" or creed could own any properly academic or professional discipline.

(Frosh 9)

Psychoanalysis, however, has never been able to shake the stigma of pseudoscience, dogmatism, and sophism associated pejoratively with its Jewish provenance. That having been said, there are still sound reasons to critique Freud's method on account of its lack of conformity with the scientific method.

Crises of Legitimacy

After World War II, psychoanalysis became a dominant approach in American psychiatry, psychoanalytically informed clinicians led most psychiatric departments in hospitals, and psychiatry residents were instructed in psychoanalytic concepts as part of their essential training. "With so many Jewish practitioners forced to flee Europe," writes Roy Porter, the US "became the world headquarters of psychoanalysis, and by the mid-twentieth century American psychiatry at large, in university departments and teaching hospitals, was heavily psychoanalytically oriented" (197). Psychiatry absorbed many of the teachings of the second and third generation of analysts. Popular schools of thought included British object relations and attachment theory, American ego-psychology and self-psychology, Freudian revisionism, and the "dyadic systems view" of the relational turn.

Beginning in the 1960s and carrying on through the 1980s, however, cognitivism, behaviourism, and psychopharmacology began to redefine the parameters of what constituted science within the field of psychiatry. Under intense interrogation, North American psychiatry struggled to prove its scientific legitimacy, while psychoanalysis began to suffer harsh criticisms from many quarters. One of the most prominent critics was philosopher of science Karl Popper (1902–1994), whose own parents had not only owned copies of Freud's books during his childhood but had also been friends with Freud's sister Rosa F. Graf (*Unended* 6; 11). Popper sought to develop "a criterion of demarcation" so that "non-science" could be distinguished from "genuine science." He insisted on the importance of repeatability and refutability (or falsifiability) in scientific studies. Rather than buttressing existing theories, scientists, according to Popper, should seek to disprove them in order to devise better ones. On these grounds, he excluded psychoanalysis, Darwin's theories of evolution, and Marxism from the realm of science.[8]

Popper argued that psychoanalysts of every stripe interpreted any state of affairs as a verification of their theory. Psychoanalysis cannot be understood as a science on Popperian grounds since its theories can be neither proven true nor repudiated; its hypotheses are untestable and unfalsifiable. The crux of Popper's objection is, according to Pushpa Misra, that "crucial concepts used in psychoanalysis provide an open field for immunizing stratagems for the support of the theory" (Misra 17). Psychoanalysts, according to this critique, masquerade as scientists when they "explain all human behaviour by their theory and count it as confirming evidence" (Misra 17). Popper insisted that psychoanalysis, like many non-scientific theories, may offer significant contributions to knowledge, but it cannot claim the support of systematically assessed empirical evidence.

In *Conjectures and Refutations* of 1963, Popper flags the insidious rhetorical nature of psychoanalytic theory:

> I found that those of my friends who were admirers of Marx, Freud, and Adler, were impressed by a number of points common to these theories, and especially by their apparent *explanatory power.* These theories appeared to be able to explain practically everything that happened within the fields to which they referred. The study of any of them seemed to have the effect of an intellectual conversion or revelation, opening your eyes to a new truth hidden from those not yet initiated. Once your eyes were thus opened you saw confirming instances everywhere: the world was full of verifications of the theory. Whatever happened always confirmed it. Thus its truth appeared

manifest; and unbelievers were clearly people who did not want to see the manifest truth; who refused to see it, either because it was against their class interest, or because of their repressions which were still 'un-analysed' and crying out for treatment.

(Popper 45)

For Popper, the explanatory power of psychoanalysis conveyed "some facts" and interesting "psychological suggestions," but in "the manner of myths," which cannot be tested (Popper 50).[9] He characterizes psychoanalysis as emerging out of a "dogmatic attitude" that "stick[s] to first impressions." A vigilant critic of dogmatism disguised as science, he recommended that psychoanalysis be replaced by a scientific "critical attitude." Unlike psychoanalysts, scientists of this discipline would be prepared to amend its principles, admit doubts, and demand tests. Whereas the dogmatic attitude aligns with faith, the critical attitude aligns with reason and the insatiable desire for accurate knowledge of the world.

Popper's critique of psychoanalysis' dogmatic orientation aligns with Paul Ricoeur's assessment of psychoanalysis as a "school of suspicion" that employs a "paranoid" hermeneutic logic. A "hermeneutics of suspicion" reads texts "sceptically" so as to detect hidden meanings lurking beneath the surface. Critics like Popper suggest that hermeneutic applications of psychoanalytic theory are much closer to religion than science in that they always seem to uncover what they have sought out to find in the first place.[10]

In response to Popper's criticism, philosopher and psychoanalyst Harry Slochower (1900–1991) addresses the role of clinical psychoanalysis as an artistic practice:

Because its subject matter is human life, applied psychoanalysis, like art, cannot and should not be a pure science. Attempts to turn it into such can only mean an impoverishment, if not a nullification, of its effectiveness. The decisive act in its approach is an act of the imagination. Its function is rather to serve as a link between science and art.

(Slochower 174)

For Slochower, psychoanalysis does not figure as a science or even a clearly demarcated discipline. Echoing Burke's understanding of rhetoric, he views it as a transdisciplinary conduit between a manifold of arts and sciences.

Several years later, in *A Critical Dictionary of Psychoanalysis* of 1968, British psychiatrist and psychoanalyst Charles Rycroft (1914–1998) attempted to account for the disparagement of psychoanalysis as a pseudoscience in his entry on "Science." While acknowledging that psychoanalysis is regularly dismissed as an unscientific philosophy, Rycroft invokes the lessons of Thomas Kuhn's (1922–1996) scientific relativism in Freud's defence:

> The proposition 'psychoanalysis is not a science' can be made true or untrue by choosing the appropriate definition of science. If one defines science in a way that makes knowledge derived from experiment and measurement an essential part of the definition, psychoanalysis fairly obviously is not one. If one defines it in terms of the attempt to establish causal relationships between events, the question hinges on whether one believes that the laws of causality (determinism) can be applied to living organisms capable of consciousness …. If one defines it, as … 'systematic and formulated knowledge,' psychoanalysis is a science, and the issue becomes one of deciding to what branch of science it belongs. (147–148)

Rycroft understands psychoanalysis as a *techne*, a system of techniques, in a sense that resonates with Aristotle's and Cicero's defences of rhetoric. From this standpoint, psychoanalysis, like rhetoric, ought to be understood as a system of knowledge and an arsenal of techniques.

Nonetheless, psychoanalysis has continued to lose traction in psychology and psychiatry departments. "While real," writes Anne Harrington, "the triumph of the neo-Freudian perspective in postwar psychiatry was fragile" (107). She contends that "American psychoanalysis rather faltered fast under the weight of a series of largely self-inflicted wounds" as "more and more critics sharpened their knives, and more and more proponents of alternative biological perspectives saw an opportunity to assert their authority" (107).

More recently, psychiatric scholar Joel Paris has questioned of the relevance of psychoanalysis to modern psychiatry and concluded,

> It is difficult to see how any of the current responses to criticism can save psychoanalysis from a continued and lingering decline. Analysis has separated itself from psychiatry and psychology by teaching its method in stand-alone institutes. The field may only survive if it is prepared to dismantle its structure as a separate discipline and rejoin academia and clinical science.
>
> (Paris 310)

While clinical psychoanalysis continues to thrive in little cul-de-sacs outside of the scientific establishment, an emerging body of research suggests that clinical psychoanalysis is a science-based practice with proven beneficial outcomes for patients (Fonagy, 2014; Misra, 2018; Shedler, 2010; Solms, 2018; Yakeley, 2018).[11] Neuropsychoanalysis, in particular, has singled itself out as a field that combines analytic insights with neurological studies. Regardless of attempts to revive the scientific legitimacy of clinical psychoanalysis, it remains estranged from the nerve centres of psychology and psychiatry. Like rhetoric, psychoanalysis continually renews its peripheral status as a third-class denizen of the republic of knowledge.[12]

The Subject of Science

French psychoanalyst Jacques Lacan's (1901–1981) seminars characterize both rhetoric and psychoanalysis as entangled with thoughts and words in motion.[13] We will explore Lacan's peculiar discourse and radical revision of Freud later in this book. But first, we must introduce Lacan's provocative ideas about psychoanalysis' unusual relationship to scientific discourse.

In "The Neurotic's Individual Myth," Lacan suggests that psychoanalysis might be best inserted into the classical trivium and quadrivium of liberal arts that emerged out of the classical Roman rhetoricians' ideas about education. For Lacan, psychoanalysis should be thought together with "astronomy, arithmetic, geometry, music, and grammar" (406). Psychoanalysis, like its disciplinary neighbours, is concerned with the cultivation of a kind of eloquence:

> It is in this respect that analytic experience is not definitively objectifiable. It always implies within itself the emergence of a truth that cannot be said, since what constitutes truth is speech, and then you would have in some way to say speech itself which is exactly what cannot be said in its function as speech. (406)

The truth of psychoanalysis is not an institutional or scientific truth but a subjective truth. What Lacan refers to as "the subject of science" signifies both the subject matter of science and the production of a subject/patient/analysand/person whose subjectivity is the irremediable by-product of a pervasive scientific worldview. "The whole of science is based on reducing the subject to an eye," writes Lacan, "and that is why it is projected in front of you, that is to say objectivated" (Lacan, *Seminar I* 80). According to Lacan, the observing subject engendered by scientific discourse is also unconsciously constituted by an almost voyeuristic network of objectifications and judgements.

For Lacan, scientific discourse deals primarily with objects and, as a result, transfigures the human subject into an object for measurement, categorization, and data collection. Because scientific analyses typically strip the subject of all distinction and uniqueness, Lacan avers that it often runs afoul by objectifying the patient's symptom and measuring it against a constructed norm. A scientific approach can provide a general answer to the patient's demand for treatment, but it does not address the particularity at stake for the patient as a singular subject:

The me [*moi*] of modern man, as I have indicated elsewhere, has taken on its form of the beautiful soul who does not recognize his very reason for being in the disorder he denounces in the world. But a way out of this impasse is offered to the subject where his discourse rants and raves. Communication can be validly established for him in science's collective undertaking and in the tasks science ordains in our universal civilization; this communication will be effective within the enormous objectification constituted by this science, and it will allow him to forget his subjectivity.

("Function" 233)

Psychoanalysis takes up the tension between science and non-science. Science is adept at providing objective solutions to certain maladies, but these solutions always come at the expense of the subject's distinct experience of the world and their own suffering. In direct contrast to scientific objectification and economic commodification, psychoanalytic treatment is organized around the cultivation of an all-too-rare intensely subjective rapport with the world.

In his very first public Seminar, which was held at Paris' Sainte-Anne Hospital in 1953–1954, Lacan distinguished psychoanalysis, as an ongoing dialectical process between analysand and analyst, from biomedical and psychological sciences that aim to draw inferences and generalize claims. If it even makes sense to view analysis "as a science," writes Lacan, it "is always a science of the particular. The coming to fruition of an analysis is always a unique case .... But with Freud the analytic experience represents uniqueness carried to its limit .... Analysis is an experience of the particular" (*Seminar I* 4). Insofar as analysis takes up scientific matters, it does so in a thoroughly unscientific (or perhaps we can call it "parascientific") fashion. "Medical diagnostics begins with the particular (the symptom)," writes Lacanian scholar Paul Verhaeghe, and moves "toward the general (the syndrome), based on a semiotic system that is entirely focused on the individual's complaints" (Verhaeghe 6). Psychoanalytic diagnostics, in contrast, "begin from the general (the incipient complaint) and proceed toward the particular (where $N = 1$), based on a system of signifiers that is part of the wider relationship between the subject and the [symbolic order]" (Verhaeghe 6). The more questions the analyst asks the patient in order to particularize their relation to their experience, the more impracticable it becomes to file their singular symptoms under an objective, universalizable syndrome of the scientific *Diagnostic and Statistical Manual of Mental Disorders*.

Lacan insisted that any approach to psychology that begins from a presumed understanding of "normality" already commits a fatal error by objectifying rather than subjectifying the patient's unique experience. Through scientific discourse, the subject is alienated from their own subjective discourse. This is one of his primary criticisms of positivist science in a clinical context.[14] He therefore prefers to characterize psychoanalysis not as a science but as a "praxis" (from the Greek for "doing") with "no other subject than that of science" ("Science" 733). Scientific modernity has engendered the modern individual who undergoes analysis. And Lacanian psychoanalytic thought necessarily recognizes this provenance, but only because psychoanalysis is not, itself, a science per se. It is something much stranger and more difficult to conceive of. Psychoanalysis is, like rhetoric, an unusual mode of doing (what Kenneth Burke would call a form of "symbolic action") that – by virtue of its liminal, parasitic status – interacts with both people and other disciplines in a fashion that brings out their uncanniness.

Chapter Breakdown

We have organized this book in the style of a sort of Möbius strip. Daniel Adleman authored the first half of the book, which is focused primarily on the influence of Freudian psychoanalysis on Burke's new rhetoric and on the far-reaching import of this conjuncture. Chris Vanderwees wrote the second half, which takes up some key rhetorical dimensions of psychoanalysis. As we worked through our chapters, we regularly shared our work with each other and discussed our drafts, so there is a wealth of connective tissue between the two sections. The cumulative effect, we hope, is a vision of rhetoric, philosophy, and psychoanalysis as profoundly implicated in each other's dramatic machinery. If rhetoric and psychoanalysis stage "other scenes" of what might otherwise be deemed properly philosophical inquiry, this interdisciplinary reverberation invites us to develop new modes of theoretical choreography for bringing these still too siloed worlds together. We hope that our book gestures provocatively in this direction.

Part I: Adleman on Burke's Uptake of Freud

Chapter One examines Burke's admiration of Freud as a para-rhetorical thinker. Burke appropriates Freud's concepts of the unconscious and free association, which he adopts and adapts for the purpose of rhetorical analysis. Even though Burke criticizes Freud for occasionally deviating from his own prescriptions when it comes to facilitating free association, Adleman contends that the full scope of Freud's influence on the new rhetoric has yet to be addressed.

Chapter Two explores Kenneth Burke's slippery concepts of "attitude" and "symbolic action," which draw a great deal of inspirational sustenance from Freud's work. Connecting Burke's work with contemporary writing on the rhetoric of health and medicine, Adleman interrogates Judy Segal's analysis of hypochondria as a "rhetorical disorder" and positions it as one of many theoretical tributaries primed for convergence with psychoanalytic pathways.

Chapter Three conducts an investigation into Burke's co-optation of Freud's concept of "identification." After undertaking a survey of Burke's modification of Freud's theories of identification, Adleman looks at Burke's psychoanalytically informed employment of identification, disidentification, and the scapegoat mechanism in his 1939 close-reading of Hitler's *Mein Kampf*. Adleman then brings some of Burke's critical rhetorical-psychoanalytic optics to bear on some of Donald Trump's scattershot rhetorical strategies. While it would be obtuse to merely label Trump as a fascist, many of his tropes and emphases resonate as aspirationally fascistic (or, as Burke might say, "fascioid").

Chapter Four highlights Freud's influence on Burke's concepts of "orientation," "trained incapacity," and "occupational psychosis." Bringing these ideas into conversation with Burke's ideas about "debunking" and "conspiracy," Adleman looks at the persuasive appeal of QAnon, a modern-day conspiracy theory that figures Donald Trump as a messianic figure poised to rescue America from a nefarious liberal plot.

Part II: *Vanderwees on the Rhetorical Dimensions of Psychoanalysis*

Chapter Five looks at the preconditions of psychoanalysis in the French clinic of Jean-Martin Charcot. Charcot's employment of photography to document his patients' symptoms emerged out of his misdirected privileging of "objective" evidence-gathering over their personal accounts of their suffering. Vanderwees documents Freud's transition away from the visual register of "scientific" photography to the acoustic register of the psychoanalytic clinic, where patients were encouraged to be eloquent about their suffering as analysts listened attentively to their free associations.

Chapter Six puts what Vanderwees calls Freud's "listening rhetoric" under the microscope in order to assess the Freudian interpretive model. While Freud models what Vanderwees refers to as a pivotal "close listening" practice (echoing the new-critical "close-reading" strategies), organized around attending to nuances of patients' utterances, other more contemporary approaches to psychology advocate for what they view as the positive role of empathy and affect in clinical counselling. Vanderwees assesses the merits of these various schools of thought.

Chapter Seven zeroes-in on Jacques Lacan's idiosyncratic rhetorical practice and his pioneering thoughts about the rhetorical tradition's relevance to psychoanalysis. While Lacan does not seem to have been aware of Burke's body of work, Vanderwees argues that his well-theorized approach to the rhetoric of psychoanalysis reverberates with many vectors of Burke's new rhetoric.

Notes

1 Derrida's "Plato's Pharmacy" was originally published in the French journal *Tel Quel* in 1968 and later collected in *Dissemination* in 1972. Barbara Johnson's English translation of *Dissemination* was published in 1983.

2 Taking issue with Adorno and Horkheimer's disparagement of Odysseus' technoscientific self-vivisection, media philosopher Peter Sloterdijk lauds him as the archetypical suave Greek orator, the resourceful Gorgiastic man of many devices. See "Odysseus the Sophist: On the Birth of Philosophy from the Spirit of Travel Stress" in *What Happened in the Twentieth Century*.

3 Freud and Jung travelled to New York to deliver lectures on psychoanalysis in 1909. This was Freud's one and only trip to the United States. Roudinesco, however, has called Lacan's anecdote into question: "I have been able to ascertain that Freud never spoke these words and that Jung, if he did tell Lacan, never said it to anyone else. It is well known that Jung was a considerable confabulator who devoted some of his time to inventing anecdotes which corresponded so well with reality that many were fooled by them. It was Roland Cahen who introduced Lacan to Jung so he could hear his memories of Freud. As a matter of fact, every historian has established that, on his arrival in the United States, all Freud said was: 'They will be surprised when they hear what we have to say'" ("Lacan, the Plague" 232).

4 Luce Irigaray and Jacques Derrida each accuse psychoanalysis (as well as philosophy) of "phallogocentrism" insofar as it privileges masculine constructions of knowledge.

5 For instance, Freud writes in *On Aphasia* that "[t]he relationship between the chain of physiological events in the nervous system and mental processes is probably not one of cause and effect. The former do not cease when the latter set in; they tend to continue, but, from a certain moment, a mental phenomenon corresponds to each part of the chain, or to several parts. The psychic is therefore a process parallel to the physiological, a 'dependent concomitant'" (55).

6 It is estimated that Freud wrote about 20,000 letters across his lifetime (Roudinesco 2).

7 See Roudinesco's *Freud: In His Time and Ours* (2016).

8 Philosopher Tom Rockmore (1942–), who has defended a constructivist view on epistemology, suggested that one might easily resist the idea that there is one science, "the science," or one form of cognitive objectivity. He challenges Popper's notion of refutability and the idea of scientific objectivity: "it is unclear that science need be falsifiable in any obvious way. ... in recent years antipositivist philosophy of science has decisively undermined the very idea that a scientific theory can be refuted. If we take the analytic philosophical attack on empiricism seriously, then it becomes very unclear how objective claims to know differ from the fact that they are accepted by the relevant practitioners of a particular domain .... As concerns psychoanalysis, and in particular dream interpretation, claims to know arise out of and are tested within the interaction between the analyst and the analysand, between the interpretation and the source of relevant information. The analyst needs to bring the proposed reading of the material in line with the material already reported and with any other material that may be reported. Objectivity in this situation means nothing more than a basic agreement between the analytic reconstruction of psychic reality and psychic reality as mainly revealed in the patient's free associations" (Rockmore 30).

9 German-born British psychologist Hans Jürgen Eysenck (1916–1997) also emerged as one of the most prolific twentieth-century critics of psychoanalysis. Eysenck attempted to measure personality and intelligence but was also one of

the fiercest critics of Freud. Eysenck wrote dozens of books and hundreds of articles, which for many years made him one of the most cited psychologists of all time only rivalled in citations by Jean Piaget and Freud (Haggbloom et al. 142). His most notable critiques of psychoanalysis appear in *The Uses and Abuses of Psychology* (1953) and in *Decline and Fall of the Freudian Empire* (1985), in which he writes that "[a]ll sciences have to pass through an ordeal by quackery. Astronomy had to separate itself from astrology; chemistry had to slough off the fetters of alchemy. The brain sciences had to disengage themselves from the tenets of phrenology (the belief that one could read the character of a man by feeling the bumps on his head). Psychology and psychiatry, too, will have to abandon the pseudo-science of psychoanalysis; their adherents must turn their backs on Freud and his teaching, and undertake the arduous task of transforming their discipline into a genuine science. This is clearly not an easy task, but it is a necessary one, and short cuts are not likely to prove of lasting value … He was, without doubt, a genius, not of science, but of propaganda, not of rigorous proof, but of persuasion, not of the design of experiments, but of literary art. His place is not, as he claimed, with Copernicus and Darwin, but with Hans Christian Andersen and the Brothers Grimm, tellers of fairy tales" (207–208). Eysenck highlights the rhetorical persuasiveness of Freud through storytelling, publicity, and literature. The scientific validity of Eysenck's own work has more recently been heavily questioned, discredited, and redacted. Following an extensive enquiry conducted at Kings College London, Eysenck's own work has since garnered accusations of data manipulation, misconduct, and racism.

10　Popper writes that "[t]his does not mean that Freud and Adler were not seeing certain things correctly: I personally do not doubt that much of what they say is of considerable importance, and may well play its part one day in a psychological science which is testable. But it does mean that those 'clinical observations' which analysts naïvely believe confirm their theory cannot do this any more than the daily confirmations which astrologers find in their practice" (Popper 49). See Ricoeur's *Freud and Philosophy: An Essay on Interpretation* (1970) for his discussion of the "school of suspicion" and Rita Felski's further exploration of the "hermeneutics of suspicion" in *The Uses of Literature* (2008).

11　See Misra, who discusses the attempts to create scientific controls and outcome research for psychoanalysis: "While the outcome of short-term psychoanalytical therapy is on par with cognitive behaviour therapy and/or interpersonal therapy, etc. the effect of long-term psychoanalytical therapy has been found to be consistently superior to other forms of therapy even after as long an interval as 6.7 years" (172).

12　Even "scientific" psychology has found itself embroiled in what many researchers now refer to as the "replication crisis" (or "reproducibility crisis"), which has raised questions about the field's own status as a science since the early 2010s. The ongoing methodological problem has grown within psychology insofar as many scientific studies have been deemed challenging or impossible to reproduce (Wiggins and Christopherson 214). The replication crisis denotes current debates surrounding possible methodological, statistical, and philosophical reforms within psychology as well as epistemological re-evaluations taking place across the "social sciences." "Remediating these matters [of the reproducibility crisis]," writes Jill Morawski, "is complicated by the fact that there remains no consensus on the roots of the problems or even whether they are problems at all" (219).

13　Lacan's defiant psychoanalytic discourse, introduction of the variable length session, and other deviations from the "standard frame" led to his excommunication from the International Psychoanalytic Association and his formation of his own school of analysis. He described psychoanalytic teaching as "thought in motion": "This kind of teaching is a refusal of any system. It uncovers a thought in motion – nonetheless vulnerable to systematisation, since it necessarily possesses a dogmatic aspect. Freud's thought is the most perennially open to revision. It is a mistake to reduce it to a collection of hackneyed phrases. Each of his ideas possesses a vitality of its own. That is precisely what one calls the dialectic" (1).

14 In a scathing critique of scientific discourse as it pertains to psychoanalysis, Lacan claims, "[I]t is not pointless to recall here that the discourse of science, insofar as it commends itself by its objectivity, neutrality, and dreariness, even of the Sulpician variety, is just as dishonest and ill-intentioned as any other rhetoric" ("Appendix II: Metaphor of the Subject" 758).

1 The Rhetorical Unconscious
Reconciling Rival Topographies

A survey of Kenneth Burke's scattered statements about the prejudices seemingly baked into psychoanalysis might lead a casual reader to assume that he was ill-disposed towards Freud and Freudian thought. In his particularly sardonic account of the socio-historical genesis of different psychological frameworks, for example, he observes that Freud's vocabulary, like Plato's, is overdetermined by its historical and geographical political coordinates. Drawing heavily on the philosophical-psychological writings of John Dewey, Burke points out that "Plato formulated the sensuously acquisitive portion of the mind after the analogy of the mercantile class, his picture of the 'spirited' faculty corresponded to the citizen-soldiers, while the 'reason' was patterned after the group empowered to make the laws" (*PC* 174). Freud's increasingly pessimistic theoretical frameworks were, by the same token, caught up in a certain "psychosis of the Strauss Waltz" on account of their provenance out of a moribund Austro-Hungarian scene, whose repressed denizens had "for many years, accommodated themselves to imperial decay" (*PC* 174).

When it comes to Aristotle's *Rhetoric*, on the other hand, Burke seems to believe that the ideas contained within this ancient text have an almost timeless quality:

> I find it regrettable that social scientists automatically ignore Aristotle's *Rhetoric*. I don't say Aristotle has given us the last word on these matters. But I submit that his actual treatment of topics is fundamentally correct. You could add new topics and develop accordingly. But what you got 2,000 years ago was the kind of approach that can be built on in principle.
>
> ("Dramatism" 327)

This piquant, but arguably unfair, contrast alone could precipitate an array of analyses juxtaposing these two infrequently compared disciplines. After all, there is a surplus of shared substance between Plato's psychological triad (*logos*, *eros*, and *thymos*), Freud's "second topography" (ego, id, and super-ego), and Aristotle's *pistis*, or "artistic" rhetorical devices (logos, pathos,

DOI: 10.4324/9781003214069-2

and ethos). Feminist Lacanian scholar Alicia Valdés has even gone so far as to suggest that there are profound homologies between Aristotle's three *pistis* and Lacan's Imaginary, Real, and Symbolic registers (Valdés 93). For Burke to pathologize Freud's paradigm while positing Aristotle's as nearly perfect bespeaks his own predilections more than anything else.

In spite of his lionization of Aristotle over Freud, Burke went to great lengths to integrate and interlace both classical rhetorical and psychoanalytic concepts into his new rhetoric. While he routinely expresses concerns about some of what he views as psychoanalysis' excesses, he is also quick to point out his indebtedness to Freud, whose approach to dreams and humour Burke repeatedly figures as quasi-rhetorical. His immense respect for Freud's innovative reading practice leads Burke to integrate psychoanalytic concepts and methods into the new rhetoric. Instead of merely juxtaposing or hierarchizing classical rhetoric and psychoanalysis, Burke strives to bring Freudian thought into the expansive new-rhetorical fold in a manner that brings out within both disciplines that which is more than themselves. Expressing frustration with contemporary rhetoricians' aversion to exploring Freud's influence on Burke's interpretative methods, Ellen Quandahl contends that "Burke both imitates and transforms Freud's practices of reading and extends the scope of their usefulness" (Quandahl 637).

The cumulative effect of Burke's transformative uptake of Freud is that it can become difficult to discern where psychoanalysis ends and rhetoric begins within his formidable new-rhetorical edifice. At times, Burke characterizes the two disciplines as though they radiate out of different sides of the same shared substance. For instance, in *A Rhetoric of Motives*, he reframes Freud's second topography as an intra-psychic "exact analogue" of a rhetorical situation: "The ego with its id confronts the superego much as an orator would confront a somewhat alien audience, whose susceptibilities he must flatter as a necessary step towards persuasion." Freud's vision of the human psyche, avers Burke, "is quite a parliament, with conflicting interests expressed in ways variously designed to take the claims of rival factions into account" (*ARM* 38). As we will explore in subsequent chapters, the trope of the fraught parliamentary wrangle resurfaces throughout his oeuvre. The parliament is, for Burke, a charged synecdoche for both the political messiness of liberal democracy and the philosophical messiness of rhetoric.

Of course, Freud is so much more than a para-rhetorical theorist for Burke. In *The Philosophy of Literary Form*, he refers to his lifelong fascination with Freud's work and the significance of his innovations. Freud's writing, he writes, is "suggestive almost to the point of bewilderment," and he imagines writing annotations in the margins of Freud's texts. Sometimes these notes would be "straight extensions of his own thinking. At other times they would be attempts to characterize his strategy of presentation with reference to interpretative method in general." Finally, "there would be glosses attempting to suggest how far the literary critic should go along with Freud and what extra-Freudian material he would have to add" (*PLF* 391) since the psychoanalytic legislature is one among a cacophony of echo chambers that hound the symbol-using, symbol-misusing animal.

Because "the Freudian perspective was developed primarily to chart a psychiatric field rather than an aesthetic one" (*PLF* 391), Burke is concerned about the potential for pedantic literary critics to uncritically adopt psychoanalytic optics and apply them to literary concerns. He certainly comes by this concern honestly. His reservations about such heavy-handed applications echo I.A. Richards' biting comments on Freud's analyses of da Vinci and Jung's analysis of Goethe. Psychoanalysts, writes Richards, "tend to be peculiarly inept as critics" (Richards 30). Writing at a time when psychoanalytic criticism was starting to gain traction in literary circles, Richards criticized psychoanalytic critics for overstepping their proper bailiwick when engaging in analyses of an artist's psychic state based on the attributes of their artistic works. Eager to redirect criticism to the contours of the work of art rather than the person that created it, Richards insists that "speculations as to what went on in the artist's mind are unverifiable" (Richards 30). The artist's psyche simply remains inaccessible to such psychologizing readings. But, perhaps more importantly, the psychology of the artist is largely beside the point for adroit artistic criticism, which should hinge on close reading practices and a sensitivity to the nuances of the work of art and its situation in the world. In this regard, Richards' approach to literary analysis, in particular, is much closer to the New Criticism of Cleanth Brooks, who advocated for an approach to literary criticism that respected the autonomy of the work of art above and beyond biographical details about the author (or the reader, for that matter).

While Burke is sensitive to the pitfalls of the intentional fallacy (i.e. speculating about the author's intentions and state of mind), he nonetheless regards Freud's architectonic as invaluable to the new rhetoric. He therefore treats psychoanalysis as though it is a kindred discipline of rhetoric and literary studies. The Freudian *oeuvre*, in Burke's hands, must be viewed as a "science of the grotesque" (*PLF* 392) and an imaginative literary edifice in its own right:

> Confronting this, Freud does nonetheless advance to erect a structure which, if it lacks beauty, has astounding ingeniousness and fancy. It is full of paradoxes, of leaps across gaps, of vistas-much more so than the work of many a modern poet who sought for nothing else but these and had no search for accuracy to motivate his work. These qualities alone would make it unlikely that readers literarily inclined could fail to be attracted, even while repelled.
>
> (*PLF* 392)

Freud's theoretical and speculative writings are so saturated with tropes, narratives, cognitive leaps, and counter-intuitive perspectives that they ought to be recognized as such and taken to heart by new-rhetorical thought. Robert Wess observes that Burke, who is always fundamentally interested in the resources of eloquence, discovers in Freud "a new kind of eloquence, the eloquence of the dream" (Wess 105). In Burke's agile hands, a zone of indeterminacy between rhetoric and psychoanalysis emerges to articulate nothing short of a poetics of the unconscious and human motivation.

Asymptomatic Symbolic Action

At an invited lecture before the American Psychological Association, Burke posits a meeting of minds between rhetoric and psychoanalysis. He begins with a dazzling exposition on what he views as the primary (more or less Aristotelian) registers of the symbolic order: logical, rhetorical, poetic, and ethical. He writes,

> Language, in its logical dimension, ranges from factual accuracy to the most highly generalized principles of self-consistency. In its rhetorical dimension, it ranges from simple acts of persuasion to complex cultural "myths" which help identify the individual with his group and thereby promote social cooperation. In its poetical dimension, language ranges from the rudimentary self-expressive outcry to the great epics, tragedies, and the like, which are enjoyed in and for themselves, for the delight in the vigorous exercise of human utterance, undertaken for its own sake, for sheer love of the art. And in its ethical dimension, language is the portrait of a personality—for whether he wills it so or not, a man's language must somehow name his number, his role, ranging from intimate family relationships to his identity with regard to class, nation, church, avocations, and the like.
>
> ("Symbol and Association" 212)

These registers correspond to Aristotelian categories of "truth, expediency, beauty, and goodness (or 'character')" ("Symbol and Association" 212). Even though "no instance of language would fall exclusively under any single one of these heads, which are not mutually exclusive, ... the four do seem to cover the ground, and are a handy empirical way of dividing up the field" ("Symbol and Association" 212).

He then brings attention to the concept of "symbolic action," which he has borrowed from Freud. In *The Psychopathology of Everyday Life*, Freud theorizes a neurotic mechanism that he refers to interchangeably as "symptomatic action" and "symbolic action." Seemingly innocuous accidents (*parapraxes*), Freud speculates, often have their origin in unconscious conflicts that seek out expression in the subject's behaviour. As an exemplary instance of such symptomatic expressions, he provides the case study of a woman who has wounded the cuticle of her left ring finger while cutting her nails on her wedding day. After guiding her through a labyrinth of associations, he helps her discover that her supposed accident was bound up with concerns about her "left-handed marriage" (*Psychopathology* 126), a turn of phrase used to characterize marriages between people of unequal social rank. Her unconscious communication, in the form of an act of self-laceration, was merely caught up in the undulations of the Strauss Waltz and awaited psychoanalytic interpretation and translation into the vernacular of everyday life.

With an interest in adopting and adapting Freud's terminology, Burke is quick to assert that "the word 'symbolic' itself can be misleading" ("Symbol" 213) because almost any word or action is suffused with symbols. "To speak of [the human being] as the 'typically symbol-using animal' in this sense is to mean that, once [a person] has emerged from the state of infancy, [their] approach to things is through a fog of words (or, if you will, [the symbol-using animal] comes to see things in the light of words)" ("Symbol" 213). In this regard, "any language (or arts such as painting, sculpture, music), could be called forms of 'symbolic action'" ("Symbol" 213), but that is not to say that it is necessarily symptomatic of a neurotic conflict; and even when behaviour is, to a certain extent, symptomatic, such analyses stand to benefit from recognizing the abyssal network of suasive forces at play in the broader symbolic milieu. Such an approach would be sensitive to the symbolic miasmas through which the symbol-using animal interprets and navigates its way through the world. Perhaps Burke's most significant divergence from Freud's concept of symbolic action resides in his emphases. While Freud underscores the unconscious intentionality of erroneous actions and other symptomatic expressions, Burke redirects the focus to the (often unconscious) symbolic actions performed at the other end of the cacophonous parliament, the utterance's orientation towards actual and imagined recipients, its audiences.

Still, Freud's own methods are of paramount importance in navigating the fog of symbols and motivations. Burke points out that, in *The Psychopathology of Everyday Life*, Freud advises those interested in tracing the symbolic import of seemingly accidental behaviours to privilege "the greater importance of associations" ("Symbol" 213) over the rigid imposition of a-priori interpretations. Sometimes, however, Freud himself would seem to fall short of heeding his own advice by insisting on overdetermined symbolic couplings rather than listening for the expanded network of associations that may come to bear on patients' dreams, slips of the tongue, and jokes. Thus, "when Freud says, for instance, that King and Queen in a dream represent the dreamer's parents, a room symbolizes a woman, a hat the male genitals, etc."

("Symbol" 215), he may overstep the proper domain of psychoanalytic symbol application. Nonetheless, Burke concludes, more than a little facetiously, "It is not within my province to dispute such interpretations even if I wanted to. I am simply recalling that Freud himself places the major emphasis on association" ("Symbol" 215). What is of paramount importance for Burke is that rhetoricians import Freud's lexicon in a nimble manner that evades the pitfalls of an overly dogmatic equation of signifiers with predetermined meanings.

Burke then expounds on the strengths and weaknesses of an associative approach to literary criticism. When critics undertake a sustained study of, say, a novel, poem, or even a literary genre, he writes,

> the tracking down of terministic correlations may take us far afield. We may get lost again and again in the labyrinthine reticulations that we discover, as soon as we systematically try tracing a term through its many contexts in a given writer's work; for we soon begin to recognize other terms that tend to recur along with it, and the charting of such secondary radiations can become exasperatingly complex. But we need not ultimately fear, since as regards these procedures we can always begin anew—for the internal relations among the terms of a work are permanently there, in fixed order, an order that makes them simultaneously a physiologically growing thing and a dead body anatomized.
>
> ("Symbol" 216)

In the process of tracking associative cobwebs, the astute literary critic will begin to discover "how the terms for natural things, for social relations, for personal attitudes, and for the mysterious or supernatural, become vibrantly interactive ... [as] psychology and literary analysis come together without confusion" ("Symbol" 216). That is to say that Burke does not wish to disavow the symbol-using animal's libidinal economy so much as recognize its constitutive entanglement with the symbolic field that constitutes its ambient atmosphere.

Gesturing to applications in domains beyond the individual psyche, Burke points out that his approach to commingling psychoanalysis and rhetoric could be deployed to improve rhetorical criticism's engagement with entire schools of writers. For instance, a rhetorician will recognize that in a certain school of thought or literary genre, "'reason' may be equated with obedience to authority or with distrust of authority, or the relation between stability and change may be 'personalized' as a distinction between 'masculine' reason and 'feminine' sentiment, or some such" ("Symbol" 216). After all, any such symbolic coupling is necessarily "loaded with social implications, as regards attitudes and corresponding programs of action" ("Symbol" 216–217). On this hybrid rhetorical-psychoanalytic matter, Burke levels his critical gaze on Freud and some of his followers for their own ideological capture within the Freudian "Strauss Waltz," which occasionally orients them towards an overhasty "equat[ion] of 'masculine' with 'active' and of 'feminine' with 'passive'" (217).

The potential for conflict between these two approaches, free association and pre-designated symbolic equations (such as the pigeonholing of femininity as passivity), leads Burke to wonder out loud, "Might each have implicit in it a mode of thought quite alien to the other? And if we consistently worked out the implications of each, might we arrive at two quite different, and even contrasting, views of reality?" ("Symbol" 217). One such rhetorical-psychoanalytic cluster that merits scrutiny, avers Burke, is the Father-King-God triad, which could be organized and interpreted according to either method:

> Obviously, they can be interrelated, since each in its way represents a principle of authority. Yet there are two quite different ways of dealing with the relationship among these terms. We might class all three of them as different species of a common genus (as I did in effect when I said that each in its way represents a principle of authority, "authority" thus standing for the element they shared in common, however different might be the particular kind of authority that distinguished each). Or we might treat one of them (say, the first), as primary, while considering the other two as derivatives or "projections" of it. Freud is clearly using this latter method when he says, "Even fate is, in the last resort, only a later father-projection"; or when he says: "Even in later years, if the Emperor and Empress appear in dreams, these exalted personages stand for the dreamer's father and mother" (a statement which, if interpreted strictly, would seem to indicate that one could not possibly dream about the Emperor and the Empress in their own right).
>
> ("Symbol" 217–218)

Burke does not go so far as to suggest that it is inherently incorrect to view emperors and deities as quasi-parental figures. But, seemingly anticipating Deleuze and Guattari's later complaints about psychoanalysis' paralysis within "the depths of the Oedipal triangle" (Deleuze and Guattari 15), he is concerned that pigeonholing them as such deprives analyses of access to the broader surfeit of associations that might reveal itself through the symbolic haze.

One such instance of overstep, according to Burke, transpires in some of Freud's literary analyses. When he applies an overdetermined hierarchy of signifiers to literary texts, Freud sometimes falls short of heeding his own advice about according primacy to the associative method. In the particularly glaring example of Freud's analysis of Dostoevsky, he attempts to apply a narrow psychoanalytic schema to the Russian author's motivations, as expressed in his fiction. In "Dostoevsky and Parricide," Freud diagnoses Dostoevsky, whom he never met, as a neurotic masochist who transposes his primary relationship with his father onto the tyrannical Tsar. Burke is especially critical of Freud's reduction of "the tremendous reality of Tsarist power to terms of a hypothetical unconscious desire on Dostoevsky's part to have participated in the killing of his murdered father" ("Symbol" 217). According to Freud's reading of Dostoevsky's coeval fiction and life, when the Russian author accepted punishment from the Tsar, his ersatz father, he was merely substituting Tsar's draconian judgement for the punishment he felt he deserved, and masochistically desired, at the hands of his biological father. This ossified psychoanalytic line of interpretation gives Burke pause because it seems to obstruct Freud from opening up to the broader historical context and "see[ing] in the realities of the Tsarist State sufficient reasons for Dostoevsky to feel like making peace with it if he could" ("Symbol" 217).

A more fruitful line of interpretation, Burke suggests, emerges out of taking Freud's original advice seriously and engaging more associatively with the Father-King-God triad. This, however, leads Burke to, once again, risk trespassing on psychoanalytic territory when he implores his audience to consider the possibility that Freud is too quick to attribute primordial status to the figure of the father over the other members of the triad, which "are said to be symptomatic surrogates for it" ("Symbol" 217). Interestingly, Burke begins by engaging in a classical rhetorical tactic, securing a measure of common ground with his would-be opponents, and articulates his measured critique in the same breath as he accords Freud his due: "Freud's hypothesis that the father is so primary, or 'primal,' that in contemporary relations between fathers and sons there is the 'echo' of a 'monstrous event,' the account of which is 'found in myths'" ("Symbol" 218), of the primal horde's convergence on the father chieftain. "Even granting this hypothesis," writes Burke, "might we not at least allow the king an existence in his own right, until deposed and replaced not by a father but by a president or some kind of super-commissar, who would exist in his own right?" ("Symbol" 218).

Even Freud would likely have to concede this point. Associatively decoupling the figure of the king from the putatively more primordial figure of the father accommodates understandings of the symbol-using animal's political circumstances above and beyond their Oedipal mooring. The king may be the nation's paternal signifier par excellence, but his dominion and manifold relationship to his subjects are so vast and idiosyncratic that they call for fine-grained analyses on their own terms. And Burke's insight applies as readily to the presence of this signifier in a psychoanalytic session as it does to its representation in works of narrative fiction.

The *Parverse* Resources of Language

Burke then zooms out and applies Freud's avowed associative approach
to the notion of God. It may well be, speculates Burke, that, *pace* Freud's
assertions in books like *The Birth of the Illusion*, the idea of God does
not necessarily derive from the idea of the father but rather "fulfils the
natural genius of language, which allows for terms of ever greater and
greater generalization, until we arrive at some term of terms, or title of
titles, that is thought to sum up the essence of things" ("Symbol" 219).
This "natural genius of language," which he refers to elsewhere as its
"entelechial" function, enlists the imagination to run with immediately
intelligible notions and take them to their extreme limits. In this case,
the religious imagination is often predisposed to scale up from empirically perceptible authority figures, such as parents, in order to construct
hallucinatory omnipotent, omniscient ones, like the gods that populate
so many religious traditions.

That, across world religions, such deities are often represented as her-
maphroditic evinces for Burke the possibility that the parental function
often serves as a more salient empirical touchstone to authority than
the paternal half of the equation. "Reduce the idea of 'god' to the idea
of 'parenthood,' then reduce the idea of 'parenthood' to terms of *sexual
imagery*, and *androgynous ambiguities* seem unescapable" ("Symbol" 220),
writes Burke. This seemingly "parental" transgender, rather than paternal, trope even surfaces right under Freud's nose in the androgynous
figure of the dreaded sphinx, whose riddle Oedipus solves on his route
to discovering that the world is a far more bewildering place than he had
ever imagined. The fact that parents temporally precede deities in the
psychic lives of young minds does not, however, suggest that all preoccupations with the gods are necessarily symptomatic of pathologies pertaining to their parents. The mind may be a far more resourceful artificer
than even Freud gives it credit for.

Burke then finishes his examination of the rhetorical tendencies of
language by applying it to other psychoanalytically charged topics. In
some instances, he suggests, these linguistic proclivities might be more
entelechial, and their provenance less neurotic, than Freud supposes. On
the topic of the occurrence of incest-related tropes in infantile ideation
and classical myth cycles, Burke proposes that this association occasionally emerges out of the naive ambiguation of different forms of love in the
infantile imagination. There is, for Burke, a potentially innocent version
of the toddler's desire to marry their parent, as this association can be
a function of their oblivious confusion about the different categories of
love in which adults engage. The flipside of infantile polymorphous per-
versity may be that there is also what we might characterize as an intersecting *amorphous parversity*, a comparatively nebulous and unperverse
cathexis in parents and other proximal figures, that does not always play

out along the precise libidinal lines envisioned by Freud. Nevertheless, unlike Jung, who seeks to replace the primacy of the erotic in Freud's thought with universal mystical archetypes, Burke does not purport to understand the true hierarchy of motives or even suggest that such a hierarchy can be divined. Rather, he seeks to complexify the picture by introducing rhetorical and linguistic motives into the Freudian parliament and forcing them to cohabitate in the fog of words and desires. Just as Lacan routes the Freudian unconscious through Saussure, Lévi-Strauss, and Heidegger, Burke conducts it through the likes of Aristotle, Cicero, and Augustine. Sadly, disciplinary inertia has largely prevented these two Copernican revolutions from being brought into contact with each other's orbits.

By the same token, sometimes the idea of parricide may be far from symptomatic of neurotic conflict. The "most thoroughly dramatic image" of the rejection of authority is the murder of an immediate authority figure. "And would not such a kill in turn be most thoroughly imagined as a murder of the first and foremost authority that the growing child had personally experienced? Whereat, you arrive at parricide" ("Symbol" 224). This personalization of abstraction may derive from deep-seated Oedipal motives. But it can also recrudesce out of the broader linguistic motives that ceaselessly animate the symbol-using, symbol-misusing, symbol-inventing animal in its forays through the obstacle-strewn human barnyard.

Freud's associative method and his concept of symbolic action inspire Burke to view the Oedipus myth as a narrative about so much more than parricide and incest. At the end of his article, he shines a quasi-Lacanian light on the subject's accession to and fraught relationship with the symbolic order: "Freud was concerned above all," according to Burke, "with the bepuzzlements that beset this [symbol-using] animal, in its development from infancy (a condition somewhat analogous to the speechlessness of other animals) into the realm of verbal articulacy (and its particular kinds of symbolic manipulation)" ("Symbol" 224). This socio-symbolic obstacle course invites rhetoricians and psychoanalysts alike to recall that the symbol-using animal is arguably much uncannier than even the fictional sphinx. Echoing Heidegger's reading of *Antigone* in *Introduction to Metaphysics*, Burke insists that the human being remains far and away the strangest of all creation. He therefore invites his interlocutors to attune themselves to the "sphinxlike riddles generated by [...] the change from infancy, animal speechlessness, to mature animal verbalizing" ("Symbol" 224).

Invoking Freud's later work in books like *Civilization and its Discontents*, he switches gears to dwell on the dire stakes of our inability to wander deftly through the fog of symbols, which is also a fog of war. Many sphinx-like "mysteries must be slain (or must be goaded by humble methodic pride, in pious impiousness, to slay themselves)," concludes Burke, so that people "can hope to cease goading one another, and being goaded by one another, to the tragically wasteful slaying of one another" ("Symbol" 224). Such a transformation necessitates a heightened sensitivity to the autonomous capacity of symbols to effect symbolic actions that are altogether deleterious to our well-being and may even fly in the face of our conscious intentions.

Over the next several chapters, we will explore key Burkean concepts like symbolic action, attitude, identification, and orientation with a view to unpacking both their psychoanalytic resonances and their underappreciated import for rhetorical theory.

2 Burke's Little Affect A

In A *Rhetoric of Motives*, Burke conducts a virtuosic survey of traditional theories of persuasion and famously concludes that rhetoric "is rooted in an essential function of language itself, a function that is wholly realistic, and is continually born anew; the use of language as a symbolic means of inducing cooperation in beings that by nature respond to symbols" (*ARM* 43). In order to articulate the extent to which "beings that by nature respond to symbols" are porous to perturbations in their symbolic milieu, he makes use of Freud's concept of "symbolic action" alongside another psychoanalytically-charged term, "attitude." This chapter will explore the interplay of symbolic action and attitude in order to think through some of the implications of Burke's psychoanalytically-suffused taxonomy.

Burke's concept of "attitude" is an uncanny and versatile rhetorical notion. Like Jacques Lacan's *objet petit a* (the hallucinatory motor of desire), it betokens the decentred subject's embodied implication in dispersed socio-symbolic atmospheres. As such, attitude is hard to pin down. It is simultaneously intensely subjective and generically impersonal, affective and symbolic, active and abstruse. And, also apropos of *objet petit a*, it has a funny way of popping out of rhetorical frameworks meant to bring into relief the symbol-using animal's complicated relationship with the symbolic ether. This chapter will undertake an examination of some of the manifold implications of Burke's numinous concept of attitude, which finds application in the analysis of everything from the manner in which ideology inheres to texts to the moorings of "psychosomatic" maladies such as hypochondria.

Performativity by Other Means

At first blush, the co-optation of Freud's concept of "symbolic action" as a new-rhetorical concept seems especially curious given the extent to which Burke migrates it away from psychoanalysis' emphasis on the chorus of voices radiating out of the speaking subject. Whereas Freud's account of "symptomatic action" describes the articulation of unconscious ideas through the subject's seemingly accidental utterances and behaviours (which are construed as utterances by other means), Burke displaces the

DOI: 10.4324/9781003214069-3

disciplinary focus away from the speaking subject to the enveloping symbolic atmosphere and uses the term to describe the impacts that symbols have on audiences qua "beings that by nature respond to symbols." As he observes, his rhetorical reformulation of the coordinates of psychoanalytic "symbolic action" to focus on what symbols do – above and beyond what they mean or where they come from – anticipates J.L. Austin's much better-known concept of the "performative" utterance, language's "illocutionary" capacity to perform actions in the world.[1]

In *A Rhetoric of Motives*, Burke traces the roots of what, in critical theory circles, is usually referred to as "performativity," the power of language to effect change in the world. He locates the genesis of this approach to language not in twentieth-century language philosophy but in antecedent currents in rhetoric, anthropology, and psychoanalysis. An integral bond between these two quasi-philosophical doppelgangers (his own approach to symbolic action and the lineage emerging out of J.L. Austin's work), avers Burke, is their emphasis on language as fundamentally *addressed* to others, on whom it exercises a multiplicity of influences.[2]

Since Socrates first disparaged philosophy's rival discipline as merely a charismatic form of pandering to one's audience, the art of persuasion has received short shrift in truth-seeking philosophical quarters on account of its focus on effects and audiences over causes and essences. Burke responds rhetorically to the perennial philosophical critique of rhetorical pandering by identifying wholeheartedly with it: "Persuasion by flattery is but a special case of persuasion in general" (*ARM* 38). "True," he continues, "the rhetorician may have to change an audience's opinion in one respect; but he can succeed only insofar as he yields to that audience's opinions in other respects. Some of their opinions are needed to support the fulcrum by which he would move other opinions" (*ARM* 38). By simultaneously describing and demonstrating the persuasive merit of rhetorical "flattery," Burke self-consciously wields the symbolic action of his discourse. Above and beyond conveying the long-standing state of affairs in this unnecessarily partisan debate, he strives to win over some of the philosophically-oriented minds crouched on the proverbial fence about rhetoric's claims to disciplinary legitimacy within a dense symbolic atmosphere. In J.L. Austin's terms, Burke's discourse is simultaneously constative (i.e. descriptive of a state of affairs) and performative (i.e. directed towards a chain of effects in the world).

The pivotal role of language's nature as not only signifying (i.e. meaning things) but also addressing (i.e. calling out to others) is, for Burke, an integral matter of shared concern between rhetoric and psychoanalysis. "The best evidence of a strongly rhetorical ingredient in Freud's view of the psyche," writes Burke, "is in his analysis of *Wit and Its Relation to the Unconscious*":

> In particular, we think of Freud's concern with the role of an audience, or "third person," with whom the speaker establishes rapport, in their common enterprise directed against the butt of tendentious witticisms. Here is the purest rhetorical pattern: speaker and hearer as partners in

partisan jokes made at the expense of another. If you "internalize" such a variety of motives. So that the same person can participate somewhat in all three positions, you get a complex individual of many voices.

(*ARM* 38)

Freud distinguishes what he refers to as "tendentious" humour from its putatively "innocent" counterpart. Tendentious jokes are barbed in that they serve as rhetorically mediated vehicles for suppressed aggression and lust to bubble cathartically to the surface of everyday life. In this regard, they essentially obey the same *motivated* signifying logic as slips of the tongue and other seemingly erroneous "symptomatic" actions. But, of course, the role of enjoyment is arguably even thornier in the case of taboo humour. Freud underlines the role of "tendentious" racist and obscene humour in facilitating the safer simulated experience of dangerous urges. This rerouting of the taboo impulse through jokes enables the consolation prize of an ersatz orgasm in the form of laughter within the safe prophylaxis of, at least somewhat sublimated, discourse.

Burke highlights a rhetorically-salient aspect of tendentious humour: the extent to which these utterances are primordially addressed to an audience. Tendentious jokes are always already directed towards variably understanding interlocutors, whose real or imagined opinions and dispositions are internalized by the joking subject, who seeks out their complicity at the expense of the joke's target (who may or may not be interpellated into the audience as well). Like his Russian language philosopher contemporaries, Mikhail Bakhtin and Valentin Voloshinov (with whose work he was not familiar), Burke seizes on the fundamental addressivity of language. But whereas Bakhtin and Voloshinov treated psychoanalysis with suspicion, Burke mobilizes psychoanalysis as a resource for thinking about ubiquitous rhetorical address (or what Bakhtin calls "dialogism"): Freud's analysis of tendentious wit shines a light on the extent to which symbolic action never transpires in a vacuum; it is animatedly dialogical. Just as a loving couple is never really alone in the bedroom (on account of the spectral audiences occupying space in their respective heads), a quip made even to oneself is always intended for a diverse internalized audience (be they real or imagined interlocutors). It would come as no surprise to Burke, then, that this counter-solipsistic motif frequently makes its way into television sitcoms and video games, usually in the figure of the sardonic character who breaks "the fourth wall" by cracking a joke or making a wry facial expression that only the distal media audience can appreciate.

Watch the Attitude

Burke picked up the rudiments of his concept of attitude from twentieth-century rhetoric pioneer I.A. Richards, much of whose work served as an antecedent to and springboard for both the New Criticism and the new rhetoric. In *Principles of Literary Criticism* (1924), Richards offers up the term as what he characterizes as a more rhetorically astute tool for accomplishing what "unverifiable" psychoanalytic literary criticism seeks to accomplish. In many ways, Richards' effort to outdo psychoanalysis without having to engage directly with it anticipates twenty-first-century currents in affect theory, whose proponents, following in the steps of Gilles Deleuze and Félix Guattari, often demonstrate an ideological aversion to psychoanalysis while engaging in a remarkably analogous theoretical activity.[3]

Offering his own rhetorical doppelganger of psychoanalytic theory for the purpose of literary criticism, Richards characterizes the mind as a network of impulses (Richards 92). Stimuli, including symbolic stimuli, condense into "attitudes" or "incipient actions" that may culminate in a range of discrete actions in the world. Impulses constantly tug at the mind and come into conflict in a manner that distresses the individual. According to Richards' conservative quasi-Freudian model, the mind achieves a desired state of equilibrium only when pulsions can be consolidated and integrated into a broader cooperative psychic effort. But affective homeostasis is always provisional since every new disruption potentially short-circuits the entire psychic system, which must constantly recalibrate its apparatus to the new stimuli. For Richards, one of the paramount values of art is that it enables the mind to achieve a balance that would not otherwise be so readily achievable.

Burke, whose dispositions towards both art and the psyche are much less conservative, frequently acknowledges that Richards' conception of attitude as "incipient action" serves as the kernel of his own understanding of the term. He nevertheless scrambles the genealogy, insisting that a pre-existing tacit understanding of attitude crops up in the work of Cicero and Augustine, both of whom understand rhetoric as often influencing people in a much subtler manner than obtrusive inducement to perform a certain action. Citing Augustine's *De Doctrina Christiana*, he writes that a man should be considered persuaded if he

> likes what you promise, fears what you say is imminent, hates what you censure, embraces what you commend, regrets whatever you built up as regrettable, rejoices at what you say is cause for rejoicing, sympathizes with those whose wretchedness your words bring before his very eyes, shuns those whom you admonish him to shun ... and in whatever other ways your high eloquence can affect the minds of your hearers, bringing them not merely to know what should be done, but to do what they know should be done.
>
> (*ARM* 50)

This affective emphasis in Roman rhetoric leads Burke to conclude that the work of Cicero and Augustine serve as correctives to Richards'

formulation: "[W]e could with more accuracy speak of persuasion to attitude, rather than persuasion to out-and-out action" (*A Rhetoric* 50). Once
he removes discrete resulting actions from the frame, the resulting picture
of symbolic action is oriented towards our symbolic atmosphere's ambient,
ever-present capacity to modify attitudes by creating a prismatic array of
seemingly "internal" states that may not even be conscious or effable.
What Lacan refers to as the symbolic order's "extimate" (i.e. simultaneously external and intimate) status, the interpenetration of the psychic
"inside" and atmospheric symbolic "outside," renders it too proximal and
too ethereal to view from any remove. This, in part, explains why Burke's
conceptualization of attitude eludes circumscription: like McLuhan's proverbial goldfish, the symbol-using animal is awash in attitudes from which
it usually has negligible critical distance.

Stylized Attitudinal Traces

In *Attitudes Toward History*, Burke launches into his survey of the attitudes that inhere to literary, philosophical, political, economic, and
theological texts and suggests that acceptance, rejection, and passivity
be understood as primordial motivating dispositions. Anticipating later
currents in affect theory and new-rhetorical genre theory (which are
already somewhat strange bedfellows), he refuses to echolocate these attitudes exclusively within the mind of the symbol-using animal. Instead,
he displaces them into the symbolic environment in order to track their
activity in literary and theoretical texts. In this regard, the vocabular-
ies found in these texts crystallize attitudes, which reveal a strategy for
encompassing a situation:

> Our philosophers, poets, and scientist act in the code of names by
> which they simplify or interpret reality. These names shape our rela-
> tions with our fellows. They prepare us for some functions an against
> others, for or against the persons representing these functions. The
> names go further: they suggest how you shall be for against. Call a
> man a villain, and you have the choice of either attacking or cring-
> ing. Call him mistaken, and you invite yourself to attempt setting
> him right.
>
> (*AH* 4)

Our "literal" terms are redolent with attitudes. So too are our fictions.
A literary text can be understood as a "strategic" or "stylized" response
to the world through the genre of tragedy, satire, or fantasy. Richards'
notion of "incipient action" is therefore stretched to encompass the manner in which each text, which comes bundled with its own constellation
of tropes and situations, condenses an elaborate attitudinal frame for con-
struing and responding to a particular situation.

Burke's approach to attitudes as strategies that encompass situations also became the kernel of "new-rhetorical genre studies," the understanding of genres as a "stylized" form of social action that functions as a response to a rhetorical situation. New rhetorical genre theorist Carolyn Miller writes of Burke's influence, "If genre represents action, it must involve situation and motive, because human action, whether symbolic or otherwise, is interpretable only against a context of situation and through the attributing of motives. 'Motive' and 'situation' are Kenneth Burke's terms, of course" (Miller 152). New-rhetorical theorists like Miller, Amy Devitt, and Janet Giltrow pursue finer-grained understandings of genre beyond the perennial generic categories (like fantasy, romance, and horror) that are frequently reproduced in contemporary bookstores and streaming video platforms. Burkean approaches to genre conceive of it as less of an imperious category imposed from above than a dynamic form of symbolic action that emerges out of the typical strategies employed by those that participate in a particular discourse community. Whereas conventional approaches to genre focus on broad categories like science fiction and fantasy, new-rhetorical genre theory isolates more specific strategic responses to a rhetorical situation in subgenres such as "feminist utopian novels" of the 1970's (Teslenko) and turn-of-the-millennium "late-Oedipal narratives" (Adleman). This more fine-grained understanding of typified strategies leads Burkean genre theorists to reflect on the tacit conversations at play between texts (or utterances) that participate in the same genre or subgenre of discourse.

Attitude and Ideology

Burke's conception of rhetorical "attitude" does so much more than aid literary scholars in categorizing genres. It also functions as a touchstone to ideological prejudices. For instance, Burke proffers the writings of Aquinas and Marx as examples of discrepant condensed attitudes towards the fairness of an economic system predicated on a class hierarchy. While both thinkers recognized the injustice of a classed society, Aquinas' writings frame this predicament "as punishment for the fall of man." Therefore, writes Burke, "his frame was designed to accept the inevitability of classes, and to build a frame of action accordingly" (*AH* 20). Marx, on the other hand, "accepted the *need of eliminating classes*, [and] hence drew the line of battle differently" (*AH* 20–21). Burke contrasts these two attitudinal drifts with that of "passive" early bourgeois sentimentality as it broke out of the deadlock of feudalism: "Following comparative victory over the nobility, the bourgeois frame merely smeared the issue out of mind. It 'rejected' class morality by 'accepting' the doctrine that the resources of private initiative were equally available to all" (*AH* 21).

Tracking these attitudinal lines, Burke characterizes this more or less "passive" bourgeois entrepreneurial position towards a classed society as a precursor to present-day libertarianism. Entrepreneurial ideology, as promulgated by contemporary libertarian and conservative economic think tanks, fetishizes the freedom of mobility nominally distributed to anyone who wishes to levitate to a more elevated class echelon but tends to turn a blind eye to the political-economic obstacles impeding the equitable distribution of such liberties. The tension between these two models of freedom breaks down "terministically" in terms of two conflicting views of freedom: the liberty to pursue one's projects, on the one hand, and the freedom from the kinds of constraints that prohibit one from pursuing such projects in the first place, on the other. Burke's emphasis on the attitudes that permeate a particular understanding of empty signifiers sheds light on the ideological valences of discrepant mobilizations of a particular cluster of keywords (like "freedom" and "class"). The most significant difference between Burke and Lacan on this score resides in their emphases. Whereas Lacan focuses primarily on the orchestration of desire within a narrative fantasy frame, Burke levels his gaze on the political-rhetorical cauldron of attitudes that influence the seemingly inscrutable behaviours of symbol-using animals.

Hexing Attitude: Burke's Project Petit A

Attitude ultimately figures into a more networked understanding of motives in Burke's work. In *A Grammar of Motives*, Burke introduces his "dramatistic pentad" to discuss "what is involved, when we say what people are doing and why they are doing it" (*GM* xv). In order to attend to the elaborate network of relations bound up in attributing motives, he characterizes such situations as elaborate dramas: "You must have some word that names the act (names what took place, in thought or deed), and another that names the scene (the background of the act, the situation in which it occurred); also, you must indicate what person or kind of person (agent) performed the act, what means or instruments he used (agency), and the purpose" (*GM* xv). This dramaturgical grammar translates into "five questions: what was done (act), when or where it was done (scene), who did it (agent), how he did it (agency), and why (purpose)" (*GM* xv). Later, he adds "attitude" to the mix in order to render what was originally a pentad into a hexad. While attitude names something like the disposition that inheres to a particular scene, the hexad is Burke's name for the enveloping dramatistic network (or *dispositif*) that conducts or produces it.

The discussion of motives often resolves into what Burke refers to as pentadic (or hexadic) ratios, with one dramatistic element or another dominating the conversation at a given time. In his spectacular *Critical Inquiry* article on the import of the Burkean watershed, Wayne Booth writes that, amongst humanities and social sciences scholars, "Burke's 'dramatism' is increasingly recognized as something that must at least appear in one's index, whether one has troubled to understand him or not" ("Kenneth Burke's Way of Knowing" 2). The under-recognized potency of Burke's paradigm resides in its pliable applicability, as a form of ideological analysis, to most any system of thought. Symbolic actions "entail conflict, conflict entails drama, and drama entails the need for dramatistic terms for our analyses" ("Kenneth Burke's Way of Knowing" 10). Burke's dramatistic elements are "fluid reagents, applicable in different 'ratios' for different problems":

> What is one agent's action is another agent's scene. A given agent can be of someone else's agency—a tool to other ends—or he can be, again, a part of someone's scene. And we shall find that philosophies and critical theories can be classified and accommodated according to their proportionate emphasis on one or another of these and the ratios among them. Scene, for example, may be elevated by materialists to become the supreme and only agent. Agent may be elevated by some religionists into supreme agent, or turned, by pantheists, into supreme scene that is supreme agent.
>
> ("Kenneth Burke's Way of Knowing" 11)

Given the widespread uptake of the dramatistic frame theory developed by Burke's student Irving Goffman in sociological circles, Booth is incredulous that Burkean dramatism is still taken up only perfunctorily and superficially, even by rhetoricians. The pentadic ratios that are regularly reified and demonstrated in static cookie-cutter fashion in rhetoric classes are, in fact, dexterous symbolic tools that engender more potent associations than they are usually given credit for.

For instance, the agent/scene ratio is in evidence in Thomas Carlyle's influential "great man" theory of history, which underscores the world-historical role of prophets, artists, and political leaders in social transformations. A more contemporary version of this approach to the agent/scene ratio would have to add the pop-cultural hagiography of trailblazing entrepreneurial media icons like Steve Jobs, Oprah Winfrey, and Elon Musk to the list. This ratio also swings the other way to underscore the malign culpability of hubristic tycoons, as demonstrated by pervasive schadenfreude directed towards the apparent sociopathy of figures like recently disgraced Theranos founder Elizabeth Holmes and Republican lobbyist Jack Abramoff.

In contrast, a pentadic analysis of Marshall McLuhan's iconic assertion that "the medium is the message" (and "massage") sheds light on McLuhan's emphasis on the "agency" of technology, which also constitutes a technological "scene" that holds sway over any individual agent's purposes for it. For McLuhan, the media environment ultimately calls the tune that the great influencer dances to. Friedrich Kittler's version of technodeterminism is even more extreme. In works like *Discourse*

Networks 1800/1900, Kittler picks up on this thread and weights the pentadic ratio even more heavily on the side of technological agency, which, he avers, determines the arc of history and overrides the authority of even the most seemingly world-historical individual actors. As Francis Fergusson points out, Burke's framework "account[s] for the analogous schools of his time without dismissing any of them" (178). It thereby creates a malleable tableau for juxtaposing them "at once sympathetically and critically" (Fergusson 178) along a networked dramatistic plane.

Dramatism as Ideological Critique

As a method for grouping philosophies and ideologies, Burke's hexad sensitizes the rhetorical imagination to the simultaneously dramatistic and cybernetic dimensions of conceptual apparatuses. The sophisticated dramaturgy that begets and inheres to complex systems of thought then services ideological analysis in a myriad of unexpected ways. *A Grammar of Motives* is peppered with insightful analyses of the sophisticated manner in which different conceptual schemes (ranging from political ideologies to philosophical systems) reflect the world, select and illuminate certain elements, and thereby deflect attention away from other possible ways of perceiving and understanding it. In his account of Western reporting on the mid-century conflicts between German fascism and Soviet communism, he updates Aristotle's rhetorical manual on the issue of representing "the enemy." Unlike Aristotle, however, Burke's interest is not to instruct readers how to incite bellicose attitudes towards audiences' political rivals. As an educator in the "interpretation of interpretation," he seeks to equip cultural navigators with the aptitude to analyse the techniques that politicians and talking heads employ to render us susceptible to bellicosity in the first place.

Levelling his gaze on the dramatism of propaganda, Burke observes that during World War II, America's relationship with Germany and the Soviet Union was a remarkably delicate balancing act. Russia's fortitude in staving off Nazi invasion "could be explained 'scenically' in terms of the Soviet political and economic structure; or one could use the act-agent ratio, attributing the power and tenacity to 'Russian' traits of character" (*GM* 16). Those identifying with the standpoint of a Western capitalist teleology were placed in a bit of a pickle. Praising Russia's political-economic accomplishments would potentially shed the wrong light on liberal capitalist triumphalism: "In deriving the act from the scene, one would have to credit socialism as a major scenic factor, whereas a derivation of the act from the agents would allow for a much more felicitous explanation from the standpoint of capitalist apologetics" (*GM* 16–17). The same could be said of emphasizing the arbitrary role of unfelicitous Russian weather (to which many Nazi soldiers succumbed in their failed effort to invade the Soviet Union) over the heroism of Allied Powers' antifascist efforts.

When America seeks to place its rivals in the crosshairs, it has a tried-and-true panoply of rhetorical tactics at its disposal: "one may deflect attention from scenic matters by situating the motives of an act in the agent (as were one to account for wars purely on the basis of a 'warlike instinct' in people)" (*GM* 17). By the same token, "one may deflect attention from the criticism of personal motives by deriving an act or attitude not from traits of the agent but from the nature of the situation" (*GM* 17). As Aristotle made abundantly clear, when a powerful government seeks to engage in militarism, it will likely induce a bellicose (or quiescent) attitude in the polity by insisting that the nation must respond to, and even put a stop to, a fearsome, inherently malevolent enemy. These frames often metamorphose into rhetorical traps for those who seek to question, undermine, or countervail militaristic propaganda. Assert that anti-war activists don't support the troops, aren't patriotic, or smack of anti-Americanism, and a lot of would-be opponents of even the most spurious wars will look the other way.

In a prescient aside on the tenuous relationship between democratic liberalism and new political developments, he insists that it is convenient for purveyors of Anglo-exceptionalism to view the United Kingdom and the United States as inherent scenic "vessels" of liberal democracy:

> And democracy is felt to reside in us, intrinsically, because we are "a democratic people." Democratic acts are, in this mode of thought, derived from democratic agents, agents who would remain democratic in character even though conditions required the temporary curtailment or abrogation of basic democratic rights. But if one employed, instead, the scene-act ratio, one might hold that there are certain "democratic situations" and certain "situations favorable to dictatorship, or requiring dictatorship."
>
> (*GM* 17)

Burke's warning of the metastases of democracy anticipates the Red Scare and the twenty-first century "War on Terror." Under McCarthyism in the 1950s, the American government cracked down on perceived dissidence with fascistic ruthlessness. Likewise, in the wake of 9/11, Bush's neoconservative War on Terror waged indefinite war on anything and anyone associated with the abstract principle of terrorism; this nebulous objective fanned out to include the targeting (through surveillance, policing, etc.) of not only those planning explosive attacks on innocent Americans but also environmental and animal rights activists, political dissidents, and even international rivals of American corporations. A Burkean frame of reference invites us to scrutinize the extent to which a government that would behave in such a draconian fashion is best understood as inherently democratic or even intrinsically virtuous.

As the ongoing War on Terror (whatever name it goes by) evinces, new technological developments render the fragile, ever-evolving democratic scene even more volatile. Writing before the existence of the home computer or cellular telephone, Burke adopted a much more sceptical frame than McLuhan about the emerging Global Village. An ever-ramifying technological environment "requires the planning of a world order" (*GM* 17). It therefore "might be thought such as to favor a large measure of 'dictatorship' in our political ways (at least as contrasted with the past norms of democracy)" (*GM* 17). Burke concludes, "If the 'situation' itself is no longer a 'democratic' one, even an 'essentially democratic' people will abandon democratic ways" (*GM* 17).

From Burke's vantage point, the incipient Global Village was a milieu that harboured the systemic potential to short-circuit ambient democratic attitudes. It goes without saying that this tension is even more seismic in the digital twenty-first century as surveillance capitalist algorithms vacuum up our data while nudging us towards certain political, economic, and aesthetic worldviews. Less chauvinistic defenders of democratic ideals might therefore privilege the act-agent ratio: "a democratic people would continue to perform democratic acts; and to do so they would even, if necessary, go to the extent of restoring former conditions most favorable to democracy" (*GM* 17). Any hypostasized notion of democracy is, after all, dangerous when employed as a cudgel against putatively antidemocratic civilizational rivals or as a banner to describe a techno-economic nexus (like, say, a social media platform) that deviates from well-established democratic principles.

Aristophanes over Aristotle

According to Burke, our symbolic milieu is constantly motivating us in a bellicose fashion. Returning to the notion of attitude as strategy, he asserts that this predicament leaves humanity with two broad paths to follow, the "tragic" path of war or the "comic" path of peace. The tragic path, which human civilization seems to be hurtling obliviously along, entails the diminishment of people's capacity to find solidary common ground with each other coupled with the amplification of humanity's technological prowess. "Up to now," writes Burke,

> human stupidity could go to fantastic lengths of destructiveness, yet always mankind's hopes of recovery could be born anew. Indeed, had you reduced the world's population to but one surviving adult, in time all the continents could again be teeming with populaces, if that one hypothetical survivor were but fairly young .... But now presumably a truly New Situation is with us, making it all the more imperative that we learn to cherish the mildly charitable ways of the comic discount. For by nothing less than such humanistic allowances

can we hope to forestall (if it can be forestalled!) the most idiotic tragedy conceivable: the willful ultimate poisoning of this lovely planet,
in conformity with a mistaken heroics of war–and each day, as the sun
still rises anew upon the still surviving plenitude, let us piously give
thanks to Something or Other not of man's making. Basically[,] this
book would accept the Aristophanic assumptions which equate tragedy with war and comedy with peace.

(*AH* xv)

Since abstractions are little more than "fossilized metaphors" (*AH* 12),
"every insight contains its own special form of blindness" (*AH* 41).[4] Thus,
even the wisest of individuals is readily deceived into dogmatism by the
operations of our symbolic ether. And dogmatism readily tips over into
partisan acrimony, militarism, and other forms of suicidal imbecility.

It therefore falls on us, according to Burke, to depetrify our thinking by
rendering ourselves attitudinally amenable to "perspective by incongruity," a "method for gauging situations by verbal 'atom cracking'" (*AH* 308).
Even if a word or concept "belongs by custom to a certain category," a
comic disposition can and will readily break with dogmatism to "wrench
it loose and metaphorically apply it to a different category" (*AH* 308).
Perspective by incongruity is much more than a matter of language for
Burke. It is, as Joseph Gusfield insists, a dynamic "exhortation to see the
limited nature of any one cognitive framework. The terminologies in
use are terministic screens that shield us from the multiplicity of possibilities. The wise observer recognizes that opposites are not so different
after all. Comedy points up the limits of intelligence and knowledge"
(Gusfield 26). In this way, "[a] new taxonomy, a new vocabulary produces
an additional angle from which to see reality. The comic enables us to
increase the use of incongruity and in this a fashion to produce new ways
of seeing, to overcome the particular blindness of our accustomed usages"
(Gusfield 26).

Attitudinalizing the Dancing, Twitching Body

As Waldermar Petermann writes in "Attitude as Equipment for Living,"
Burke's reinterpretation of the concept of attitude, even at this early stage
of his career, is "not quite as unambiguously just a state of mind or an
abstract strategy for handling a class of situations. From time to time,
a more basic physical connection emerges" (Petermann). In books like
Attitudes Toward History, for instance, "attitude and bodily action are also
described as counterparts, which makes an interpretation of bodily act as
manifested attitude possible" (Petermann).

There is necessarily "a bodily dimension of attitude" (Petermann), but
the relationship remains a somewhat opaque one because symbolic action
does not break down along hygienic Cartesian lines. Sometimes, as in

Richards' formulation, persuasion engenders an incipient action in the addressee, who performs the action with conscious intentionality. For example, when an Instagram poster sees that a respected acquaintance has characterized their favourite sweater as unattractive or outdated, they may suddenly feel impelled to alter or delete the photo; and perhaps they then rush to the store to replace it with a more fashionable garment. At other times, an attitude's relationship with a certain course of action may be less perceptible or intelligible. Maybe the poster does not do anything about their sweater or photo but superegoically "internalizes" the slight, temporarily acquiring a heightened sensitivity to such sartorial criticism until such time as they have gotten over the insult.

Sometimes, as a result of the symbolic action of sartorial criticism, one's bodily act (like a grimace or a twitch) may even become wired to a barely conscious attitude. Burke, here, uses the metaphor of dancing to describe the bodily expression of an attitude: one's body dances to the tune of a corresponding attitude (*AH* 339). For example, the self-conscious Instagram poster may claim (even to herself) not to care about the sartorial criticism but nonetheless develops a tick every time she wears the sweater or encounters the aforementioned acquaintance in public. This variety of embodied expression is remarkably close to Freud's notion of symptomatic action in that the body *performs* the underlying "neurotic" concern as though it has a mind of its own.

Nevertheless, for Burke, Freud's understanding of symbolic action as symptomatic of underlying neuroses is often at risk of missing the mark. A broader spectrum of rhetorical variables must be brought into consideration in order to appraise the motivational structure of symbolic actions. Using Descartes' flawed understanding of the mind/body divide as a leaping off point, Burke sets up his own antinomial version of the human subject-animal body dialectic: "If the human being is a symbol-using animal, some motives must derive from [their] animality, some from [their] symbolicity, and some from mixtures of the two. The computer can't serve as our model (or 'terministic screen'). For it is not an animal but an artifact." (*LSA* 63). Situating the symbol-using animal as a creature that can appear alternately neurotic, bestial, or hyperrational, depending on the spectator's vantage point, Burke wants to maintain an open space for associations and stave off overhasty circumscriptions of what it means to be a simultaneously resourceful and clumsy animal placed within a suasive ecosystem of bodies, symbols, sentiments, technologies, authorities, and interpretations.

Rhetorical Dis-ease

In *The Philosophy of Literary Form*, Burke takes up the matter of "psychogenic illness" as an example of "a 'symbolic' act on the part of the body." What the easily-swayed hypochondriac experiences as an irrefutably ill body may be dancing to the tune of "a corresponding state of mind quite as the formal dancer reorders his externally observable gesture to match his attitudes" (*PLF* 10–11). That is to say that the hypochondriacal subject is caught up in and obliviously moving to the beat of symbolic rhythms that they might not even consciously hear. According to Burke, to merely isolate such an attitude as "neurotic" or "hysterical" would miss the socio-symbolic forest for the experiential trees.

In *Health and the Rhetoric of Medicine*, Judy Segal draws on Burke's account of the uncanny "symptomatic" relationship between the mind, body, and symbolic environment in order to analyse the phenomenon of hypochondria from a rhetorical vantage point. Segal argues that "[t]he hypochondriacal body may, [...] in some literal sense, have a mind of its own. Or perhaps, [it] may dance an illness it does not have." (Segal 76). After reading an online discussion thread of a particular ailment, a self-diagnosing subject may be so persuaded that they are ill that the doctor's repeated insistence to the contrary will fall on deaf ears. The supposedly autonomous body itself may even join the dance by behaving as though it is sick in spite of a groundswell of medical evidence that all is well.

This contorted nexus of auto-persuasion leads Segal to conclude that, rather than militating against psychological frameworks, an astute rhetorical approach "complements existing accounts of hypochondria" (76). In keeping with Burke's litany of different registers of language in "Symbol and Association," Segal recites her own survey of different disciplinary approaches to the sphinx-like riddle of hypochondria: "As a medical problem, hypochondria is intractable; as a psychological problem, it is mysterious; as a psychiatric problem, it is perhaps too easily biologized; as a social problem, it is amorphous" (Segal 76). However, as a rhetorical problem, it is "bounded, interesting, and suggestive" (76).

Segal's exposition on "hypochondria as a rhetorical disorder" seizes on Burke's theory of ambiguity as a motivating force: "Instead of considering it our task to dispose of any ambiguity by merely disclosing the fact that it is an ambiguity," writes Burke, "we rather consider it our task to study and clarify the resources of ambiguity. For in the course of this work we shall deal with many kinds of transformation and it is in the areas of ambiguity that transformation takes place" (*GM* xix). Unlike Aristotle, who was willing to cede a great deal of theoretical territory to philosophy when it came to matters of truth and falsity (and seemed to believe that the separation of disciplinary purviews was a relatively hygienic one), Burke, like most denizens of modernity, avers that opinions about truth and fiction are riddled with ambiguity. Just as the perception of truth, for Lacan, is structured like a fiction, Burke understands it as structured by opinion. And the ambiguity that permeates matters of opinion serves as a resource for persuasion. After all, if a hypothetical panel of experts with seemingly unassailable authority is incapable of adjudicating a matter (like, for example, COVID-19 vaccination or mask protocols) with relative certainty, a deluge of opinions may flood the scene and cloud the lay observer's perception of the issue. Even then, matters that appear relatively certain in the register of scientific inquiry may be altogether unclear at the level of common sense or everyday empirical perception.

Segal conducts a genealogy of hypochondria and notes that the term derives from the ancient Greek correlative to female hysteria. While psychoanalytically-tilted historical perceptions of hypochondria as a form of hysterical neurosis are buttressed by cultural representations in the early novels of Philip Roth and Woody Allen films, she argues that rhetorical optics shed a different light on the phenomenon as inextricably bound up with authority and persuasion within an overarching dramatistic "scene for hypochondria" (Segal 83).This hypochondriacal symbolic environment bombards the bewildered individual with media representations, pharmaceutical advertisements, discussion threads, and other influences that invite them to entertain the notion that they may be ill.

There are even fake grassroots "astroturf" websites that large pharmaceutical corporations set up to persuade curious Google navigators that they may suffer from a particular treatable ailment (from depression to erectile dysfunction). When the anxious lay researcher, persuaded by this cacophonous rhetorical scene, brings their concerns to their licensed medical professional, they may be told that their experience of illness is illegitimate; it is merely "in their head." Segal contends that "[b]ecause the patient lacks authority of diagnosis, any argument in the course of the doctor-patient interview can compromise the[ir] *ethos* or presenting character" (Segal 81). From the standpoint of the medical system, they have insufficient expertise to refute the doctor's diagnosis based on DIY research, some of which is tilted towards impelling them to redouble their efforts to change the doctor's mind. When they repeatedly fail to persuade medical professionals in the position to validate their concerns, their intransigent protests may undermine the legitimacy of their experience of their own body as out of sorts. This dysfunctional feedback loop may, in turn, amplify their anxiety – and, with it, an array of "psychosomatic" symptoms – when the doctor dismisses them as simply being possessed of (or by) an overactive imagination.

For the uneasy patient, this destabilizing state of affairs is "clinically troubling, not least because the hypochondriac may at any point be 'legitimately' sick. Just as paranoids are sometimes being followed, so hypochondriacs are sometimes very ill. It seems that both parties in the conversation of hypochondriac and physician have some self-doubt" (Segal 81). Segal observes that the crises of persuasion and authority that inhere to medical designations of hypochondria also pertain to an array of ailments that are difficult, even for medical professionals, to recognize and diagnose. For example, patients who suffer from fibromyalgia, chronic fatigue, and chemical sensitivity often have to contend with a great deal of uncertainty and ambiguity on account of the ease with which these disorders go unrecognized or misrecognized by doctors and epidemiological tests (Segal 75).

It goes without saying that these contradictions bubble to the surface of collective experience with a vengeance in the COVID-19 era in that the ailment is both "novel" and constantly mutating; so too is the symptomatology. As a result, both the medical establishment and the media are constantly catching up to the reality. From masking regimens to vaccination protocols to the diagnosis of long COVID, the scene is replete with seemingly irresolvable ambiguities that potentially undermine the credibility of any party that presumes to know what precisely is going on with any measure of certainty. Every authoritative utterance that turns out to have been made on the basis of faulty conjecture only undermines the ability of future authorities to efficaciously disseminate prescriptions and expect them to be followed. Part of the problem resides in the general public's, as well as our governments', faulty understanding of science, which necessarily proceeds in fits and starts as it exposes itself to the possibility of error.

Of Instagrammatology

Another potentially pathological rhetorical feedback loop that Segal explores is that of what she refers to as "aesthetic hypochondria: the nagging feeling that one doesn't look as well–or as good–as one might" (Segal 87). Aesthetic hypochondria is a "dis-ease of the surface–which includes both the pathology currently known as 'body dysmorphic disorder' and a more pervasive skin-deep version of the sense that things are not right." "Cosmetic surgery," she continues, is one method "by which unattractiveness is absorbed into the medical realm and made a treatable condition about which one may worry and obsess" (Segal 87). In the age of reality television and ubiquitous social media, young people, especially young women, are constantly put in the position of evaluating their appearance in relation to real and fabricated peers, icons, and strangers whose appearance is mediated through software, cosmetics, and surgeries that have morphed beauty standards increasingly in the direction of such aggressive interventions on "Mother Nature."

Segal's formulation of the collocation "aesthetic hypochondria" betokens the symbol-using animal's maladroit employment of and by an increasingly persuasive media environment. As *New Yorker* youth culture journalist Jia Tolentino writes in "The Age of Instagram Face," over the last decade, a new "cyborgian" face has started to emerge in the mediasphere: "It's a young face, of course, with poreless skin and plump, high cheekbones. It has catlike eyes and long, cartoonish lashes; it has a small, neat nose and full, lush lips. It looks at you coyly but blankly, as if its owner has taken half a Klonopin and is considering asking you for a private-jet ride to Coachella" (Tolentino). This "distinctly white but ambiguously ethnic" Instagram Face, writes Tolentino, emerges out of a social media milieu that "has its own aesthetic language." The "ideal image," she claims, "is always the one that instantly pops on a phone screen. The aesthetic is also marked by a familiar human aspiration, previously best documented in wedding photography, toward a generic sameness" (Tolentino).

Tolentino observes that the human body "is an unusual sort of Instagram subject: it can be adjusted, with the right kind of effort, to perform better and better over time" (Tolentino). Because social media is equipped with a personal marketing director's wet dream of filters with which to modify one's appearance, most any user can digitally modify their bodies to make them appear thinner in some places and rounder in others. They can render their eyes larger or change their colour. They can make their lips fuller and more luscious. The potential for aesthetic manipulation in accordance with ever-ramifying hegemonic beauty ideals is being amplified by an increasingly powerful array of digital tools. Whether alterations are made to the skin or the pixels, all roads lead to Instagram face.

Whether they enter the marketplace as online daters, job candidates, or aspiring influencers (arguably the most explicitly rhetorical category in online culture), young people are finding themselves increasingly seduced into the digital-cosmetic machinations of social media platforms that potentially invite them into a slipstream of aesthetic hypochondriacal uneasiness, self-curation, and self-manipulation. This *unheimlich* manoeuvre on bodily apperception is propelling large numbers of young women, in particular, to plastic surgery clinics, where they are receiving Botox injections, eyelid surgeries, wrinkle fillers, liposuction, and butt implants. Tolentino writes of becoming possessed of the eerie feeling "that technology is rewriting our bodies to correspond to its own interests—rearranging our faces according to whatever increases engagement and likes." This alienation from our increasingly agentive media regime leads her to ask an unsettling "rhetorical question" of her readership: "Don't you think it's scary to imagine people doing this forever?" (Tolentino).

Notes

1 In *Gender Trouble* (Routledge, 1990) and *Bodies that Matter* (Routledge, 1996), Judith Butler popularized the use of "performativity" to describe the performative construction of gender roles. One advantage of employing "symbolic action" rather than "performativity" in a wide variety of contexts is that, in everyday discourse, "performative" has increasingly become synonymous with mere "performance," as in insubstantive "performative activism."

2 In his favourable review of Austin's influential *How to Do Things with Words*, Burke maps Austin's performative-constative distinction (i.e. what language does vs. what it signifies) in terms of his own extant dramatistic-scientistic distinction: "Austin begins with two terms, only one of which ('performative') is dramatistic. The other ('constative') is clearly designed to be on the 'scientistic'(T-F) slope" ("Words as Deeds" 248).

3 Writing of Deleuzian affect theorists like Brian Massumi and Eric Shouse, Ruth Leys characterizes "[t]he new affect theorists' tendency to reject psychoanalysis or to try to reconceptualize it" as a function of their recognition that "our relations to the world are, in large measure, visceral, embodied, and affective" rather than representational (Leys 458 n.)

4 This formulation of the dialectic of blindness and insight was immensely influential on Paul de Man, who borrowed this turn-of-phrase in *Blindness and Insight: Essays in the Rhetoric of Contemporary Criticism* (1983). See Martin McQuillan's *The Political Archive of Paul de Man: Property, Sovereignty, and the Theotropic* (2012) for a more explicit account of their relationship.

3 Identification, Disidentification, Scapegoating, and War

In this chapter, we take up Kenneth Burke's adoption and adaptation of the psychoanalytic notion of *identification*. His provocative incorporation of this concept into the new rhetoric is his most well-documented purloinment from Freud, who coined the term (*Identifizierung*) and employed it somewhat elastically over the course of his career. But whereas Freudian identification is locked into the gravity field of the Oedipus complex, Burke generalizes the concept, connecting it with not only identity formation but also persuasion, shared substance, cooperation, conspiracy, and rhetoric's perennial ethical mission in the struggle to find common ground in spite of the myriad forces that divide us against each other. This chapter culminates in a close reading of Burke's critique of Hitler's *Mein Kampf*. Reading Hitler's book as a nefarious, masterful work of sophistry (in the pejorative sense), Burke brings identification into resonance with other psychoanalytic concepts such as projection, perversion, association, and paranoia in order to assess Hitler's efforts to seduce the German public into buying into his crypto-Catholic Pied Piper mission to scapegoat Jewish people for Germany's abject circumstances in the wake of the military and economic spasms of the early twentieth century.

The Lines of Identification

In her account of Burke's retooling of Freud's concept of identification, rhetorician Diane Davis writes, "Burke based his theory on Freud's, and the overlap is readily discernable" (Davis 124). Even in Freud's hands, identification is a remarkably malleable mechanism that undergoes a number of elaborations across a range of different texts. In *Group Psychology and the Analysis of the Ego*, Freud conducts a brief survey of the metamorphoses of identification in his work and the life of a person. At bottom, identification is "the earliest expression of an emotional tie with another person" (*Group* 105). Connecting this emotional bond to an early stage of the Oedipal complex, Freud asserts that a very young boy "will exhibit a special interest in his father; he would like to grow like him and be like him, and take his place everywhere. We may say simply that he takes his

DOI: 10.4324/9781003214069-4

father as his ideal" (*Group* 105). At this early stage of sexual development, a young boy's propensity to identify with his father is fundamentally ambivalent: the father is simultaneously his aspirational ideal and his rival for the mother's affections. As Davis frames the matter, "identification by definition involves seizing the other's place, ousting the other from the position that 'I,' having devoured the other, now presume to occupy. According to Freud, wherever there is identification, there is already and intrinsically war" (Davis 124 n.). The byzantine entanglement of identification, identity, and war will, of course, be of immense interest to Burke as well.

The Freudian conception of identification is also connected to the work of mourning and, by extension, character formation. In *Mourning and Melancholia*, Freud claims that the experience of loss galvanizes a regression that "establish[es] an *identification* of the ego with the abandoned object" (*Mourning* 248), which is then internalized. After, for example, the death of a loved one, the unmetabolizable internalized object "becomes a substitute for a libidinal object-tie" (249). In *The Ego and the Id,* Freud moves identification beyond mere defence mechanisms by connecting it with "the form taken by the ego" in identity formation; this variety of identification, taking in and internalizing aspects of other people, "makes an essential contribution towards building up what is called. . . 'character'" (*The Ego and the Id* 28).

Freud's vision of the identificatory architecture of the personality leads Anna Freud's school of ego psychology to organize its mode of therapy around ego support. Ego psychologists therefore interpret Freud's dictum "*Wo Es war, soll Ich warden*" as "Where the id was, there the ego will be." In his early writings, Lacan dedicates a great deal of space to attacking ego psychology's investment in reifying and supporting the fledgling ego. Rather than normalizing the ego, Lacan insists on characterizing it as the ultimate symptom of moribund identifications, some of which must give way (or at least be brought into relief as such) if the analysand is to break out of some of their most intractable impasses. While he agrees that the ego is constituted through a variety of identifications, he takes aim at the identificatory constitution of the ego, recognizing it as a problem of alienation that analysands should be aided in recognizing and traversing. "By contrast with the ego and the illusory sense of fictional selfhood it supports," writes Adrian Johnston, "the psychoanalytic subject of Lacanianism is an unconscious kinetic negativity defying capture by and within ego-level identificatory constructs. The Lacanian enunciating subject of the unconscious speaks through the ego while remaining irreducibly distinct from it" (Johnston).

Over the scope of Freud's career, the concept of identification becomes malleable and pervasive. Beyond the immediate scope of the Oedipal drama, writes Freud, an individual's identification with another "may arise with any new perception of a common quality which is shared with some other person" (*Group* 137). Drawing on all of the aforementioned understandings of identification, Jean Laplanche and Jean-Bertrand Pontalis observe that the concept seems to "overlap a whole group of psychological concepts" (Laplanche and Pontalis 206). These include "imitation, *Einfühlung* (empathy), sympathy, mental contagion, projection, etc." (Laplanche and Pontalis 206). They define identification in a general vein as the "psychological process whereby the subject assimilates an aspect, property, or attribute of the other and is transformed, wholly or partially, after the model the other provides" (Laplanche and Pontalis 205). As we will see, Laplanche and Pontalis' general definition arguably comes closest to Burke's de-Oedipalized, rhetoricized variation on Freud's concept.

The Purloined Sub-Stance

Laplanche and Pontalis's definition of identification serves as a useful aperture to Burke's lionization of it as an inherently rhetorical concept. Burke seizes on identification because he recognizes it as a polyvalent rhetorical principle that underlies all acts of persuasion. Like Freud writes Davis, he understands "identification as a social act that partially unifies discrete individuals, a mode of 'symbolic action' (as Burke would say) that resides squarely within the representational arena (or the dramatistic frame)" (Davis 125). But he disentangles identification from its Oedipal moorings in order to generalize it as a rhetorical principle that permeates the scene of persuasion at both the molar and molecular level. Writes Davis, "Burke agreed with Freud that humans are motivated by desire at least as much as by reason, but he ditched the Oedipal narrative, arguing that the most fundamental human desire is social rather than sexual" (Davis 124–125).

As he is wont to do, Burke adopts a psychoanalytic concept and then, in practically the same breath, delves into the rhetorical archive to exhume its putative pre-psychoanalytic roots. Leaping over Freud, he harkens back to his original master, Aristotle, to echolocate the pre-Freudian genesis of the concept of identification in the rhetorical tradition. Citing Aristotle's assertion that it is easier to praise Athenians amongst Athenians, he extrapolates the identificatory roots of persuasion: You persuade others insofar as you can speak their "language by speech, gesture, tonality, order, image, attitude, idea, identifying your ways with [theirs]" (*ARM* 55). The array of attributes that the symbol-using animal may find itself assimilating and incorporating into its socio-affective repertoire is, apropos of Laplanche and Pontalis, almost infinite. But the accent in Burke is on persuasion. Above and beyond the fact that the symbol-using animal ceaselessly integrates this identificatory shrapnel into its psychic apparatus, where it takes root and ramifies in the form of egoic architecture, identificatory seductions are the basis of most all acts of persuasion. In a media atmosphere that is constantly beckoning, interpellating, and moving us in different directions, these identifications (be they role models, name brands, occupations, sports teams, or ethnicities) are the hooks that the symbolic ether latches onto our motivational collars; and, by the same token, they are the suasive snares that we, however knowingly, deploy to latch onto the collars of those in our socio-symbolic orbit.

Socrates viewed identificatory rhetorical appeals as mere "flattery" by way of pandering to an audience's irrational prejudices. He seized on rhetoric's infidelity to the unwavering eidetic Truth in order to undermine the sophist Gorgias' claims that rhetoric, like philosophy, should be understood a proper discipline. But Burke subverts the Socratic disciplinary hierarchy by underscoring rhetoric's primacy as a mechanism that subtends all communication, including philosophy. Always the cunning rhetorician, he cleaves to Socrates' critique in order to find common ground with philosophy and philosophers. Rather than shying away from the philosopher's gibe, he embraces "flattery" as a general principle of rhetoric and one that philosophers should not be so quick to write off:

> Persuasion by flattery is but a special case of persuasion in general. But flattery can safely serve as our paradigm if we systematically widen its meaning to see behind it the conditions of identification or consubstantiality in general. And you give the "signs" of such consubstantiality by deference to an audience's "opinions." For the orator, following Aristotle and Cicero, will seek to display the appropriate "signs" of character needed to earn the audience's good will. True, the rhetorician may have to change an audience's opinion in one respect; but he can succeed only insofar as he concedes to the audience's opinions in other respects. Some of their opinions are needed to support the fulcrum by which he would move other opinions. (Preferably he shares the fixed opinions himself since, "all other things being equal," the identifying of himself with his audience will be more effective if it is genuine).
>
> (*ARM* 55–56)

Far from Socrates' pretences of a quasi-objective philosophical dialogue, Burkean rhetoric attends to the subjectivity of its interlocutors with a view to drawing out meaningful commonalities. Persuasion is simply not possible without some level of connection between participants. This "shared substance" may be a partly conscious common cause, some ineffable aesthetic compatibility, or merely a synchronized vibration. And even when two philosophers are engaged in a rationalistic dialogue about fundamental essences, mere opinion – which Socrates disparaged as the ignominious province of rhetoric – is the necessary starting place along any conversational terrain.

Having established identification's pre-existence as a rhetorical principle, Burke nonetheless diffracts it through a distinctly psychoanalytic prism. Decoupled from the orator's conscious intentions, Burke's "new rhetoric" is oriented towards the identifications and disidentifications that constitute the symbol-using animal's largely unconscious suasive milieu. And, importantly, the instrumental use of identification in order to get one's way is merely a special case. Generalized identification is often its own autopoietic end within a symbolic milieu, "as when people earnestly yearn to identify themselves with some group or other." When individuals engage in such identifications, writes Burke, they "are not necessarily being acted upon by a conscious external agent, but may be acting upon themselves to this end. In such identification there is a partially dreamlike, idealistic motive, somewhat compensatory to real differences or divisions, which the rhetoric of identification would transcend" ("Rhetoric Old and New" 203). He therefore distinguishes the new rhetoric from its predecessor in terms of its new emphases on ambient communication, identification, and the unconscious: "The key term for the old rhetoric was 'persuasion' and its stress was upon deliberate design. The key term for the 'new' rhetoric would be 'identification,' which can include a partially 'unconscious' factor in appeal" ("Rhetoric Old and New" 203).

Any pretence of a self-conscious subject engaging in transparent intentionality flies out the window. When rhetoric is conducted through the Freudian looking glass, discourse is fractalized and rendered "dreamlike." And so, too, is the self-aware individual:

> There is an intermediate area of expression that is not wholly deliberate, yet not wholly unconscious. It lies midway between aimless utterance and speech directly purposive. For instance, a man who identifies his private ambition with the good of the community may be partly justified, partly unjustified. He may be using a mere pretext to gain individual advantage at public expense; yet he may be quite sincere .... Here is a rhetorical area not analyzable either as sheer design or as sheer simplicity.
>
> (*ARM* xiii–xiv)

Burke's understanding of rhetoric as both instrument and milieu brings it extraordinarily close, once again, to the study of ideology or what Lacan calls fantasy. Even when we traffic in mere opinion, without so much as an intentional assertion about where the truth resides, we participate in the weaving and fortification of a symbolic tapestry that is replete with suasive force. This suasive undercurrent, which is bound up with identification, often lurks beneath the surface of consciousness and permeates even the most solipsistic stories that we tell ourselves about ourselves.

Burke (with Freud) against Freud

In *A Rhetoric of Motives*, Burke begins his argument in favour of identification, as the rhetorical device *par excellence*, with an exposition on the shortcomings of psychoanalytic optics in diagnosing the motives underlying representations of violence. Looking at psychoanalytic attempts to theorize violent cinema's relation to the psyche, Burke observes that certain psychoanalytic thinkers (whom he doesn't name) seem to leap to conclusions in diagnosing the violent drives that lead to the creation of cinematic depictions of violent acts, which they claim radiate out of humanity's unconscious violent drives. Casting a glance across the Freudian field, Burke avers that "objections arise when certain kinds of speculation (of a psychoanalytic cast)" emphasize "the primacy of vengeance and slaughter as motives (and looking upon friendly or ethical motives purely as a kind of benign fiction for harnessing these more nearly 'essential' impulses), such thought is really more like the *forerunner* of modern militarism than its *critic*." Often, he continues,

> The analysts will show such zeal, [on] behalf of killing as the essential motive, that they will seek many ingenious ways of showing that a work was motivated by the desire to slay some parental figure who suffered no such fate at all, in the imagery of the plot as interpreted on its face. They apparently assume that to show "unconscious" parricidal implications in a motive is by the same token to establish parricide as the motive. Where a play is explicitly about parricide, one might feel some justification in complaining if we would see behind it merely the choice of a parental symbol to represent some motivation not intrinsically parricidal at all, but using parental identifications as "imagined accidents" that personify it. But whatever may be the objections in such cases, they would not apply at all in cases where there is no explicit imagery of parricide, and one must by exegesis hunt out parricide as motive.
>
> (*ARM* 18)

We can perhaps hear I.A. Richards' voice murmuring in the background of Burke's critique. Like Richards, Burke chastises these unnamed psychoanalytic thinkers for hastily imposing violent Oedipal-parricidal schemes onto fictional narratives that should lend themselves to more complicated and nuanced lines of interpretation on their own terms.

In his engagement with Freud, Burke is driven by more than just a desire for faithful attunement to the drives underlying the texts in question. He also wants rhetoric, as a theory of influence (as it inheres to the symbol-using animal's dramatistic network), to be adequate to the task of accounting for "a wider scope" (*ARM* 20) of human motivation. Burke tasks himself with attending to disidentificatory motivation "in the order of killing, of personal enmity, of factional strife, of invective, polemic, eristic, logomachy" (*ARM* 19). These are all "aspects of rhetoric that we are repeatedly and drastically encountering, since rhetoric is *par excellence* the region of the Scramble, of insult and injury, bickering, squabbling, malice and the lie, cloaked malice and the subsidized lie"

(*ARM* 19). But he also seeks to highlight the other end of the motivational spectrum in order to account for more benevolent (and nonmalevolent) orientations. Such identificatory optics must include everything from "sacrificial evangelical love, through the kinds of persuasion figuring in sexual love, to sheer 'neutral' *communication* (communication being the area where love has become so generalized, desexualized, 'technologized,' that only close critical or philosophic scrutiny can discern the vestiges of the original motive)" (*ARM* 19).

Defenders of psychoanalysis would, of course, be quick to point out that Burke's identificatory communion may be accounted for by Freud's notion of Eros, or union, which exists in persistent tension with Thanatos, the death drive. This claim certainly holds a certain amount of water in many instances. Still, Burke moves beyond the ambit of Freud's approach to Eros and Thanatos by insisting, *pace* Freudian psychoanalysis, that identification qua union is more primordial than discord: "We need never deny the presence of strife, enmity, faction as a characteristic motive of rhetorical expression. We need not close our eyes to their almost tyrannous ubiquity in human relations; we can be on the alert always to see how such temptations to strife are implicit in the institutions that condition human relationships" (*ARM* 20). However, given that these institutions are essentially collaborative networks, "we can at the same time always look beyond this order, to the principle of identification in general" (20) since there is no strife, enmity, or faction without a measure of underlying agreement about the terms of division. "Because of our choice, we can treat 'war' as a '*special case of peace*'" in that war is "a *derivative* condition, a *perversion*" (*ARM* 20). Supplementing psychoanalytic accounts of the psyche's primarily sexual and violent unconscious impulses, the Burkean unconscious is also flooded with primordial modes of connection, communion, and cooperation.

Burke's understanding of war as a *perverse* aberration of cooperation is arguably not so much psychoanalytic (though he obtrusively borrows this term, too, from Freud) or metaphysical as political and "metarhetorical." On this point, he argues that

> to begin with 'identification' is, by the same token, though roundabout, to confront the implications of *division*. And so, in the end, men are brought to that most tragically ironic of all divisions, or conflicts, wherein millions of cooperative acts go into the preparation for one single destructive act. We refer to that ultimate *disease* of cooperation: *war*.
>
> (*ARM* 20)

From this hopeful standpoint, he understands war "not simply as strife come to a head, but rather as a disease, or perversion, of communion. Modern war characteristically requires a myriad of constructive acts for each destructive one; before each culminating blast there must be a vast network of interlocking operations, directed communally" (*ARM* 20). And communion, for Burke, is cognate with communication, which is, in turn, cognate with rhetoric.

The Burkean Pharmacy

In the lead-up to World War II, Burke got his hands on Hitler's autobiographical *Mein Kampf* and read it with morbid fascination. Amidst the clamour of Americans calling for the book's banning, he vociferously objected, viewing *Mein Kampf* as an exemplar of sophistic abuses of identification and disidentification. Burke was chagrined by his fellow American antifascists, many of whom insisted on blanketly disavowing the book rather than reading it carefully and analysing it as a case study in the perversion of democracy for tyrannical ends. What few commentators attend to is the extent to which Burke's critique of Hitler's malicious "sophistry" mobilizes not only Freud's lexicon of identification, perversion, association, and projection but also, surprisingly, Socrates' ancient critiques of sophist rhetoric (as philosophy's unethical mimic).

At the beginning of his essay, Burke points out that proponents of banning Hitler's book are correct to view it as noxious. It is precisely on account of the insidiousness of Hitler's rhetoric that Burke calls for it to be exposed as sophistic charlatanism, and he does so in terms that artfully echo Socrates' critique of rhetoric in *Gorgias*. Just as Socrates compares rhetoric to a form of "cookery" masquerading as medicine, Burke calls Hitler a snake oil salesman whose book is a "well of Nazi magic; crude magic, but effective" (*PLF* 191). He therefore implores his fellow antifascists to join him in analysing the bewitching "'medicine' this medicine man has concocted" so "that we may know, with greater accuracy, exactly what to guard against, if we are to forestall the concocting of similar medicine in America" (*PLF* 191).

Once again, Burke employs consubstantiation as a tactic in order to join ranks with Socratic philosophy and bring it into the new-rhetorical fold. He finds a measure of common ground with Socrates' antirhetorical critique of the Sophists, whom the great philosopher chastised for prioritizing persuasion and commerce over Truth. However, rather than adopting the view that rhetoric is either, at worst, sophistry or, at best, philosophy's docile handmaiden, he employs rhetoric as a para-philosophical, para-psychoanalytic close reading practice in order to critique mendacious fascist rhetoric as a manipulative corruption of the discipline's political-philosophical compass. What his analysis discovers is that Hitler figures himself as a kind of newfangled Platonist, one that identifies the "villainous Jew" as the snake-oil "orator" (*PLF* 195) that would "seduce" (*PLF* 195) innocent Germans and "poison their blood" (*PLF* 195). But unlike Derrida's version of "Plato's Pharmacy" (which culminates in the image of Plato's dissolution under the weight of the impossible task of separating truth from fiction and poison from cure), what me might call "Burke's Pharmacy" culminates in something like a rehabilitation of Plato as a critic of Nazi sophistry.

The bedrock of Hitler's persuasive strategy, claims Burke, is a seductive economy of identifications and disidentifications that necessitates close interrogation. "Hitler found a panacea," writes Burke, "'a cure for what ails you,' ... that made such sinister unifying possible within his own nation" (*PLF* 192). This sinister act of political hucksterism was organized around the construction of a quasi-religious centre, "geographically located, towards which all eyes could turn at the appointed hours of prayer" (*PLF* 192). Writes Hitler, "Only the presence of such a center and of a place, bathed in the magic of a Mecca or a Rome, can at length give a movement that force which is rooted in the inner unity and in the recognition of a hand that represents this unity" (Hitler qtd. in *PLF* 192–193). The unifying hand would belong to Hitler, Munich would serve as the "materialization of his unifying panacea" (*PLF* 192), and the German people's rallying cry would be the extirpation of "a common enemy" (*PLF* 193).

Unshared Substances

While contemporary theories of "the scapegoat mechanism" are often attributed to Rene´ Girard's ground-breaking studies of mimesis in works like *Deceit, Desire, and the Novel*, Girard actually borrowed the term from Kenneth Burke's *Permanence and Change*. Burke describes what he calls the "scapegoat mechanism" as a quasi-psychoanalytic defence mechanism that emerges out of a social group's dysfunctional relationship with turbulent undulations in its environment. In *Permanence and Change*, he compares popular forms of racism to the ancient Athenian practice of "scapegoating." The ancient Greeks hallucinated that they could ritually purge plagues that befell their polity by magically funnelling them into the vessel of a goat, which could then be ushered out of the city state. In what Burke viewed as an analogous form of sorcery in his own time, mid-century American racists conveniently attributed widespread societal ills to the presence of non-Caucasians and foreigners, which the racist imagination sought to purge or subdue in order to make America great again.

Burke composes several necropolitical allegories to describe the life-world of the economically and socially disenfranchised racist. The standard racist hastily blames racialized people for ills brought upon them by an increasingly unjust mode of capitalism offering little in the way of a social safety net. One of Burke's most disturbing and evocative parables is his narrative about a rat placed in an electrified maze by a cruel experimental psychologist. When the cruel vivisectionist electrocutes the rat, "the conditions of the experiment ... do not enable the rat to perceive the experimenter's part in the enterprise at all" (*PC* 15). Just as the abused animal responds in a seemingly "pathological" fashion to the experimenter's invisible electrical shocks by looking for invisible enemies in their Skinner mazes, a certain brand of racist, according to Burke, foolishly misrecognizes the source of their torment at the hands of a callous and volatile world. Due to the ease with which the racist imagination singles out racialized minorities, it will thoughtlessly fall back on the scapegoat mechanism – as a sort of obverse fetishism (detesting, rather than desiring, the object in question) – in order to explain away complex, often inscrutable, economic or political ills in terms of the actions of a hated individual or group.

In his careful analysis of *Mein Kampf*, Burke underscores the pivotal role of scapegoating in Hitler's sophistry. The German people's supposed shared substance is their pure Aryan blood, which accords them a mystical racial dignity. The execrable "common enemy" of the German people, according to Hitler, is the Jew, "the international devil materialized, in the visible, point-to-able form of people with a certain kind of 'blood'" (*PLF* 194). Having "thus essentialized his enemy, all 'proof' henceforth is automatic" (*PLF* 194). The figure of the "international Jew stock exchange capitalist" (*PLF* 195) was blamed for Germany's economic and social undulations. It would be pointless, adds Burke, to reason with the Hitlerian antisemite and "point to the 'Aryan' who commits the very crimes against poor and working Germans that Hitler attributes to the 'international Jew.'" From the standpoint of such a scapegoating imagination, these ideological complications merely serve as "proof that the 'Aryan' has been 'seduced' by the Jew" (*PLF* 195). Every reasonable retort can be rationalized and assimilated into the conspiratorial racist narrative.

Underlying Hitler's tendentious logic is the need to employ the Jew as a "[p]rojection device" (*PLF* 202). Here, Burke once again borrows a term from Freud's lexicon of defence mechanisms. Hitler's act of projection onto the Jewish scapegoat allows him to "hand over his infirmities to a vessel, or 'cause,' outside the self, one can battle and external enemy instead of battling an enemy within. And the greater one's internal inadequacies, the greater the [number] of evils once can load upon the back of 'the enemy'" (*PLF* 203). Hitler's political expediency resided in his cunning displacement of the perceived illness in the body politic, at a time of scarcity and discord, onto the fabricated figure of the malign Jew. This projection of negativity conveniently affords "*a noneconomic interpretation of economic ills*" (*PLF* 204; Burke's emphasis), whereby he was able to focus the German people's attention on the putrid, contagious *Jewish* modality of finance while deflecting it from the putatively unparasitic forces of Aryan finance with which the *Führer* was clearly more comfortable.

Hitler's Courtly Romance with the German *Volk*

Burke's interests in psychoanalysis, narrative, and propaganda attune him to the fact that Hitler's seduction narrative is replete with "sexual symbolism" (*PLF* 195): "The masses are 'feminine.' As such, they desire to be led by a dominating male. This male, as orator, woos them–and, when he has won them, he commands them. The rival male, the villainous, Jew, would on the contrary 'seduce' them. If he succeeds, he poisons their blood by intermingling with them" (*PLF* 195). If the economy of courtship plays out in such a fashion that the paternal Platonic orator fails to win over and command the effete body politics, the perverse Jewish sophist deceives the unknowing *Volk* into spreading their proverbial legs for him. According to Hitler's German faery-tale logic, the scheming, monstrous Jew is then able to infect the figurative and literal German bloodstream with his toxic substance. "Whereupon, by associative connections of ideas," Burke writes, "we are moved into attacks upon syphilis, prostitution, incest, and other similar misfortunes, which are introduced as a kind of 'musical' argument when he is on the subject of 'blood-poisoning' by intermarriage or, in its 'spiritual' equivalent, by the infection of 'Jewish' ideas, such as democracy" (*PLF* 195). Here, we should pay attention to Burke's critique of Hitler's mendaciously constrictive web of associations: the *Volk*'s toleration of the Jews' infiltration of the Fatherland can register only as a slippery slope into a cesspool of bodily, political, and spiritual contamination.

But hate and love coagulate both perversely and persuasively in Hitler's discourse. Even though "Hitler's book certainly falls under the classification of hate, ... the rationalized family tree for this hate situates it in a quasi-Christian form of 'Aryan love'" (*PLF* 199). Mobilizing a love for the unpolluted bloodstream of the German people, Hitler's "caricatured version of religious thought" (*PLF* 199) is geared towards the possibility of the downtrodden German nation's "symbolic rebirth" (*PLF* 205). Hitler enlists the German public to cooperate, out of its love for the Aryan bloodline, in recognizing the parasitism of the odious Jew. "The projective device of the scapegoat," writes Burke, "coupled with the Hitlerite doctrine of inborn racial superiority, can again get the feel of *moving forward*, towards a *goal*" (205) of progress towards a secular Promised Land. Always deflecting from an economic interpretation of primarily economic ills, he consistently "ends his diatribes against contemporary economic ills by a shift ... to the 'true' cause, which is centred in 'race'. While the Aryan race is 'constructive,' the Jew is inherently 'destructive'" (*PLF* 204). Therefore, the Aryan project to extirpate its semitic enemy is motivated by self-preservation, brotherly love, and the benevolent drive to unity. "The Aryan, as the vessel of *love*, must *hate* the Jewish *hate*" (*PLF* 204).

In order for Germany to properly congeal as a folkish organism, Hitler believed he had to function as its unifying "inner voice." As a synecdoche for the German *Geist*, Hitler's voice functioned as both the German Christianic conscience and its sadistic superego. Nonetheless, the dysfunctions of the parliamentary system remained a massive impediment to Hitler's efficient leadership over the body politic. About this aspect of Hitler's Pied Piper project, Burke engages in much the same variety of autobiographical motivational analysis for which he critiques Freud. In Burke's defence, however, his reading practice is closer to the New Criticism in that it cleaves to the language, tropes, and lines of signification proffered by the text. However, in contradistinction to the reading practices of New Critics like Cleanth Brooks, he does not shy away from the "intentional fallacy" of divining the author's motivations from his words and life circumstances.

In a spectacular act of "interpretation of interpretation," Burke diagnoses Hitler's diagnosis of the Hapsburg Empire's multiple personality disorder as a consequence of his personal experience of Vienna as a young man. For Hitler, Vienna was an echo chamber of vices. Young Hitler, "suffering under the alienation of poverty and confusion" (*PLF* 200), had been dismayed to find in post-war Vienna "the city of poverty, prostitution, immorality, coalitions, half-measures, incest, democracy (i.e. majority rule leading to 'lack of personal responsibility'), death, internationalism, and anything else of thumbs-down sort the associative enterprise cared to add on this side of the balance" (*PLF* 200). This feckless decadence inhered most of all to the image of the parliament, which, "at its best, is a 'babel' of voices" (*PLF* 200). Hitler had been revolted by the ineffectual "wrangle of men representing interests lying awkwardly on the bias across from one another, sometimes opposing, sometimes vaguely divergent" (*PLF* 200). Thus, he "came to take this parliament as the basic symbol of all that he would move away from" (*PLF* 200). If Munich was to become Hitler's Rome, the rotten circus of Viennese parliamentary democracy was his Babylon.

Through Burke's eyes, Hitler's demagoguery figures as a malevolently poetic form of symbolic action that demands careful analysis. Masquerading as the Pope of Germany, a newfangled Platonic orator, a paradoxically anti-Jewish psychoanalyst, and a pseudo-Nietzschean epidemiologist of the spirit, Hitler masterfully assumes rhetorically adroit positions designed to enlist the German people to his cause. Burke's account of Hitler's fixation on the Truth of German blood, his aversion to messy parliamentary wrangling, and his projection of societal ills onto racialized scapegoats figure the *Führer* as simultaneously a cynical sophist and a facile Platonist, one whose schema of the world is engineered to persuade a democratically-led public to identify with fascist totalitarianism. His savvy rhetoric speaks to the deflated German public's desperate need for a scapegoat at a time of disunity, widespread morass, economic collapse, and decimated imperial ambitions. The cunning manner in which Hitler attributes the Viennese "moral decay" to the figure of the loathsome Jew opens onto an associative web that magically explains away so many of Germany's infirmities. The Jew "thereupon gets saddled with a vast amalgamation of evils, among them being capitalism, democracy, pacifism, journalism, poor housing, modernism, big cities, loss of religion, half measures, ill health, and the weakness of the monarch" (*PLF* 205). The cluster of societal ailments that Hitler attaches to his rival Jewish courtier renders the figure of the Jew the enemy of Aryan salubrity and the ultimate obstacle to Germany's achievement of its heroic destiny.

Echoes of Fascism

Since Donald Trump's election and ignominious failure to win a second term in office, many journalists and academics have wondered aloud whether he should be understood as a fascist. Political scholars like Sheri Berman and Matthew Feldman suggest that it makes more sense to characterize him as an aspiring authoritarian who has more in common with sleazy kleptocratic thugs like Italy's Silvio Berlusconi than militaristic dictators in the mould of Mussolini or Hitler. While it might be simplistic to brand Donald Trump a fascist, his rhetoric certainly draws power from the fascistic logic of the scapegoat that so concerned Burke in the 1930s.

In "The Rhetoric of Trump's Struggle," David Masiel observes that Trump's discourse "supplants the singular enemy with the comparatively unwieldy, three-headed monster of illegal Mexican labor, unhinged Muslim terrorism, and corrupt big government supported by its free-loading constituents" (Masiel 3). These scapegoats for American detumescence deflect away from more substantive political-economic investigations by creating ready-to-hand targets for xenophobic rage. Even though the American government does have an obligation to be concerned about issues like terrorism, immigration, and political corruption, "he's not talking about economic policy any more than his words on terrorism are talking about foreign policy" (Masiel 3). Building a wall around America, banning Muslims from entering the country, and locking up Hillary Clinton may sound to some like panaceas to deeply engrained social maladies. They certainly translate well into the rhetoric of Tweets and political t-shirts. However, such draconian measures would be all but impracticable for even the President of the United States to actually execute.[1] Still, Trump seemed remarkably unperturbed by the abyss that separated his claims from his powers and frequently doubled down on such impossible promises, or what some would call "mere rhetoric."

This disconnect leads Masiel to point to another aspect of Trump's penchant for engaging in non-political solutions to political problems. Pointing to his "no bullshit swagger, his decidedly un-politic tendencies to make outrageous statements" (Masiel 4), he characterizes Trump as a "carnival barker" who is prodigiously adept at directing his audience's attention. While the heirs apparent of the Clinton and Bush political dynasties trotted out pre-scripted talking points through 2015 and 2016, Trump shot from the hip. Masiel continues, "Trump's America responds to his rhetoric because they long for a strong leader, crave a person who can stand up to a ruling elite that is nonresponsive to their concerns. This is a ruling elite that most Americans both envy and despise" (Masiel 5).

The term "fascism" derives from the Italian word *fascio*, which means "bundle of sticks." Mussolini's fascists came to associate the term with the ancient Roman symbol of a bundle of rods tied around an axe. Roman lictors, who were the magistrate's bodyguards and proto-policemen, used these rods to enforce his will through force. The *fasces* trope connoted strength through unity. While a single rod is easily broken, a dense bundle is almost unbreakable (especially when it doubles as an offensive weapon). Hitler certainly qualified as a fascist in this regard. He choreographed an elaborate political-theological dramatistic scene that situated him as a crypto-Catholic messianic dictator that could serve as a figurehead for German racial-ethnic unity. The Hitlerian fascia systematically ran through the German Leviathan and coordinated the submission of much of Europe.

President Trump, on the other hand, derived political-theological support from an uncanny amalgam of evangelical fervour, QAnonian folly, and public fascination with his refusal to play by the sterile rules of political discourse. While Trump may not be a fascist leader, he certainly appeals to "an American version of a fascistic longing for order, clarity, and dignity" (Masiel 5).[2] "This functions," Masiel continues, "despite the obvious truth that Trump's appeal reeks of American individualism on steroids, of punchline politics, and the cult of celebrity" (Masiel 5). That so many Americans could invest their hopes in a television game show host who promised to apply his best-known catchphrase – "You're fired!" – to the moribund liberal democratic status quo speaks volumes about the desperate predicament of the nation two decades after what was supposed to be the dawn of a new American century.

Future Fascisms

The German people's susceptibility to the panaceas that this "medicine man" (*PLF* 191) invited them to consume was, according to Burke, predicated on Hitler's rerouting of a universal, primordial drive to unification at a time of profound disarray and late-imperial autoimmune spasms. Burke therefore admonished his fellow anti-Hitlerians for engaging in trite disavowals of Hitler's legitimately "exasperating, even nauseating" (*PLF* 191) text rather than submitting it to careful rhetorical scrutiny.

When well-intentioned critics no longer conduct close readings, they are ultimately "contributing more to our gratification than to our enlightenment" (*PLF* 191) while snake-oil salesmen on both sides of the Atlantic continue to market their wares to those inclined to listen.

Burke is quick to point out that Hitler was essentially a "skilled advertising man" (216), a fascist proto Don Draper with a shrewd understanding of "the power of spectacle" (217). As a persuasive sophist, Hitler was an obscene manipulator, and *Mein Kampf* was "the testament of a man who swung a great people into his wake" (*PLF* 191). Burke thus proposed, in the lead-up to America's involvement in World War II, that antifascist critics dispense with gratifying displays of book burning by other means. Instead, he enjoined them to read Hitler's words and to read them carefully, "not merely to discover some grounds for prophesying what political move is to follow Munich" but "to discover what kind of 'medicine' this medicine-man has concocted that we may know, with greater accuracy, exactly what to guard against if we are to forestall the concocting of similar medicine in America" (*PLF* 191).

While Trump did not actually write his autobiographical *The Art of the Deal* himself, he did appear to have written many of his own Tweets. One could only wonder what Burke would have to say about Twitter's cancellation of Trump's account right before the election. The platform that had afforded his rise to power at long last pulled the plug on his ascent. Because of Burke's hopeful investment in the Enlightenment project to emancipate humanity through the cultivation of critical humanistic tools, he vigilantly subscribed to the belief that aspiring progressive communities are always better off reading texts closely and interpreting them carefully than excommunicating them from polite conversation for fear they might contaminate the fold. It stands to reason that he would likely be critical of the social media platform's censorship of such an important, albeit buffoonish, individual's political discourse.

Then again, the modern-day Internet often resonates as many steps removed from Enlightenment-era fantasies of civilizational progress through technology and humanistic discourse. As contemporary loci of both superegoic censorship and impulsive parliamentary wrangles, platforms like Twitter, Facebook, TikTok, and Weibo engender a symbolic fog that, for many participants, occludes access to even the pixelated simulacrum of a viable democratic agora. Burke and Freud would both likely view the immense sway of social media in the digital twenty-first century with an admixture of morbid fascination and dread. As to whether the state of our digital atmosphere, with all of its snares and phantasms, would bring Burke closer to Freud's pessimism about the symbol-using animal's civilizational arc, we could only speculate.

Notes

1 It goes without saying that even if Trump had somehow managed to erect a wall around the entire southern border of the United States, such an impressive act of mobilization would not have accomplished much more than a xenophobic spectacle of securitization.

2 In "Magic for a People Trained in Pragmatism: Kenneth Burke, *Mein Kampf*, and the Early 9/11 Oratory of George W. Bush," Jason Thompson characterizes former President George W. Bush as a closer approximation of the fascist model of leadership on account of his more effective mobilization of the American public at the beginning of his disastrous "War on Terror."

4 Beyond the Pressure Principle

Disorientation, Debunking, and Conspiracy

In this chapter, we explore Burke's treatment of concepts like orientation, trained incapacity, occupational psychosis, debunking, and conspiracy. These new-rhetorical concepts were, like so much else in Burke's repertoire, influenced by Freud's later speculative work on the pleasure principle and that which lies beyond it. In his far-reaching exposition on orientation, trained incapacity, and occupational psychosis in *Permanence and Change*, Burke examines these ideas as rhetorical counterparts to canonical Freudian concepts. He is especially invested in assessing the roles of different regimes of interpretive training in preparing the symbol-using animal for the vicissitudes of the world that it will encounter. Oftentimes, these orientations equip us to engage with particular economic, political, or bio-ecological environments. When our atmospheric conditions change, they exert pressures that lead us to alter some of our interpretive frameworks. Since not all of these pressures and paradigms are conscious, we often discover too late that our modes of training, and the worldviews out of which they emanate, incapacitate us when it comes to tackling the exigencies of a turbulent world. Burke's uptake and transfiguration of the psychoanalytic field, especially Freud's late work on repetition (in *Beyond the Pleasure Principle* and *Civilization and Its Discontents*), engenders theoretical optics that shed meaningful light on the contemporary circulation of online conspiracy theories like Pizzagate and QAnon.

Burke begins *Permanence and Change* with an exploration of "orientation" as a rhetorical concept. Operating at the intersection of the lifeworld (how the world is presented to consciousness) and the worldview (how we conceive of the world and the opinions we form about it), orientation, for Burke, signifies our fundamental interpretive optics on an often treacherous environment. In order to bring the suasive dimensions of orientation into relief, he examines a variety of situations in which nonhuman animals are confronted with the symbolically-charged modes of human deception. For example, a trout that succumbs to the lure of a baited hook but ultimately escapes (or gets thrown back) will perhaps, by virtue of its instinct for self-preservation, develop "a more educated way of reading the signs" (*PC* 5) and becomes better equipped to recognize such snares down the

DOI: 10.4324/9781003214069-5

road. "It does not matter," he adds, "how conscious or unconscious one chooses to imagine this critical step—we need only note the outward man-ifestation of a revised judgement" (*PC* 5). In this sense, "All living things are critics" (*PC* 6) in that we all develop automated semiotic subroutines meant to assist in the difficult task of pattern recognition.

What separates humanity from "this sophisticated trout" (*PC* 6) is our prodigious "powers of abstraction," which allow us to "greatly extend the scope of the critical process" (*PC* 6). While nonhuman animals engage in a rudimentary form of "criticism" that allows them to distinguish food from bait and friend from foe, only the symbol-using animal is oriented towards engaging in more sophisticated modes of second-order criticism:

> Though all organisms are critics in the sense that they all interpret the signs about them, the experimental speculative techniques made available by speech would seem to single out the human species as the only one possessing an equipment for living beyond the criticism of experience to a criticism of criticism. We not only interpret the char-acter of events ... we may also interpret our interpretations.
>
> (*PC* 11)

The symbolic ether is simultaneous our most powerful critical tool and our most bewildering symbolic fog. "The very power of criticism," writes Burke, has allowed humanity "to build up cultural structures so complex that still greater powers of criticism are needed before [we] can distinguish between the food-processes and bait-processes concealed beneath [our] cultural tangles. [Our] greater critical capacity has increased not only the range of [our] solutions, but also the range of [our] problems" (*PC* 12).

Our disorientation within the symbolic fog often leads us astray. Burke invites the reader to contemplate "what conquest over the environment we have attained through our powers of abstraction, of generalization" and "the stupid national or racial wars which have been fought precisely because these abstractions were mistaken for realities" (*PC* 13). After all, he adds, "No slight critical ability is required for one to hate as his deepest enemy a people thousands of miles away. When criticism can do so much for us, it may have got us just to the point where we greatly require still better criticism" (*PC* 13). By condensing its genius in abstract systems of thought, the symbol-using animal has also inadvertently canalized itself through tangled networks that frequently culminate in self-destructive, world-destructive behaviours. There is, in other words, a destructive drive lurking within technoscientific instrumental rationality. This fossilization of thought into alternately homicidal and suicidal pathways calls on crit-ics to engage in the kind of rhetorical "atom cracking" required to stave off tragedy.

He therefore frames *logos*, the power of reason, as both humanity's crowning achievement and our most "irrational" second instinct. Such quasi-instinctual predilections flip over into a treacherous form of "trained incapacity" when our context changes and we misrecognize a new situation as fundamentally resembling an old one. A rapidly changing economy, media environment, or climate zone is a potential minefield in this regard. Not only is it impossible to cultivate a god's-eye view on the socio-symbolic ether, but our immediate environs also condition us to universalize and operationalize our hitherto successful strategies for engaging with a particular version of the world. When we succumb to hermetically sealed hermeneutics, the ossification of our worldviews and practices renders us ill-adapted to the vicissitudes of a volatile, constantly metamorphosing world.

Burke refers to the orientational lifeworld as an "occupational psychosis." Attributing the phrase to John Dewey, he employs "psychosis" here in the now antiquated sense of one's "psychic state" rather than its contemporary sense of a schizoid mental breakdown. And he employs the term to signify our "occupations and preoccupations," states of mind that emerge out of inurement to a particular station in the world (such as a job, economic class, or ethnic identity). As a "bundle of judgements" about "how things were, how things are, and how things may be" (*PC* 15), the occupational psychosis is more than simply a state of mind. It is a "moral network complex beyond all possibilities of charting" (*PC* 305). This internalized constellation of "ethical structures" is "self-perpetuating" to the point that "it is probably carried into the most casual bit of slang" (*PC* 305).

When the parameters of the overriding world, or one's position within it, invisibly change, one's encrusted orientational bubbleworld may flip over into a disorienting form of "trained incapacity." A cryptocurrency investor's lucrative risk-taking behaviour in 2019 may bankrupt her in 2022. By the same token, a college student's racist joke that has his fraternity brothers rolling in the aisles may cost him his job and reputation when he, or someone else, shares it over Twitter. So much about the significance of such utterances and activities is less a function of the signifier-signified relationship than the labyrinthine vascular system of the world within which it lands.

On this matter, once again, Burke compares the symbol-using animal's predicament to that of other nonhuman animals caught up in a cruel psychology experiment:

> Pavlov's dog had acquired a meaning for bells when conditioned to salivate at the sound of one. Other experiments have shown that such meanings can be made still more accurate: chickens can be taught that only one specific pitch is a food-signal, and they will allow bells of other pitches to ring unheeded. But people never tremble enough at the thought of how flimsy such interpreting of characters is. If one rings the bell next time, not to feed the chickens, but to assemble them for chopping off their heads, they come faithfully running, on

the strength of the character which a ringing bell possesses for them. Chickens not so well educated would have acted more wisely. Thus it will be seen that the devices by which we arrive at a correct orientation may be quite the same as those involved in an incorrect one. We can only say that a given objective event derives its character for us from past experiences having to do with like or related events.

(*PC* 14)

Against the grain of received Kantian wisdom about the inherently self-emancipatory qualities of education, Burke insists that symbol-using animals quickly become symbol-misusing, maladaptively conditioned animals when the enveloping scene changes the significance of their symbolic actions. An occupational "way of seeing," remarks Burke, "is also a way of not seeing – a focus on object A involves a neglect of object B" (*PC* 49).

Burke continues with a comment that reverberates as remarkably prescient in the age of COVID-19: "A ringing bell is in itself as meaningless as an undifferentiated portion of the air we are breathing. It takes on character, meaning, significance (dinner bell or door bell) in accordance with the contexts in which we experience it" (*PC* 10). When the dinner bell is furtively transformed into a murder bell at the drop of a hat, the chickens' "past training [causes] them to misjudge their present situation. Their training has become an incapacity" (*PC* 10). For Burke, our socio-symbolic "second nature" makes us a lot more like his allegorical chickens than philosophies of human exceptionalism tend to allow for. He therefore implores us to attune ourselves to the ever-present possibility of such disconnects between our socio-symbolic orientation and substantive contextual differences as we migrate from milieu to milieu. Of course, in the age of COVID-19, "the air we are breathing" has been embedded with new material-semiotic folds that call on all of us who breathe to reorient ourselves towards our hitherto invisibilized enveloping atmosphere.

Debunking and Rebunking the Air We Are Breathing

A preoccupational lifeworld that especially concerns Burke is the station of what he refers to as the "debunker." Debunking is the semi-automated unreflective practice of vigilantly exposing the fatuousness (or we might even say the motivated "tendentiousness") of one's opponent's arguments while preserving a more stable plateau for oneself. In our present-day parlance, debunking is usually associated with undermining illogical arguments, conspiracy theories, and other forms of snake oil charlatanism. But Burke's version of debunking is arguably closer to the rhetorical activity of the adamant conspiracy theorist than those bent on exposing his errors.[1] That is because Burke's critique of debunking is focused not so much on the truth or falsity of the views being promulgated as the debunker's dogmatically adversarial orientation, their a-priori *drive to debunk*. The overbearing pulsion to expose error and duplicity (i.e. to debunk "sophistry") bespeaks a rigidly uncharitable attitude about the motivations animating one's opponents in an argument. This stalwart ethical orientation impels the symbol-using animal to absolutely decimate the other side's rhetorical house of cards.

As an overriding disposition, debunking figures as another perversion of cooperation in that it takes pathological precedence over the pursuit of common cause with our interlocutors. About this dysfunctional orientation, Burke writes,

> I think that the typical debunker is involved in a strategy of this sort: He discerns an evil. He wants to eradicate that evil. And he wants to do a thorough job of it. In order to be sure he is *thorough enough*, he becomes *too thorough*. In order to knock the underpinnings from beneath the arguments of his opponents, he perfects a mode of argument that would, if carried out consistently, also knock the underpinnings from beneath his own argument.
>
> (*PLF* 171)

Debunking emerges out of a fundamentally uncharitable "tragic" attitude, as Burke refers to it in his account of "comic correctives" in *Attitudes Toward History*. Whereas didactic propaganda of the debunking variety tends to entail "polemical, one-way approaches to social necessity" and other people's motivations, an ethical "comic" approach necessitates a more nuanced and ambivalent, "charitable attitude towards people" when deploying one's resources for the "purposes of persuasion and cooperation" (*ATH* 166).

Debunking, when taken to the extreme, manifests itself as a tragic "trained incapacity" to read others through a charitable lens. According to Burke, such uncharitable brush strokes have their roots in early modern political theory:

> We may note the emergence of the debunking attitude in the works of Machiavelli and Hobbes. Machiavelli tended to consider the "ungrateful, deceitful, cowardly, and greedy" aspects of men not as an aspect of their "fall," but as the very essence of their nature. Lying was not a deviation from the norm, it was the norm. Beneath this strategy, to be sure, there was a humane motive. Machiavelli felt, I believe, that since virtues are by very definition rare, they are a frail structure upon which to build a state. But if you could found a state upon vice, you would have a firm foundation indeed. And in an age of marked instability, Machiavelli was searching vigorously for firmness, a kind of beneath-which-not. Similarly, Hobbes based his arguments for political authority upon the "nasty" and "brutish" nature of men,

who required an absolute monarch to hold their essential meanness in check. You may trail this mode of thought down through the paradoxes of Mandeville. And finally, in Adam Smith, it becomes benign, as Smith worked out a structure whereby the sheer accumulations of mutually conflicting individual greeds added up to a grand total of social benefit.

(*PLF* 169)

"In brief," Burke concludes, "the history of debunking is interwoven with the history of liberalism" (*PLF* 169). While fascistic debunking takes the putative enemy's baseness as a foundational tenet, standard conservative and liberal modes of debunking seem to be predicated on "our own" collective greed. As liberal and conservative uptake of Adam Smith's influential account of "the Invisible Hand" (which purportedly saves us from the consequences of our atomization) evinces, both brands of political-economic ideology share the foundational belief that capitalism magically transfigures selfishness into "social benefit." So much about the ethical compass of Western civilization is, according to Burke, rooted in the hallucinatory equation of systemic greed with cooperation.

This "tragic" modality of occupational psychosis, whether it be fascist or liberal, also readily tilts into what we might call "conspiracy theory" when the "marked instability" of the world creates ruptures in our socio-symbolic tapestry. On the issue of the disoriented symbol-using animal's drive to "discover" conspiracies hiding beneath the surface of vertiginous networks of influence, Burke writes that a complex social formation described by one observer as innocent cooperation will be artificially stabilized by the debunker as a nefarious conspiracy. From this conspiracy-transfixed standpoint, the debunker may aver that any form of social cohesion is necessarily a malign plot:

> Sovereignty itself is conspiracy. And the pattern is carried into every political or social body, however small. Each office, each fraternal order, each college faculty has its tiny conspiratorial clique. Conspiracy is as natural as breathing. And since the struggles for advantage nearly always have a rhetorical strain, we believe that the systematic contemplation of them forces itself upon the student of rhetoric.
>
> (*ARM* 166)

Dwelling on the etymology of "conspire," which literally signifies "breathing together," Burke invites rhetoricians to contemplate overdetermined conspiracy thinking as a disorientation bound up with the drive to debunk one's potential adversaries. Rather than undertaking the difficult work of echolocating common ground within a co-inspired shared space, the conspiracy theorist is convinced in advance of the other side's malignity.

The conspiracy theorist is a debunker because they have their finger on the trigger when it comes to seeking out and unmasking plots which may not exist as such. As a counterpoint to debunking, Burke prescribes a more ambivalent comic frame of reference in relation to the "unresolvable ambiguity" (*GM* 24) of our suasive environment. "Instead of considering it our task to dispose of any ambiguity," writes Burke, "we rather consider it our task to study and clarify the resources of ambiguity. For in the course of this work we shall deal with many kinds of transformation and it is in the areas of ambiguity that transformation takes place" (*GM* xix). Sensitive to the ambiguities that subtend so many received wisdoms about plots and cabals, the rhetorically astute observer would be reluctant to assume a posture of certainty about the conspiratorial orientation of a relatively opaque social nexus. Burke's wariness is not because conspiracies do not exist but because such a rigid commitment to certainty about them overdetermines too much about how we engage with our ambient symbolic haze, about which (at least much of the time), sadly, very little can be certain. Apparent conspiracies tend to remain impenetrable and irresolvably ambiguous. We can and should speculate about and seek to get to the bottom of them. However, Burke would have us extend our critical feelers in a much more nuanced fashion. It is impossible to see clearly through the symbolic fog, yet we have little choice but to learn to dwell nimbly with uncertainty, proceed circumspectly when the light seems to break through, and take calculated risks when something smells off.

As Burkean theorist Elizabeth Weiser frames the matter, Burke advocates for a "comic" posture that engages in neither the paralytic occupational psychosis of "upholding the status quo" nor the profligate debunkery that tilts towards "merely tearing down the existing structure" (Weiser 22). Just as occupational psychosis engenders trained incapacity in the face of the marked instability of the world, the debunker's cynical, accusatory disposition (about the sinister modality of cooperation in which others are participating) maladaptively precludes the possibility of cooperation at the outset. After all, the conspiracy theorist's drive to impose their truth on the scene alienates both those who are reluctant to take the plunge into conspiracy thinking and those who are accused of being in on the plot in one fell swoop.

The Fantasmatic Substance of Conspiracy Thinking

Political theorist Michael Barkun defines a conspiracy belief as "the belief that an organization made up of individuals or groups was or is acting covertly to achieve some malevolent end" (Barkun 3). Conspiracy thinking, writes Barkun, is a predisposition to "interpret events and circumstances as the product of malevolent conspiracies, a tendency to impose a conspiratorial narrative on salient affairs" (Barkun 4). When such a perception of the world is based on fossilized misinterpretation rather than the cautious assessment of authoritative evidence, it tends to be organized around three principles that pervade most every conspiracy theory: "nothing happens by accident," "nothing is what it seems," and "everything is connected" (Barkun 3–4). The conspiracy theorist debunks status-quo common sense and exposes uncanny secrets to the light of day. In Burkean terms, their web of analytic associations, replete with fossilized metaphors, is inadequately *free* to speak to the social field's impenetrable ambiguity and its resistance to totalization within a conspiracy-theoretical field. The conspiracy theorist does not recognize the ineffable status of what Lacan would call the social field's Real dimension, the extent to which our words and other symbols necessarily fail to speak comprehensively to what we perceive as the underlying Truth.

As we glossed in the previous chapter, Burke implores his readership to view Hitler as the far right-wing conspiracy theorist par excellence. To this end, Burke employs Freud's later ideas about repetition compulsion, in tandem with Aristotle's notion of entelechy, to articulate the contours of Hitler's dangerous conspiratorial rhetoric. In *Language as Symbolic Action*, Burke brings the conspiratorial brand of occupational psychosis into resonance with entelechy, the principle of movement towards the perfection of a proper end. He characterizes Freud's notion of "destiny compulsion" as "the thought that the sufferer unconsciously strives to form his destiny in accordance with this earlier pattern" (*LSA* 509). This formulation of a principle of automatism leads Burke to ask, "Why should such a 'destiny compulsion' or 'repetition compulsion' be viewed as antithetical to the 'principle of perfection'?" (*LSA* 509). After all, an individual that is entrenched in his occupational psychosis may engage in a form of magical thinking, "exerting almost superhuman efforts in the attempt to give his life a certain form, to so shape his relations to people in later years that they will conform perfectly to an emotional or psychological pattern already established in some earlier formative situation" (*LSA* 509).

According to Burke, this hybrid rhetorical-psychoanalytic variant on repetition compulsion is evident in the conspiracy theorist's obsessive invocation of the "perfect villain" (*LSA* 509). "The Nazi version of the Jew," writes Burke, "is the most thorough-going instance of such ironic 'perfection' in recent times" (*LSA* 509). Hitler's projection of all that holds German society from fulfilling its proper destiny onto the "perfectly" malevolent figure of the Jew begets unanswerable questions about Hitler's state of mind and intentions. "The distinguishing quality of Hitler's method as an instrument of persuasion," writes Burke, may lead one to ask "whether Hitler is sincere or deliberate, whether his vision of the omnipotent conspirator has the drastic honesty of paranoia or the sheer shrewdness of a demagogue trained in Realpolitik of the Machiavellian sort" (*PLF* 210).[2]

At the end of the day, Burke contends, we need not engage in such a speculative "either–or" exercise (*PLF* 210) about Hitler's intentions.

What he cares most about is the rhetorical-psychoanalytic mechanism that makes Hitler's fascist conspiracy theory tick: "Have we not by now offered grounds enough for or contention that Hitler's sinister powers of persuasion derive from the fact that he spontaneously evolved his 'cure-all' in response to inner necessities?" (*PLF* 211). Germany, in a state of economic, political, and spiritual turmoil, was perfectly poised to receive the snake oil that Hitler was marketing in the form of the Jewish scapegoat. Burke wanted his readers to acquaint themselves with his particular brand of hucksterism so that they could both recognize it for what it was in the lead-up to World War II and equip themselves to take on the quasi-fascistic American demagoguery that he believed was looming over the horizon.

Citing Freud's speculative account of civilization's prehistory in *Totem and Taboo*, Burke observes the classically psychoanalytic paranoid dimensions of Hitler's conspiracy theory. Burke looks to Freud's remarks about ancient tribal Oedipalized attitudes towards patriarchal rulers. Ancient tribal people's rulers were once deemed to be omnipotent deities, to whom they ascribed "power over rain and shine, wind and weather, and then dethrone them or kill them because nature has disappointed their expectation of a good hunt or ripe harvest" (Freud qtd. in *PLF* 214). By the same token, "a paranoiac names a person of his acquaintance as his 'persecutor', ... thereby elevat[ing] him to the paternal succession and brings him under conditions which enable him to make him responsible for all the misfortune which he experiences" (*PLF* 214). And, importantly for Burke, paranoia is a much more common psycho-rhetorical phenomenon than we tend to give it credit for. It is, to a certain extent, an inherent by-product of our symbolic environment's interactions with potentially alien and dangerous phenomena.

Piggybacking on Burke's insights into "primitive" magical thinking, Slavoj Žižek elaborates on this paranoid economy of good and evil supernatural paternal functions in Hitlerian discourse. According to Žižek's account, Hitler's brand of conspiracy theory hinges on a dualistic fantasy system. This paranoid symbolic texture has a benevolent stabilizing dimension (corresponding to the good father or deity function) and a malevolent destabilizing aspect (corresponding to the devil function). Wielding the "beatific side" of fantasy, Hitler rendered himself the good German father, who conjured "the dream of a state without disturbances, out of reach of human depravity" ("Invisible Ideology" 28). The obverse of this fantasy of the benevolent, unifying father is the "fantasy in its destabilizing dimension" ("Invisible Ideology" 28). This other pole mobilizes "all that 'irritates' me about the Other, images that haunt me of what he or she is doing when out of my sight, of how he or she deceives me and plots against me, of how he or she ignores me and indulges in an enjoyment that is intensive beyond my capacity of representation" ("Invisible Ideology" 28).

Žižek insists that "the fundamental lesson of so-called totalitarianism" is the "co-dependence of these two aspects of the notion of fantasy" (28). "The foreclosed obverse of the Nazi harmonious *Volksgemeinschaft*," or "Germanic people's community," writes Žižek, "returned in the guise of their paranoiac obsession with the Jewish plot" (28). The magical thinking of a perfectly harmonious, rational, meaningful, unified, cooperative German nationalist project is predicated on the equally magical thinking of a malevolent, inhuman, parasitic, irrational, licentious, conspiring, overproximal pest in the national ointment. Everything that impedes the actualization of this Imaginary of German greatness is condensed in the fantasy of a Satanic Jewish plot. This distorted figure of the aberrant Jew is a symptom of a fantasy system that aims to vouchsafe the smooth functioning of the *Volk*'s national sovereignty machine.

Paranoid Normaladies

In an effort to genealogize the history of conspiracy thinking, political theorist Jodi Dean views the emergence of the 9/11 truth movement as a somewhat new modality of conspiracy theory that nonetheless piggybacks on long-standing rhetorical elements. Pointing to truthers' facility with an emerging online environment, she describes this conspiracy theorizing community as "symptomatic of a larger sociocultural development that involves a new constellation of questioning, doubt, credibility, and certainty" (*Democracy* 148). This crisis of rhetorical ethos involves a scrambling of digital denizens' capacity to adequately discriminate when it comes to attributing expertise and recognizing irresolvable ambiguity. Dean avers that a cacophony of online narratives affords a "volatile mix of certainty and skepticism" (*Democracy* 148) in place of an authoritative "official story" about the terrorist plot. Without an unimpeachable, omniscient expert to explain away the "truth" about 9/11, the 9/11 truth movement seeks to assume the role traditionally filled by journalists and scholars in debunking propaganda and exposing political corruption.

Burke actually described a precursor to the ethos-wielding strategies of modern-day conspiracy theorists in the "disturbing strategy" employed by "conservatives" and "reactionaries" (*PLF* 175) of his day to debunk their opponents' arguments:

> It would seem that they are no longer bothering to seek good arguments; rather, they are content to seek any arguments, if only there be enough of them kept running through the headlines, an avalanche of arguments, condemnations, prophecies of dire calamity, "statistical proofs," pronouncements by private and institutional "authorities," a barrage, a snowing under, a purely quantitative mode of propaganda. Are there no eagles among their publicized utterances? Very well; then let them be instead a swarm of mosquitoes. Before you could refute

this morning's, there is a new batch out this afternoon. Anything, everything, if only it all points in the same general direction.

(*PLF* 175)

The debunker's occupational psychosis, when it comes to navigating and wielding the avalanche of quantitative propaganda, necessitates the disavowal of inconvenient ambiguity and nuance. All expert accounts are funnelled into a rhetorical algorithm that points conclusions "in the same general direction." The truther barrages their interlocutor with authoritative-sounding statistics, analyses, and reports. This rhetorical technique, often referred to as "the Gish gallop," deluges the conspiracy doubter with so many data points that they will be helpless to refute the pattern they form. The only reasonable conclusions that can be drawn, the 9/11 truther has decided in advance, is that bomb detonations, not airplane crashes, caused the Twin Towers to collapse and that Bush and Cheney were, beyond a shadow of a doubt, in on the terror plot from the beginning. It bears repeating that Burke and Dean are not so naïve as to suggest that conspiracies do not exist. What they take issue with are the conspiracy theorist's pathological tincture of certainty (about their own prized narratives) and scepticism (towards certain authorities) as well as the "swarm[ing]" methods he employs to persuade others that no other explanation is possible.

From Pizzagate to QAnon

Many contemporary conspiracy theories remediate a lot of the strategies that Burke adumbrates in his reading of *Mein Kampf* (which may, in part, account for their fascist resonances). But they are also motivated by what Burke would characterize as an increasingly agentive algorithmic "scene" for conspiracy thinking. Since around the time of Trump's rise to power, online conspiracy theories like QAnon have been amplified by an algorithmically-charged social media milieu that has most of us running around like headless chickens. QAnon is itself a mega-conspiratorial algorithm that sucks up and co-opts extent conspiracy theories (such as the 9/11 truth movement, sovereign citizen campaigns, paranoid accounts of 5G networks and mind control, and "Plandemic" narratives). But arguably, the conspiracy theory that is closest to the navel of the QAnon fever dream is often referred to as "Pizzagate." Pizzagate refers to the belief that a sinister group of liberal elites – usually including the likes of Hillary Clinton, George Soros, and Bill Gates – operated a child trafficking ring under a Washington, D.C. pizza parlour called Comet Ping Pong. On an image board called 4Chan, a shadowy figure known only as Q sent out reports (known as "Q Drops") of a gathering storm of Trump-allied forces that was gearing up to arrest the perpetrators of these and other obscene crimes against humanity.

Although Pizzagate-proper may have largely fallen by the wayside, the fantasmatic logic that subtends its scapegoat-messiah structure persists with a vengeance. While the liberal Democratic devils (some of whose Jewishness is frequently underscored) now inhabit the parasitic position once occupied by Jews in Hitler's conspiracy theory, Trump tends to occupy the position of messianic saviour, who will "make America great again." This quasi-Hitlerian economy of poison and panaceas of the body politic is especially redolent in QAnon discourse. In "The Plan to Save the World," "Joe M," a fervent QAnon influencer and contributor to the bestselling book *QAnon: An Invitation to the Great Awakening*, describes the Deep State's long-standing, elaborate conspiracy to keep America down:

> Every president after Reagan was one of these Deep State criminals, and their empire grew even stronger. With each bad president came new depths America and the world would sink. The world collapsed into darkness. Do you need me to tell you how? Destroyed factories, declining job numbers, sicker people, opioids, destruction of Iraq, Syria and Yemen with pointless war, displacement of people into Europe, Isis, terrorism, collapsed governments, poverty and genocide.
>
> (M 7)

In a fashion that echoes Hitler's snake oil, Joe M. posits Donald Trump as the remedy to America's profligate disrepair: "Good patriots in the US military, and their global partners asked Trump to run for president so that they could take back control of America legitimately without alarming the public" (M 8). Trump somehow prevailed over the Deep State when "he overcame the voter fraud and won .... [H]e was a patriot and he was loved and admired by the public. He was not interested in joining the cabal, mainly because they hated America and he did not agree with them on that point" (M 8). In true debunking fashion, he magically exculpates Trump from the evils of the world, which he projects onto a tight-knit cabal of liberal elites and the Deep State. Of course, if Joe were to look closely at the publicly-available archive of Trump's well-documented sins, it would rapidly, as Burke puts it, "knock the underpinnings from beneath his own argument."

According to Joe, divine justice is (or at least was) imminent. Trump and his allies have been furtively coordinating the arrest of corrupt criminals such as "famous politicians, actors, singers, CEOs and celebrities. People who have earned our trust, respect and admiration. They have done very bad things that are all fully known and documented, and they will be severely punished" (M 8). Q's followers are, according to Joe, "among the first to realize that our petty partisan divisions are just trivial distractions, and we are all enslaved by a hidden enemy." He continues, "We realize that the problem was never Capitalism or Socialism, Democrat or

Republican, black or white, Muslim or Christian" (M 8). At face value, Joe's call to overcome "petty partisan divisions" sounds almost quasi-socialist. Joe, like more sober critics of the American way of life, points to a deep rot at the heart of the American Leviathan. But in Joe's version of *The Matrix*, Donald Trump has been working tirelessly behind the scenes to root out a hydra-headed "hidden enemy," one whose extirpation will magically set America aright.

Crippled Epistemology

Internet disinformation researcher Kate Starbird points to a significant difference between contemporary social media conspiracy theories like QAnon and pre-social media conspiracy theories. The "echo chamber" of information begets what she refers to as a "crippled epistemology." While conspiracy theorists often figure themselves as diligent researchers that are driven to debunk popular delusions, many more astute observers recognize their trained incapacity to dwell with uncertainty and refrain from drawing conclusions about matters that are occluded from plain view. Their "belief in conspiracy theory 'alternative narratives' does not imply mental illness, but is instead indicative of a 'crippled epistemology' due in part to a limited number of information sources" (Starbird). These resources are fed to the theorist by, among other things, recommendation algorithms and bad-faith actors within an online rhetorical scene for conspiracy that ceaselessly reinscribes the conspiracy theorist within the circuit of their trained incapacity to see the world otherwise.

Starbird's research suggests that this counterintuitive diminution of our access to knowledge of the world is exacerbated by the illusory perception of a diverse information diet, when, in fact, our data is often drawn from a deceptively narrow number of reservoirs. She describes today's online environment as a "breeding ground" of conspiracy thinking. On the one hand, "the same content appears on different sites in different forms"; on the other, "believing in one conspiracy theory makes a person more likely to believe [in others]." Thus, "a 'critically thinking' citizen seeking more information to confirm their views about the danger of vaccines may find themselves exposed to and eventually infected by other conspiracy theories with geopolitical themes, with one conspiracy theory acting as a gateway to others" (Starbird).

Former Google computer scientist Tristan Harris lends credence to Starbird's analyses and describes how aspects of QAnon culture emerged out of Facebook's algorithmic architecture. Looking at Facebook's recommendation tendencies, he observes that once a Facebook user shows interest in a particular conspiracy theory, "Facebook groups cross-recommend other conspiracy theories" since "the algorithms that optimize for engagement can't distinguish between healthy, conscious, wise thoughtful engagement and essentially radicalizing, alienating, and isolating people from their families" (Harris). The overriding orientation of Facebook's machine-learning recommendation system is to attract, maximize, and monetize attention. Whether users are engaging in casual voyeurism, complaining about the weather, or reading about a Clinton-Soros sex trafficking operation is a secondary consideration. "To Facebook's algorithm," asserts Harris, "it's the same thing, as long as it increases the amount of engagement" (Harris).

The analyses undertaken by Starbird and Harris suggest that contemporary updates of media-rhetorical literacy will have to consider the trained incapacities that emerge out of these paranoid pathways. The rabbit holes that they describe should be understood as pathological only because they precipitate a surplus of associations that are oppressively unfree, and the conspiracy theorist tends not to apprehend the extent to which their algorithmic environment, this digital-rhetorical scene for conspiracy thinking, conducts them along media channels that continually consolidate their encrusted mode of debunkery.

Due in large part to the pervasiveness of social media and streaming video sites, conspiracy theories are no longer fringe elements of popular culture. If anything, their impact on popular orientations has never been stronger. Media scholar Benjamin Bratton observes,

> From 5G conspiracy theories to mask protests to self-destructive super-spreader events that keep the economy on lockdown, the disconnect between rational policy and what people think and do is dangerously pronounced. This disconnect won't go away all by itself once the virus runs its course. It is not just exemplary of the annus horribilis of 2020, it is inseparable from the Western response to the pandemic and the realities that it makes clear. In relation to the fraught politics of surveillance, the intricate question of what should be the appropriate structures of planetary-scale sensing and computation, as opposed to its current one, presents itself under the shadow of conspiracy theory as the default mode of folk politics.
>
> (Bratton 195)

In the age of planetary-scale social media, the impact of these digital-rhetorical psychoses is not reducible to the discourse of "just a few crazies." Bratton insists that "the number of people who you know that will refuse or have refused to get vaccinated for utterly spurious reasons will surprise you, if not shock you" (Bratton 189). Trained incapacity is a feature, not a bug, of the dramatistic infotainment ecosystem.

This increasingly prevalent default mode of conspiratorial folk politics, avers Bratton, "is driven by several interlocking motives: epistemic (one's understanding of what is going on), existential (feelings of being safe and in control), and social (maintenance of a positive image of oneself and social group)" (Bratton 190).[3] There is nothing unreasonable about experiencing these essentially Maslovian needs. Nevertheless, like Burke and Žižek, Bratton is concerned that our desires are increasingly conducted through a libertarian fantasy screen that obscures the extent to which even the most autonomous human life is primordially "an epidemiological and informational entanglement" (Bratton 191). Our overarching Western libertarian narrative creates such a potent symbolic fog that it deludes many of us into believing that we are economically, biologically, ontologically, and politically atomized entrepreneurial subjects rather than multiply consubstantial denizens of a shared economy and ecology, including the very air we breathe. The pandemic makes a mockery of both Invisible Hand narratives and our flimsy pretences of autonomy. Nonetheless, the sticky residue of our neoliberal training for an imagined entrepreneurial universe clings tenaciously to the scene and deters us from seeing the world otherwise.

The Coming Storm

In 2016, Pizzagate came to a head. Image boards and social media platforms were circulating accounts of a Clinton-run child sex ring operating out of Washington, DC pizza restaurant Comet Ping Pong's basement. On December 4, 2016, Pizzagate follower Tim Welch became so fed up with online accounts of Clinton atrocities that he decided he had to put a stop to them once and for all. Welch grabbed his AR-15 rifle and headed to Comet Ping Pong to set the imprisoned children free. When he showed up, he fired several shots in the restaurant, only to discover that Comet Ping Pong had no basement. Upon discovering that there were no abused children to be found, a detumescent Welch turned himself into the police.

"Four years later," writes Michael Miller, "thousands of people would follow Welch's fevered path to Washington, drawn from across the country by an ever more toxic stew of disinformation and extremism, including Pizzagate's successor: QAnon. This time, instead of a pizzeria, they would target the U.S. Capitol." Daniel Bessner and Amber A'Lee Frost dwell on the array of characters who showed up at the assault on the Capitol to scrutinize the cultural fabric of the constellation of aspiring activists that seems to have coagulated around Q:

> [Q] adherents don't share economic interest, culture, or even a political program. Rather, many people joined Q because of their alienation and disconnection from a system they view as illegitimate. To provide their ever-more precarious lives with meaning and an explanation for American decline, Q adherents congealed under a series of bizarre Internet conspiracy theories that unite a right-wing, anti-elitist, but

nevertheless authoritarian sensibility that is organized around narratives that link pedophilic cabals, racism, antisemitism, fears of "cultural Marxism," Satanism and, of course, absolute faith in the singular, salvific, and millenarian figure of President Donald J. Trump.

(Bessner and A'Lee Frost)

Like so many regular Germans in the lead-up to World War II, the people who showed up to the Capitol were rebounding from a bewildering cascade of ruptures: 9/11, the so-called War on Terror, the 2007/8 financial meltdown, the ever-widening gulf between the wealthy and the poor, and the pervasive "feeling of impotence in a political system that was supposed to be a democracy." They so desperately required a snake oil solution to their epistemic, existential, social, and economic discontent that they found a hallucinatory solution to their trained incapacity in the form of an old scapegoat-messiah circuit.

Trump is no Hitler. But his quasi-messianic status should impel us to reflect on parallels in their appeal to general populations in a state of turmoil. Reflecting on Hitler's brand of magical thinking, Burke dwells on Hitler's overtures to national unity through the racist, xenophobic "devil function" attached to the figure of the Jew. Burke observes that the fascist "snake oil" of Nazism serves as a missed encounter with the Real of Germany's disrepair in the aftermath of World War I:

> But this unity, if attained on a deceptive basis, by emotional trickeries that shift our criticism from the accurate locus of our trouble, is no unity at all. For, even if we are among those who happen to be "Aryans," we solve no problems even for ourselves by such solutions, since the factors pressing towards calamity remain. Thus, in Germany, after all the upheaval, we see nothing beyond a drive for ever more and more upheaval, precisely because the "new way of life" was no new way, but the dismally oldest way of sheer deception – hence, after all the "change," the factors driving towards unrest are left intact, and even strengthened. True, the Germans had the resentment of a lost war to increase their susceptibility to Hitler's rhetoric. But in a wider sense, it has repeatedly been observed, the whole world lost the War – and the accumulating ills of the capitalist order were but accelerated in their movements towards confusion. Hence, here too there are the resentments that go with frustration of men's ability to work and earn.

(*PLF* 220)

The short circuit in the Hitlerian scapegoat mechanism constituted a pernicious positive feedback loop: the German economy was in tatters, the forlorn public was desperate for a legible explanation and a practicable solution (preferably one that radically exculpated them), and the citizenry was invited to direct its rage, pain, and violent jouissance towards an execrable cathartic vessel. But when they proceeded along this path, the original crises that Hitlerian magical thinking was meant to rectify were only exacerbated.

This conspiratorial psychosis, according to Burke, speaks to people's desperate epistemological need to understand an inscrutably oppressive world. Hitler's antisemitic conspiracy theory "provided a 'world view' for people who had previously seen the world but piecemeal" (*PLF* 218). The success of Hitler's sophistry leads Burke to ask, "Did not much of his lure derive, once more, from the bad filling of a good need? .... [Were the Germans] not then psychologically ready for a rationale, any rationale, if it but offer them some specious 'universal' explanation" (*PLF* 218) of the freefall to which the Teutonic world had succumbed?

Just as Burke predicted, the more effort the Nazis dedicated to purging the alleged parasites on the body politic (parliamentary democracy, Jews, the Roma, homosexuals, etc.), the worse everyone's predicament seemed to get as "the accumulating ills of the capitalist order were but accelerated in their movements towards confusion" (*PLF* 218). The Hitlerian bait-and-switch of the "bad filling of a good need" led many to misrecognize the source of their discontent in all-too-tendentious prefab scapegoats. Once much of the country is on-board, fascistic snake-oil salesmen need only cynically gesture towards their scapegoats – as manufactured acute causes of deeper collective ills – in order to galvanize a bewildered public into spasms of psychotic confusion and mimetic violence.

If the assault on the Capitol was a sort of missed encounter with the political traumas that beset the American body politic, we would be wise to heed Burke's advice about the magnetic allure of the scapegoat mechanism at moments of national crisis. In the mid-twentieth century, he speculated that a fascistically inclined salvific figure might emerge to offer similar snake oil to traumatized, deracinated Americans. Seemingly anticipating a better organized, more efficacious version of Trump, he writes, "At that point, a certain kind of industrial or financial monopolist may, annoyed by the contrary voices of our parliament, wish for the momentary peace of one voice" (*PLF* 220). Mobilizing the public's confusion and discontentment, Burke's imagined authoritarian ruler would hoodwink some and strongarm others into paving his way to the presidency.

In this regard, Trump may well have been a warm-up for the pseudo-populist, fascistic leader of the future whom, as Burke speculates, "might, under Nazi promptings, be tempted to back a group of gangsters who, on becoming the political rulers of the state, would protect him against the necessary demands of the workers" (*PLF* 220). He would market populist snake oil to the people while doing the bidding of the 1%, occasionally throwing a tokenistic bone to xenophobes, religious zealots, and conspiracy theorists. If such a disciplined, savvy, charismatic American fascist were to emerge, "His gangsters, then, would be his insurance against his workers." But, once the genie has been let out of the bottle, Burke asks, "who would be [our] insurance against his gangsters?" (*PLF* 220).

Notes

1   The epithet "conspiracy theory" is also, of course, employed to discredit accounts of the world that the utterer would prefer to disavow for tendentious reasons. The petroleum lobby has, for example, routinely accused the environmental movement of trafficking in conspiracy theories. See Adleman, Daniel. "Where We Go One, We Go All: QAnon and the Mediology of Witnessing." *Communication +1* vol. 8, no. 1, 2021.

2   Of course, Freud's urparanoid subject was Daniel Paul Schreber. In *My Own Private Germany: Daniel Paul Schreber's Secret History of Modernity*, Eric L. Santner explores Schreber's psychotic descent into conspiratorial theories about the rot at the heart of the order of things, and Freud's reading thereof, as a sort of primal scene of modernity.

3   See Karen M. Douglas et al. "The Psychology of Conspiracy Theories." *Current Directions in Psychological Science*, vol. 26, no. 6, 2017, pp. 538–542. Bratton seems to be invoking their theoretical scaffolding without citing their paper.

5 Charcot and Freud

From Clinical Gaze to Free Association

Towards the Transference

"The relations between rhetoric and medicine," writes Judy Segal, "are various and webbed" and one could "start rhetorical investigation anywhere, and you can get everywhere from there" (Segal 2). In this chapter, we examine the pre-history and emergence of psychoanalysis in order to explore Freud's radical divergence from the methods of his physician contemporaries and forebears. His departure enacted a paradigm shift from the visual to the auditory register as he placed unprecedented emphasis on listening carefully to the words of his patients. This chapter will mobilize Burke's notion of "perspective by incongruity" to explore the unlikely emergence of Freud's revolutionary concept of "free association" out of the literary, philosophical, and therapeutic milieu of his time.

Psychoanalysis emerged at the end of the nineteenth century as an attitudinal shift in the clinician's approach to knowledge and authority in relation to transference. Each school of psychoanalysis theorizes transference differently, but the notion might be plainly understood as the analysand's unconscious ways of relating to the analyst through strong emotions, assumptions, identifications, and projections over the course of treatment. In 1893, Freud originally described transference as the analysand's displacement or projection onto the analyst, which gradually falls away over the course of treatment with the realization of the "false connection" or "illusion" that may be structured through previous experiences or through a transferal "on to the figure of the physician the distressing ideas which arise from the content of the analysis" ("The Psychotherapy" 302–304). Freud theorized transference as both an impediment to and vehicle of treatment that the analyst must respond to deftly. By the same token, he warned analysts of the dangers of "countertransference," their often counterproductive emotional reactions to their patients.

"[O]ne of the most powerful means of persuasion in the hands of physicians," writes Sarah Bigi, "is their professional ethos, or authority" (67). Lacan describes a common transference phenomenon that transpires when the analysand believes the analyst to be in the authoritative position of the

DOI: 10.4324/9781003214069-6

sujet supposé savoir, or what Alan Sheridan has translated as the "subject supposed to know." This variety of transference emerges out of the analysand's presumption that there could be a subject who possesses knowledge of the problems at stake in their treatment. "As soon as the subject who is supposed to know exists somewhere," contends Lacan, "there is transference" (*Seminar XI* 232).[1] The analysand may assume that the analyst understands the truth of their ailment, the solution to their presenting problem, or the secret meaning of their dream. But this is an illusion, albeit a productive one, made possible by Freud's unlikely invention of psychoanalysis at the turn of the century.

Getting an Eyeful: Freud at the Salpêtrière

There is a long book that remains to be written on the significance of Freud's departure from the authoritative methods of his famed mentor, neurologist Jean-Martin Charcot (1825–1893). At the heart of Freud's innovations in treating patients with "nervous illnesses" or hysteria was his emphasis on listening to his patients. As Georges Didi-Huberman and Daphne de Marneffe observe, Freud's deviation from Charcot's approach marks an important shift from an emphasis on "objective knowledge" gleaned from a forensic gaze to the "subjective knowledge" produced by the presence of an attentive ear. This shift from the eye to the ear and from the forensic to the locutionary opened the possibility of free association as a therapeutic practice and transference as a libidinal dynamic between analyst and patient.

Cynthia Chase notes that Freud described transference in two different senses. There is the patient's transference towards the analyst, but also the transference of affect from the unconscious to the preconscious. "The same word," Chase writes, "designates a relationship to a person, a kind of *action* and a mode of expression, the condition of an idea's entering consciousness, a condition of knowledge" (212; emphasis in original). If transference is revealed in various forms of resistance to free association, then it becomes "an action destined to defeat a knowledge of transference, and to refuse the knowledge that *transference* is the condition of knowledge [emphasis in original]" (212). Freud sought to cultivate an acoustic space for listening to manifestations of the unconscious in expressions of transference articulated through the analysand's symbolic action of free association. At every turn, his emphasis on listening overturned the prevailing norms that accorded primacy to clinical techniques of observation, classification, and documentation of patients' symptoms.

In late nineteenth-century Vienna, patients' words fell largely on the deaf ears of senior medical practitioners, who had little patience for listening. The medical establishment's emphasis was not on attending to the speech emanating from the suffering body but on locating symptoms in an anatomical aetiology. As a junior physician, Freud would have been exposed to a medical atmosphere fraught with the therapeutic pessimism of neurological experts that sought to comprehend and classify illnesses rather than ameliorate them. The science of mental disturbances near the end of the nineteenth century was still wedded to the predilection that one had to get at the deceased patient's brain between the ears, crack open the skull, dig around in the flesh, and get a gander at the insides in order to retrospectively understand the illness. Élisabeth Roudinesco gives us a sense of the *fin de siècle* medical attitude with which Freud had to contend:

> The growing influence of Viennese hospital-based medicine, linked to the profusion of patients from all over the German speaking world, went hand-in-hand with an attitude particular to certain members of the medical establishment who were more interested in research, autopsies, and anatomo-pathology than in the therapeutic relationship. For them, the fascination with death took precedence over the desire to cure or to care for suffering bodies. At the time, the most advanced clinical art consisted in examining the body of a dying patient to identify the signs of illness that only an autopsy would reveal. (40)

The living patient suffering from mental disturbances was essentially an inconvenience to the empirically motivated brain pathologist, whose métier was opening up cadavers.

After graduating from medical school in 1882, Freud worked and studied with psychiatrist Theodor Meynert, who was also a neuroanatomist schooled directly in the approach characteristic of pathologist Carl von Rokitansky. Rokitansky is perhaps best known for his routine performance and supervision of tens of thousands of autopsies, averaging 2 per day, 7 days per week throughout his 45-year career (Markel 12). These autopsies were often carried out in operating theatres for students to observe and learn from the spectacle of dissection. Known for his insistence that all psychic disturbances could be located primarily in organic matter of the fore-brain, he observed that "[t]he historical term for psychiatry, i.e., 'treatment of the soul,' implies more than we can accomplish, and transcends the bounds of accurate scientific investigation" (v). In other words, physicians had little hope of, let alone interest in, healing maladies of the mind or spirit. With the aim of establishing psychiatry as an anatomical science, Meynert provided students like Freud with labelled diagrams of the brain. But he demonstrated little concern for what patients had to say about their distress (Roudinesco 41).

Freud became less interested in dissecting cadavers with a scalpel and much more preoccupied with dissecting the patients' discourse through listening and interpretation. Yet before he began to listen, Freud would have to pass through the theatrical spectacle of suffering at Paris' Salpêtrière Hospital, where incurable "madwomen" – including epileptics, hysterics, sex workers, and the poor – were held for treatment and study. The hospital housed a diverse population of 5000 patients, which provided an opportunity for medical researchers to document, study, and compare illnesses. At the hospital, Charcot became a central figure in the world of neurology for his research and became famous for his lecture demonstrations on hysteria. Under his leadership, the Salpêtrière became "the Mecca of international neurological study" (Goetz et al. 327). Still, in spite of all of the hospital's advancements, Charcot acknowledged that it remained a "grand asylum of human misery" (qtd. in Kumar et al. 47).

In *Invention of Hysteria: Charcot and the Photographic Iconography of the Salpêtrière*, Georges Didi-Huberman provides one of the most thorough analyses of Charcot's directorship of neurological research and describes the suffering at hospital at the end of the nineteenth century as "a kind of feminine inferno" and a "nightmare" (xi). Before shaking the epistemological basis of neuropathology through lending an ear to his patients, Freud had to first, in the words of Didi-Huberman, "get an eyeful … [o]f women's bodies, in all of their states" (80). When he arrived to study in Paris with Charcot at the Salpêtrière in 1885, not only did Freud encounter new methods for working with nervous illnesses through techniques of hypnosis and suggestion, but he was also witness to an image factory complete with advanced photographic technologies designed to document patients and their symptoms.

Clinical Photography and Charcot's Fantasy of Objectivity

In the late nineteenth century, the camera was revered for its purported ability to capture the world as it was without conducting it through the interpretive prism of an artist's sensibility. Albert Londe, Charcot's director of the photographic department of the Salpêtrière in the 1880s, referred to the photograph as "the scientist's true retina" (qtd. in Didi-Huberman 32) on account of its ability to function as a prosthetic eye. With the help of physicians Désiré Magloire Bourneville and Paul Regnard (who was also a photographer), Charcot employed photography to systematically categorize and catalogue the symptomatology of hysteria and epilepsy in *Iconographie Photographique de la Salpêtrière* in 1877 several years before Freud's visit. Referring to Charcot's photographic laboratory, Didi-Huberman writes that "Freud was the disoriented witness of the immensity of hysteria *in camera* and the manufacturing of images [emphasis in original]" (xii). Charcot employed photography as a routine laboratory tool that was meant to support his belief in neurological determinism and confirm the validity of his classifications of hysteria. Attempting to master hysteria as an analytic object, Charcot's research accrued persuasive force through the public's pervasive belief in the objective status of the knowledge gleaned through photographic documentation.

In her article exploring the differences between Charcot's and Freud's approaches, Daphne De Marneffe summarizes the well-documented accounts of Charcot's assessment of patients. He would seat himself at a table and call patients to the room for visual evaluation. He would then have them undress completely while an intern would read a summary of the patient's case. The intern would test the reflexes of the patient while the master remained mysteriously pensive. Charcot would call in another patient and then another, assessing them with the same intent look, and quietly make comparisons between each patient while making notes or sketches (Kumar et al. 47). Photography was his preferred method for confirming and documenting his observations: "Charcot found in photography the appropriate tool for representing the distillation of general symptom characteristics from the observation of many cases" (de Marneffe 78), writes de Marneffe. "By capturing various hysterical poses on film and then superimposing negatives from different cases, a general picture of the syndrome was created that expunged individual difference" (de Marneffe 79).

Rejecting allegations that the appearance of hysteria could be influenced, or even generated, by his own suggestion through what we could call the symbolic action of the clinic, Charcot characterized photography as a technology that ensured scientific neutrality:

> Behold the truth .... It would seem that hystero-epilepsy exists only ... as has sometimes been said, at the Salpêtrière, as if I had forged it through the power of my will .... But, truth to tell, in this I am nothing more than a photographer; I inscribe what I see.
>
> (qtd. in Didi–Huberman 29)

Charcot's method allowed him to document and archive the manifestations of hysteria through photography's evidentiary frame. Since he could not observe the brain as it functioned inside the living patient's cranium, he instead located the brain's effects on the symptomatic body through a clinical gaze routed through photography, which afforded the clinician an ostensibly true and objective record of reality.[2]

Charcot's practice of photographing living patients recasts dissection through a clinical gaze. Lauren Jane Barnett argues that, historically, "[t]he knowledge that underlies the clinical gaze – the knowledge of diseases held by the doctor or clinician – is largely developed by looking at cadavers" (38). Charcot's photography of hysterics instantiated the gaze as a form of disciplinary authority that produced knowledge from a position that anticipated the future outcome of the autopsy. Under the objectifying clinical gaze, the patient's subjectivity is eschewed while their body and behaviour become a passive spectacle produced for the sake of medical observation.

Barnett argues that while the clinical gaze may objectify both the doctor and the patient,

> the doctor wields the gaze and is thereby elevated to the status of the specialist. Such an elevation creates a power dynamic in which the doctor exerts power over the patient: the power to use the gaze to objectify the patient, to discover the disease, and to cure or treat the disease. As the doctor learns through the gaze, the patient is objectified and essentialized to only those body parts the doctor deems relevant. (35)

Charcot's method sidesteps the patient's experience or interpretation of her own symptoms since the doctor as authority is understood to possess a superior understanding of her suffering. The *Iconographie Photographique de la Salpêtrière* does contain verbatim transcriptions of patients' utterances and allusions to past traumas, but these transcriptions are discussed only in the context of medical measurements and summaries without even any direct comment or interpretation from attending doctors at the hospital.

In the *Iconographie*, Charcot and his colleagues interpret the meaning of patients' behaviours through the creation of diagnostic labels of symptoms. Jann Matlock describes the photographs and reports as they are presented within the *Iconographie*:

> The published and unpublished reports of the master create a silence in the daily surveillance records, as if no one but Charcot might have anything to say about these patients. Their cases are reduced to epithets: 'hysteria,' 'he's afflicted with hystero-epilepsy,' 'appears to be affected by general paralysis.' There are no causes, no descriptions of symptoms, no records of what the women might have had to say about these bodies out of control. The differential diagnoses give no space to accounts of what may have brought these women into the asylum .... Their names and the volume gave the doctors license to practice on them. Their diagnoses, exchange for their names, authorized a certain kind of gaze upon their symptoms. (135)

In this sense, Charcot remained close to traditions of anatomy and dissection supported by pathologists such as Rokitanksy and Meynert. But Charcot did not seem to appreciate his implication in the generation of the phenomenon that he documented.

Didi-Huberman highlights the rhetorical force of Charcot's photographs of hysterics:

> If everything seems to be in these images, it is because photography was in the ideal position to crystallize the link between the fantasy of hysteria and the fantasy of knowledge. A reciprocity of charm was

instituted between physicians, with their insatiable desire for images of Hysteria, and hysterics, who willingly participated and actually raised the stakes through their increasingly theatricalized bodies. In this way, hysteria in the clinic became the spectacle, the *invention of hysteria*. Indeed, hysteria was covertly identified with something like an art, close to theater or painting. (xi)

Didi-Huberman's account foregrounds not only the visual and performative spectacle of Charcot's depiction of hysteria but also the transferential relationship between doctor and patient that was hiding in plain view. "Most critically," writes de Marneffe, "the doctors did not take into account the emotions and motives of their women patients, or the interaction of patients' emotional agendas and their own investigative procedures" (89). From a scientific standpoint, Charcot's blindness to the transformative affects of his intensely choreographed photographic scene radically undermined his status as a neutral, objective observer.

Charcot's studies on hysteria seem to exemplify Lacan's formula for desire as it might become apparent in the transference: "Desire full stop is always the desire of the Other. Which basically means that we are always asking the Other what he desires" (*My Teaching* 38). Lacan puts this notion another way through emphasis on the Italian question of *che vuoi?*, which literally translates as "What do you want?" Lacan's formulation of the question, "What does the Other want from me?" describes, among other things, the analysand's frustrated transference towards the analyst as the *subject supposed to know* the truth of their situation.

In the context of the Salpêtrière, doctors photographed bodies with their own fantasies of hysteria in mind, while the hysterics demonstrated illness as part of their transference towards fulfilment of the doctor's desire to accumulate medical knowledge. There were clearly unacknowledged transference feedback loops at work between patients and doctors. The more the patient reinvented her symptoms as a symbolic action for the accumulation of knowledge, the more certain illnesses worsened. The symptoms of the patients were transformed into an iconographic text rendered for the purpose of study, speculation, and interpretation. But the classificatory-diagnostic project lacked a curative or therapeutic dimension.[3]

What Charcot and his team of physicians and photographers at the Salpêtrière failed to recognize is that they were not necessarily capturing truth or objective knowledge but were, rather, always engaged in a rhetorical construction and interpretation of the truth from the position of what Lacan called the "university discourse." Lacanian psychoanalyst Bruce Fink describes this form of discourse as "systematic knowledge" that becomes an "ultimate authority, reigning in the stead of blind will, everything having its reason." Fink suggests that "the university discourse provid[es] a sort of legitimation or rationalization of the master's will" (*Key* 33). The flurry of photographic documentation produced at the Salpêtrière had all the dignified trappings of a rational nexus of objective scientific procedures even as this dense network of practices systematically blinded itself to its own arbitrary baked-in prejudices.

Surrounded by photographic media that share so much in common with the mirror, Charcot was unable to reflect upon his own lack of reflection. "It is ironic," writes R.D. Laing in *The Voice of Experience*, "that such scientists cannot see the way they see with their way of seeing" and that "[t]o the purely objective point of view, everything is an object and only real relations and correlations are objective ones" (15). The limitation to any position of scientific objectivity, whether it be Charcot's approach to the hysterics or contemporary psychological experiments, is that such a position is rarely introspective or reflexive but, rather, assumes its own authority. For Laing, such a position of objectivity often fails to account for subjectivity:

> The act of objectification, and the stance of objectivity, are not objective objects. They cannot be seen by a way of looking whose distinctive competence is precisely to bring the desubjectivized objective events into focus. The scientific objective world is not the world of real life. It is a highly sophisticated artifact, created by multiple operations which effectively and efficiently exclude immediate experience in all its apparent capriciousness from its order of discourse. (15)

In this light, Charcot's stance of objectivity, his understanding of photography as a purely scientific process, and his objectification of patients on film converged in the form of an ideological assemblage that excluded the immediate subjective experience of the patient, not to mention the doctor's insidious influence, from scientific scrutiny. It should come as no surprise, then, that Charcot was unable to account for the patient's transference to the doctor when positing his own clinical role as that of a neutral and authoritative observer. He had blinded himself with science.

Freud's own eulogy for "the father of modern neurology" foregrounds the fact that Charcot's claim to objective knowledge demonstrably privileged the visual register's role in constructing the "objective truth" of hysteria:

> [H]e had the nature of an artist—he was, as he himself said, a '*visuel*', a man who *sees*. Here is what he himself told us about his method of working. He used to look again and again at the things he did not understand, to deepen his impression of them day by day, till suddenly an understanding of them dawned on him .... He might be heard to say that the greatest satisfaction a man could have was to

see something new – that is, to recognize it as new; and he remarked
again and again on the difficulty and value of this kind of 'seeing'.

(Freud, "Charcot" 12)

Although Freud admired Charcot, translated his works, named his oldest
son after him, and wrote him a glowing obituary, he had to depart from
his teacher's "vision" in order to forge an escape hatch from the dead-end
of seeing the same patterns over and over.

Freud's transition from studying physiology and neurology to inventing
psychoanalysis constituted a paradigm shift that opened up a new spectrum of possibilities for the treatment of patients. "Freud brings out with
admirable candor," writes de Marneffe, "the link of compassion and interest (both qualities of a personal relationship) to a sense of respect for the
patient"; he "has listened to his patients, and their utterances have 'dic-
tated' to him an approach" (98–101). Less than ten years after his studies with Charcot, Freud and Breuer published *Studies on Hysteria*, which,
not unlike the *Iconographie Photographique de la Salpêtrière*, presents detailed
accounts of many clinical cases. But this text diverges significantly from
Charcot in that the authors privileged the female patients' verbal testi-
mony over doctors' visual observations and photographic images of their
bodies. Freud mapped a path out of the extrospective and suggestive visual
method of Charcot towards an introspective, dynamic, and interpretive
listening practice that would send ripples through every psychotherapeutic
and clinical counselling session in his wake.

Streams, Lines of Flight, and New Perches

In psychoanalysis, the analyst listens carefully to the analysand's speech
in order to attend to its meandering and divergent paths. What we refer
to as psychoanalytic "close listening" is predicated on the analysand's free
associations, which the analyst "reads" for the purpose of clinical information gathering. The analysand's transference emerges out of this deluge
of speech. Freud's idea for the use of free association in the clinic has its
basis in distinct intellectual tributaries that converged at the end of the
nineteenth century.

Before the literary modernists popularized the term "stream of consciousness," several psychological theorists, including Scottish philosopher Alexander Bain (1818–1903), had already proposed the notion that
senses, feelings, thoughts, and speech tended to flow together as though in
continuous currents, streams, or rivers. According to Kenneth Burke, the
construction of a new metaphor such as this one functions as "a device for
uniting under one head movements which were generally considered in
complete isolation from one another" (*PC* 89). Burke wrote that perspective by incongruity results in "unsuspected connectives" that create novel
"relationships between objects which our customary rational vocabulary

has ignored" (*PC* 90). Since we can only approximately characterize the experience of our own inner thoughts through figurative descriptions, the metaphorical stream of consciousness gave shape to early attempts to articulate the cascading processes of the mind as they were experienced.

Although the first employment of the phrase is often erroneously attributed to American psychologist and philosopher William James (1842–1910), Bain first coined the phrase "stream of consciousness" as a psychological metaphor in his book, *The Senses and the Intellect*, published in 1855. Throughout this text, Bain describes the mind in terms of its energy, movement, and flow: "The concurrence of sensations in one common stream of consciousness ... enables those of different senses to be associated as readily as the sensations of the same sense" (359).[4] According to Bain, all senses flowed together to create our experience of perception, memory, narrative, and temporality.

His description of stream of consciousness in action anticipates Freud's concept of free association:

> Our past life, therefore, be conceived as a vast stream of spectacle, action, feelings, volition, desire – intermingled and complicated in every way, and rendered inherent by its unbroken continuity. It is impossible, however, to associate equally all the details, so as to recover them at pleasure; only the more impressive facts remain strong together in recollection. The larger epochs and the stirring incidents readily come to our recollection, when we go back to some early starting point; while the minor events failed to appear on the simple thread of sequence in time, and are recalled only by the presence of other circumstances that serve to link them with the present. (453)

Long before Freud, Bain laid the foundation for conceptualizing consciousness as a flux of thoughts, affects, actions, memories, and desires. His theories also anticipated Freud's concepts of repression and free association.

Just prior to the publication of James' *The Principles of Psychology*, French philosopher Henri Bergson (1859–1941) published *Time and Free Will* (1889), which engaged with Bain's work and proffers a similar notion of flow, *durée réelle* or *durée pure* [actual duration or pure duration], as a way to describe the dynamic protean movements of consciousness in relation to memory, perception, and temporality. According to Bergson, chronological or historical time is a fiction, an imaginary and homogenous construction: "The fundamental illusion consists in transferring to duration itself, in its continuous flow, the form of the instantaneous sections which we make in it" (149). He contended that we are immersed in a "general stream of becoming" and that "[i]n reality there is no one rhythm of duration; it is possible to imagine many different rhythms which, slower or faster, measure the degree of tension or relaxation of different kinds of consciousness and thereby fix their respective places in the scale of being" (77; 207). In *Creative Evolution*, Bergson suggests that we perceive duration as "a stream against which we cannot go" (45) and further developed this notion of temporality in relation to the experience of consciousness as a dynamic "course of time"; he writes, "[T]he flow of time might assume an infinite rapidity, the entire past, present, and future of material objects or of isolated systems might be spread out all at once in space" (12). Anticipating Freud's concept of free association (and later influencing Deleuze's philosophy of becoming), Bergson's theory of pure duration describes consciousness as continuously drifting from one state to another as it experiences the unfolding of time.

Bergson and William James became friends over the course of their careers, wrote each other letters, and carefully read each other's works (Atkinson 62). In *The Principles of Psychology* of 1890, James proposed a Bergsonian framework for describing the kinetic nature of consciousness. Echoing Bain's earlier portrayals of conscious experience, he writes that consciousness is not a discontinuous experience cobbled together from discrete components:

> Consciousness … does not appear to itself chopped up in bits. Such words as 'chain' or 'train' do not describe it fitly as it presents itself in the first instance. It is nothing jointed; it flows. A 'river' or a 'stream' are the metaphors by which it is most naturally described. *In talking of it hereafter, let us call it the stream of thought, of consciousness, or of subjective life.*
>
> (233; James' emphasis)

James also whimsically likens consciousness to "a bird's life" insofar as mental activity appears to be composed of alternating "flights and perchings" (James 236). He suggests that the "resting-places" or "substantive parts" of the mind are typically occupied by "sensorial imaginations … [which] can be held before the mind for an indefinite time, and contemplated without changing" (James 236).

The "places of flight" or "transitive parts" are engaged with "thoughts of relations, static or dynamic" (James 236). These "flights" are prevalent between the mind's contemplative interludes of rest and ultimately "lead us from one substantive conclusion to another" (James 236). He proposed that the rhythm of language and punctuation expresses this alternating condition of thought. "There is not a conjunction or a preposition, and hardly an adverbial phrase, syntactic form, or inflection of voice, in human speech," writes James, "that does not express some shading or other of relation which we at some moment actually feel to exist between the larger objects of our thought" (238).

From Bain to Bergson to James, the metaphor of the stream of consciousness opens up a number of critical "perspectives by incongruity" that reframe the forensically static brain as a force of dispersion and momentum. Bain's description connected the movement of a body of water to the experience of the flux of thoughts, sensations, and memories. This hitherto unarticulated figuration picked up speed as it moved through the work of Bergson and James, establishing a cascade of associations that would spill over productively into Freud's psychoanalytic clinic.

Trains of Thought

Given that Freud cited Bain's ideas in his own works and was also familiar with James' *The Principles of Psychology*, he was probably aware of the concept of stream of consciousness when he set to work developing his own theory of free association.[5] Clinical psychoanalysis hinges on this flow, this outpouring of the analysand's speech, which gives shape to whatever is running through the person's mind. The analytic session is a charged rhetorical scenario, a vibrant dialogical scene within which the analysand attempts free association while the analyst maintains a listening presence.

The phrase "free association" is actually A.A. Brill's early English translation of Freud's German *freier Einfall*, which literally means "free irruption" or "sudden idea," a state of mind which allows ideas, words, or images to pour out spontaneously and then be spoken aloud. Freud's free association employs the stream of consciousness as a psychoanalytic process. The analysand's engagement in this improvisatory speech act with the support of the analyst allows them to hear their inner voice spoken out loud. Such an impromptu invocatory effort requires another person's presence. Free association provides analysands an opportunity to extemporize interior life, express thoughts and feelings out loud, and encounter their own desire in a new light.

In his recommendations for beginning treatment, Freud described his technical preference for seating arrangements in the consulting room as to have "the patient to lie on a sofa while [the analyst] sit behind him out of his sight" ("On Beginning" 133). Freud advised analysts not to take notes during sessions since this could distract them from the task at hand; it was better to take notes immediately after the analysand's appointment. With the removal of the face-to-face relation, Freud shifted his clinical epistemology from looking and observing to hearing the analysand's inner voice and attending to the rivulets of their discourse.

In Lacanian terms, the analysand's use of the couch, a remnant of the hypnotic method out of which psychoanalysis evolved, disrupts everyday forms of communication so that they may more easily hear the overdetermined symbolic aspects of their discourse.[6] Freud did not want to divert the free-associative symbolic aspects of the analysand's free associations with his own facial expressions or distract with his own body language. He writes, "Since, while I am listening to the patient, I, too, give myself over to the current of my unconscious thoughts, I do not wish my expressions of face to give the patient material for interpretations or to influence him in what he tells me" ("On Beginning" 134). Freud wanted to limit the interference of the visual register with the analysand's flux of associations. Whereas Charcot's project to create a unified, generic picture of the hysteric is stuck in what Lacan would call the Imaginary register of the impossibly whole unified image, Freud emphasized what Lacan refers to as the "Symbolic" dimension, the fragmented, dispersed polysemic utterances that never cohere into a unified picture of the self.

In order to facilitate an environment conducive to the free-associative flux, Freud advises the clinician to develop a "rapport" with patients, exhibit curiosity through "a serious interest," and listen sympathetically but dispassionately. This logistical architecture lays the groundwork for the patient's transferential connection and provides tactful openings for the analyst to share occasional interpretations ("On Beginning" 139–140). He suggests that what emerges in the analysand's discourse, rather than overbearing directives from the analyst, ought to guide the direction of the therapeutic process. The material with which the analyst begins treatment, Freud claimed, "is on the whole a matter of indifference – whether it is the patient's life-history or the history of his illness or his recollections of childhood .... [T]he patient must be left to do the talking and must be free to choose at what point he shall begin" (Freud, "On Beginning" 134). The patient's outpouring of speech, which had been almost irrelevant for Charcot, now directed the course of treatment.

Freud's listening treatment follows the course of the analysand's thoughts and feelings as they voice them. His innovations allowed the analysand to take the lead without any stipulation as to the point of departure or predetermined emphasis on what subject matter was acceptable. The analyst ideally goes with the flow. As a guiding thread to help the analysand get started in treatment, Freud proffers the metaphor of railway travel:

> So say whatever goes through your mind. Act as though, for instance, you were a traveller sitting next to the window of a railway carriage and describing to someone inside the carriage the changing views which you see outside. Finally, never forget that you have promised to be absolutely honest, and never leave anything out because, for some reason or other, it is unpleasant to tell it.
>
> ("On Beginning" 135)

According to Freud's update of Plato's cave, the visual register still plays a role, but the patient now plays the role of witness; and what they endeavour to articulate is an almost ineffable spectacle of inner experience. But the relatively new technology of train travel is also an operative metaphor. The patient draws on memory traces to make connections with intersecting tracks of thought during free association. This train of signifiers proceeds without any conscious selection of the route. There is a sense in which both the analyst and patient are merely along for the ride.

In free association, language is, as Burke puts it, "a species of action ... and its nature is such that it can be used as a tool" (*LSA* 15). The analysand wields free association as an instrument of self-expression and interpretation but also as a demand to be heard by the analyst. The astute analyst therefore adopts a "close listening" orientation that is akin to the New Criticism's close reading practice. When it comes to interpreting symptoms, the close listener, for the most part, refrains from interfering and allows the analysand's discourse to reveal its own rhetorical logic in slips of the tongue, evasions, repetitions, etc.

Peter Barry characterizes close reading as a practice that may detect "poised ambiguity" in the text. The critic could either aim interpretations to "produce *dis*unity, to show that what had looked like unity and coherence actually contains contradictions and conflicts which the text cannot stabilize or contain" or "take a text which appeared fragmented and disunified and demonstrate an underlying unity" (77). The hermeneutic and rhetorical endeavour of psychoanalytic interpretation also hinges on the analyst's attention to unity and disunity in discourse and transference. We must acknowledge that the aim of analysis is not necessarily to help the analysand find meaning but rather to help them become acquainted with their meaning-making machinery.

Since the analysand's free association produces an array of rhetorical displacements in the transference, the analyst must listen closely for the analysand's rhetorical devices, such as ellipsis (omission), metonymy (part for the whole), and periphrasis (indirectness), each of which may reveal unconscious defences and censorship at work in discourse. "Free association and the transference," writes Paul Earlie, "reproduce the two key modes of rhetoric as *techne*: rhetoric as persuasion and rhetoric as interpretative tool" (225). Given that analyst and analysand are engaged in a dynamic exchange of persuasion and interpretation, Freud's deployment of free association in the clinic as a form of "listening rhetoric," which Wayne Booth describes as "[t]he whole range of communicative arts for reducing misunderstanding by paying full attention to opposing views" (*The Rhetoric of Rhetoric* 10). Only, in this case, the opposing views emerge out of the almost infinite lines of interpretation the analyst could adopt towards the patient's discourse.

For Booth, listening and speaking are two sides of the same rhetorical coin. The listener must hear as many sides of the conflict as possible before offering a response. "Whenever we manage to listen first and continue listening," he writes, "we are far superior as rhetors than when we aim our words at targets that don't exist" (21). The rhetorically-astute listener knows when to facilitate rather than impose an interpretive frame. They are adept at "join[ing] and progress[ing] together" with others in order to learn more about the issues at stake rather than engage in a kind of "win rhetoric" meant to pin down the objective truth from a certain vantage point (*Rhetoric* 149). The analyst's practice of *listening rhetoric* entails paying close attention to the analysand's speech and hearing their discourse from as many angles as possible with the hope of generating a fuller perspective of the presenting problems. For Booth, listening rhetoric is a complex process orchestrated in the service of encountering an experiential universe that is totally heterogeneous to one's own: "I am not just seeking a truce; I want to pursue the truth behind our differences" (46). Rather than listening for what one knows or relatable moments in the analysand's discourse, the analyst must attempt to adopt an impartial stance (or at least a stance that functions that way, rhetorically speaking). Only through such a radical neutrality will they have a chance at detecting and eliciting the unknown and unexpected associative rhetoric of the analysand's speech. The analyst's task is often reducible to asking questions or creating openings in order to help the analysand clarify, parse, or elaborate on what they have said along a lubricated associative path. Still, in psychoanalysis, as in rhetoric, the coordinates and criteria of good listening remain remarkably undertheorized.

Although he insisted on the unknowability of certain aspects of the unconscious, Freud was constantly trying to engage his analysands through an interchange of speaking and listening. He attempted to underscore the ways that cognitive dissonance could arise from contradictory viewpoints that coexist in the analysand's mind. Kenneth Burke provides a brief example of this brand of psychoanalytic symbolic action at work:

> An 'unconscious' resentment against A might be so displaced that it reveals itself as a resentment against B. And 'condensation' can take place when, if A is associated in your Unconscious with B, you might have a dream in which various traits of both A and B are combined in a single image.
>
> (*LSA* 66)

The power of free association derives, in part, from its openness to contradictions and aporias that militate against common-sense understandings of truth and reality. Freud believed that the analyst's task often involves listening together with the patient so as to aid them in hearing their own articulation of otherwise censored wishes.

Psychoanalyst Christopher Bollas favours the phrase "free talking," which he characterizes as a form of speech that proceeds without predetermination from thought to thought, idea to idea, topic to topic, or story to story (9). The analysand impossibly tries to say everything that comes to mind with as little censorship or suppression as possible. Bollas draws attention to the rhetorical scenario in which the free aspect of the analysand's associations come into conflict with inhibitions and resistance:

> [F]ree association is always a 'compromise formation' between psychic truths and the self's effort to avoid the pain of such truths. Ironically enough, however, free talking deploys the mental process of the analysand, revealing the struggle inherent to thinking one's self .... Psychoanalysis does not provide ready answers to patients' symptoms or lives. Instead, it supplies a relationship that allows the analysand to hear from his or her own unconscious life, and Freud's insistence that the most valued material is to be found in the seemingly irrelevant – a kind of trivial pursuit – worked from modernist assumptions that to comprehend an object (a historical period, a novel, a person) one must study it in its ordinary sense, not pre-judged by hierarchical assumptions. (10–11)

Like Freud, Bollas underscores the fact that free association is never completely free in that it inevitably encounters internal resistance. But the patient can, over time, cultivate proficiency as a close listener in order to attend to the content and form of their own speech as it articulates their desires, drives, memories, and experiences.

Following Lacan's formulation that one's desire is the desire of the Other, Mladen Dolar suggests the voice ought to be understood within the structural web of transference: "there is no voice without the other .... the voice is something which tries to reach the other, provoke it, seduce it, plead with it; it makes assumptions about the other's desire, it tries to influence it, sway it, elicit its love" (27–28). In the clinic, the analysand's voice encounters an obstacle course of impediments. Unlike James' notion of the stream of consciousness, Freud's babbling brook cannot always follow paths of least resistance. "[O]ne of the first things one notices as a practitioner," writes Fink, "is that the analysand's associations seem to be anything but free" as a person may "dance circles around certain topics rather than go directly towards them, or to veer away from them altogether when the memories and thoughts associated with them are overcharged" (*Fundamentals* 10n13). The analysand's free speech unavoidably runs up against unexpected or repudiated desires. Even as their discourse canalizes the flow of painful thoughts and feelings, it also vehiculates defence mechanisms that stem the tide.

In ordinary conversation, we may attempt to speak pragmatically while excluding interfering ideas that we deem insignificant or non-sensical. But Freud suggests that during free association, we "must never give in to these [inner] criticisms" and must strive to speak freely "precisely because [we] feel an aversion to doing so" (135). During free association, propriety and instrumental pragmatism must be dispatched (within the limits of our powers) so that a charged word, image, or sense might lead to another without any apparent connection. Lacan recommends that the analyst maintain a listening presence that "leaves the subject free to have a go at it" (1958/2006 535). The first object of concentration may be exhausted and give way to a seemingly arbitrary connection, a curious expression might spring forth through a tangential idea, or a bit of subjective truth may surge from the body. Psychoanalysis aims to dredge the river of memory for salient connections that can be reinserted into subsequent associations, which may epiphanically flip over from incongruity into congruity.

Notes

1 Lacan devoted *Seminar XIII* to encouraging his listeners to think through the dynamics of transference, knowledge, and love at stake between Socrates and his student Alcibiades in Plato's *Symposium*.

2 For Foucault, the conditions of the medical gaze rely upon a cold neutrality and the opportunity for the researcher (in this case the clinician with the laboratory aid of the camera) to acquire access to study the object at stake (in this case the patient). The conditions necessary to achieve the possibility of objectivity integral to medical knowledge and institutional standards for validity further rely upon an assemblage of power, order, and authority that ultimately disperse and define bodies, actions, behaviours, and discourses. See Foucault's discussion of the clinical gaze in *The Birth of the Clinic* (1963/1994) as well as in *Psychiatric Power: Lectures at the College de France, 1973–1974* (2003/2006).

3 De Marneffe raises an important assertion regarding the discrepancy between Charcot and Freud in their capacities for listening: "On the sociological level, one obstacle to Charcot's listening to his patients was that they seemed so different: they were women, they were poor, and they were sick. In a period when class, gender, and mental illness were considered more rigid categories than they are today, the disparities between the scientist and his subject gaped very large. To listen to (poor, sick) women's accounts, to see them as something other than 'babbling,' and to use these as scientific evidence was to throw into confusion accepted notions of knowledge and power .... Charcot's claim to the position of neutral observer would have been put into question. The fact that for a did listen to his patients' accounts may rest in part on the fact that he saw a different group of patients, patients who were not warehoused en masse in an asylum but were able to visit his consulting room and to pay his fees" (105).

4 Bain also referred to the stream of consciousness as a "cerebral highway" (359).

5 Freud cited Alexander Bain's work in *Jokes and Their Relation to the Unconscious* of 1905 and in his 1910 paper, "The Antithetical Meaning of Primal Words," but it is not entirely clear if he drew the notion of free association from Bain's descriptions of stream of consciousness. Eugene Taylor highlights the relationship between Freud and James and how these authors influenced each other's respective works in "William James and Sigmund Freud: 'The Future of Psychology Belongs to Your Work'" in *Psychological Science* vol. 10, no. 6, 199, pp. 465–469.

6 For Lacan, the Imaginary is the aspect of psychic and social experience formed through narcissistic identification with one's own mirror image and with others who one perceives through a lens of sameness or similarity. This identification results in the formation of the ego or an "I" and allows the person to maintain some illusory sense of identity, selfhood, autonomy, and wholeness ("The Mirror Stage" 76). The Imaginary is the realm of images and imagination, but

also of deception and lure. It is deceptive because it is a surface of everyday appearances and presents what is readily visible while concealing the underlying structure of the patient's symptoms. When Lacan refers to as the "other" with a small "o" is the imagined other, the projection of the ego as specular image, or simply the other as another individual. This "little other" might also be conceptualized as the subject's projected alter ego who desires what the subject desires and therefore produces an aggressivity based on the assumption of sameness. As a result, Imaginary relations are frequently conducted through rivalry. "[T]he important point," writes Lacan, "is that this form [in the mirror] situates the agency known as the ego, prior to its social determination" ("The Mirror Stage" 76). Ultimately, the mirror stage produces the subject's ego as a necessary fantasy that establishes relations to others and structures the experience of social reality. For the analyst, we could say that the Imaginary is always operative in countertransference to the analysand. Not to be confused with Burke's notion of symbolic action, the Symbolic encapsulates the rhetorical and linguistic dimension of communication in relation to an Other with a big "O," the superego, and the law. Bruce Fink suggests that we could also think of Symbolic relations as "the way people deal with ideals that have been inculcated in them by their parents, schools, media, language, and society at large, embodied in grades, diplomas, status symbols, and so on" (*A Clinical Introduction* 33). Lacan refers to the big Other of the Symbolic as one's own idiosyncratic relation to language and the designation of radical difference (not similarity as in the Imaginary) that cannot be integrated with identification. Each subject experiences the Other in a distinct way. This Other is not known in advance (and is unconscious). For Lacan, one of the aims of psychoanalysis is to help shift the distressing relation that an analysand may have in regards to the Other in the form of parents, the law, or social and cultural ideals. When the analysand free associates over the course of the analysis, the Symbolic structure in relation to the Other may be revealed gradually through the repetition compulsion of their discourse along with glimpses of their own unconscious desire.

6　All Ears

Psychoanalysis and the Rhetoric of Listening

The Listening Cure

Psychoanalysis is most colloquially referred to as a "talking cure." The expression was coined by Josef Breuer's patient Bertha Pappenheim (whom Freud and Breuer refer to as "Anna O." in *Studies in Hysteria*). In *Psychoanalytic Listening*, Salman Akhtar directly addresses the question of talking and its relationship to listening:

> Psychoanalysis is a listening and talking cure. Both elements are integral to clinical work. Listening with no talking can only go so far. Talking without listening can mislead and harm. And yet, the listening end of the equation has received short shrift in analytic literature. (xiv)

Throughout his career, Freud provided several recommendations on listening techniques. Nevertheless, British and American psychoanalytic literature in the following decades emphasized hermeneutics of interpretation over listening and, with the exception of a short burst of interest in the 1980s, dedicated little attention to different possible methods for listening to patients' discourse.

Akhtar highlights this "long silence" on the topic of analytic listening and observes that post-Freudian textbooks and monographs say almost nothing new about listening as a psychoanalytic technique (22–23). There are just a few notable exceptions, including Theodor Reik's theory of the analyst's "third ear," which we will explore later in this chapter. However, in Austrian physician Otto Fenichel's encyclopaedic *Psychoanalytic Theory of the Neurosis* of 1945, for instance, the topic of listening is largely absent. We might conclude that Fenichel was occupied with the pursuit of masterfully objectifying the struggles of analysands through taxonomy, diagnosis, and interpretation. By the same token, in Polish neurologist and psychoanalyst Herman Nunberg's *Principles of Psychoanalysis* of 1955, there are few reflections on principles of listening; instead, the text focuses on topographic and dynamic conceptions of the unconscious, instincts, the ego, anxiety, defences, character structure, and analytic theory. British

DOI: 10.4324/9781003214069-7

psychoanalyst Charles Rycroft's *A Critical Dictionary for Psychoanalysis* of 1968 similarly explicates dozens of psychoanalytical terms, but there is no entry on "listening." These authors frequently aim to generalize the particular symptoms of individual analysands for the sake of communicating psychoanalytic principles and concepts that analysts might then map onto information gathered in subsequent sessions. But listening remains a blind spot in theories of psychoanalysis and clinical counselling.

Listening is the bread and butter of analytic practice, and yet it is given short shrift in encyclopaedias, dictionaries, and textbooks of psychoanalysis. To this day, there is little in the way of a framework for what psychoanalytic listening actually entails. Clinicians are often preoccupied with listening for the purpose of categorizing cases in order to be able to speak in "psychoanalese," as Reik calls it. The rhetorical coordinates of any discipline limit and contort our capacity to listen with a radical openness to speech. If we take psychoanalytic listening as a rhetorical practice, it must be thought in terms of what Kenneth Burke calls a "scene" of rhetoric or what Wayne Booth refers to as a "rhetorical domain," a locus of "rhetorical standards that contrast sharply with the standards embraced by those in other domains" (Booth 18). As a discourse community, each school of psychology and psychoanalysis places different interpretive emphases on affect, language, object relations, transference, and the importance of human development. Some clinicians have a tendency to become obsessed with mastering cases, presumptuously assuming the position of expert on the legitimate meanings of patients' words and symptoms.

Listening from a position that tries to understand, intellectualize, or categorize cases can be deceptively counterproductive. Chiding philosophers for engaging in a similar game of misrecognition, Jean-Luc Nancy asks, "Isn't the philosopher someone who always hears (and who hears everything), but who cannot listen or who, more precisely, neutralizes within himself, so that he can philosophize?" (1). When we assimilate the analysand's discourse into a developmental model, a psychological framework, or a philosophical system, we are no longer listening, except to confirm what we already know. Lacan's insistence that "there is no other resistance to analysis than that of the analyst himself" speaks to the analyst's own potential incapacity to actually listen to the words of the analysand sitting before them (1958/2006 497).

In this chapter, we survey conceptualizations of deep psychoanalytic listening, or what we have called "close listening," which is not couched in the security of understanding, the safety of clinical categorization, or the objective truth of diagnosis. Freud recommended the practice of *gleichschwebende Aufmerksamkeit*, a form of close listening commonly translated to English as "evenly suspended attention." Following Freud and Lacan, we advise that analysts develop protocols for maintaining a cautious underlying posture of awareness about the limitations of pre-digested institutional knowledge that claims the status of objectivity about the meaning of individual patients' utterances. We seek to conceptualize and advocate for a psychoanalytic listening that would militate against the tendency to generalize the particularities of the patient's discourse in favour of a listening posture that relinquishes almost all demands except that the patient speak. When particularities of the patient's discourse come into relief during the psychoanalytic session, the analyst who has cultivated this form of attention might then guide the analysand towards remembering, repeating, and working through their own understanding of their history. The analyst lends their ear to the analysand's discourse to set in motion a complex associative economy, one that subtly guides the analysand in scrutinizing the significance of their own chains of signification. This form of listening runs against the grain of many contemporary doctrines of "empathetic" clinical practice, which we will also examine. In what follows, we explore this Freudian notion of attention, investigate what has been written about it, and examine how psychoanalysis conceptualizes, shapes, and tropes analytic listening practices.

Playing It by Ear

There is an old Dutch joke about a painter with a single ear. The painter, who is sensitive about his appearance, needs to hire an assistant for an upcoming exhibition. Wanting to test candidates' attention to detail, he says to his first candidate, "Your resume shows that you do very objective work. I only have one question for you, when you look at me, what do you see?" The candidate nervously provides the obvious answer, "Sir, I cannot help but notice you have only one ear." The painter erupts in anger and chases the candidate from the room before calling in the next one. When the second candidate sits down for the interview, the painter says, "Your resume shows that you are strong in emotional intelligence. I only have one question for you: when you look at me, what do you see?" This second candidate had been eavesdropping from the waiting room and has the idea to offer empathy: "Well, Sir, I noticed the wound you have there and thought it must have been so painful and upsetting to lose your ear." The painter explodes again and sends the candidate running out the door. The exasperated painter calls in the third candidate and raises the inevitable question, "Now, your resume says you bring a fresh perspective to the workplace so then give me your perspective. When you look at me, what do you see?" The third candidate proudly responds, "Sir, I was looking very carefully and noticed that you are wearing contact lenses." The painter is astonished with the third candidate's immediate eye for detail: "It is incredible that you could make out from across the room that I am actually wearing contact lenses. How is this possible?" "Well, Sir," says this candidate, "you would need two ears for a pair of glasses."

Although the joke features a painter who is preoccupied with what the other notices about his appearance, we can also detect that it unexpectedly delivers an instructive comment about listening.[1] Our painter demands an answer from his interlocutors but is angered by their objective, empathetic replies, all of which lead to the emergence of the truth in plain sight about the missing ear. Each of the interviewees attempts to persuade the painter with replies that raise an important question: What does the painter want? In this context, it appears that the painter who is lacking an ear might wish for a prospective candidate to lend one of their own. The painter does not seek objectivity, empathy, or an alternative perspective but, rather, always desires something else. He demands a reply from the candidates, each of whom reflects back his sore spot in slightly modified form. The painter's demand that the candidates report what they see might actually conceal a desire to be heard differently.

An Archaeology of Listening

The etymology of "listening" should fascinate psychoanalysts and rhetoricians alike. The Old English *hlyst* refers to the sensory experience of hearing and also to the ear as an organ. It is the verb and the noun, the act and the object. It is to hear and the ear. This root implies being attentive, keeping silent, and giving one's auricle to the other. The Old English *lystan* and the Dutch-German *lusten* are the roots not only of "listening" but also of "lusting." The Middle English *lest* and *lyst* carry connotations of pleasure, joy, appetite, and inclination. The verb form suggests pleasing, leaning, liking, longing, caring, choosing, wishing, and desiring. It is no wonder one of the most common complaints couples' therapists hear is "My partner does not listen to me," which might as well be shorthand for "my partner does not desire me." We now hear more easily such connotations in the lack laden adjective, "listless." The Middle English nouns *liste* and *leste* pertain to art, craft, wisdom, skill, stratagem, and wile. It is tempting to plunge down the rabbit hole of coincidental etymology and observe that this sense of listening resonates as a discipline, a system of techniques that should, for both rhetoricians and psychoanalysts, be understood as an auditory praxis.

This web of associations related to listening invokes the Greek concept of *techne*, a form of making, doing, or know-how. In Greek, there is also *akoustikos* or acoustics, which lexicographers say probably derives from *akoein*, a word that connotes hearing, but also designates marking or perceiving. Listening involves intention and attention, the aural and the oral, the auricular and the oracular, and the auditory and the invocatory. Further English derivatives such as *liest* and *lyce* convey the notion of a border, limit, boundary, or edge, while "list" denotes a hem or a strip of cloth that might be employed as a filter ("list, n1"). Accordingly, it is tempting to theorize everyday listening as an act of processing sonorous utterances and submitting them to semiotic filters.

In *Listening*, philosopher Jean-Luc Nancy reminds us that the French *écoute* invokes scouting and spying. He also points to the phrase *être à l'écoute*, which originates from the lexicon of military espionage and refers to "tuning in" (4). This is where paranoia intersects with acoustics for the speaker that fears the incursion of another's ear. Through the eavesdropper, we are alerted to the relationship between listening and the secret. It is in this context that Nancy asks a salient question for psychoanalysis and rhetoric: "What secret is at stake when one truly *listens*, that is, when one tries to capture or surprise the sonority rather than the message?" (5). Influenced by Lacan's work, Nancy encourages us to hear the Symbolic associative aspects of the sonorous chain of signifiers rather than to listen for the Imaginary of the speaker's intended meaning.[2] In the service of rescuing listening from the pitfalls of hallucinated understanding, Nancy suggests that we listen for the polyvalent and even asignifying aspects rather than assume that we understand the speaker's intention. This is why the attentive psychoanalyst does not impose their understanding on the patient's discourse. Instead, they attend to clues in prosody, speech patterns, gaps, and evasions.

When we examine the roots of "hearing," as in the Old English *híeran* or German *hören*, we discover longstanding lines of signification involving the sensory perception of sound. Hearing overlaps with listening insofar as one might exercise the auditory function in hearkening efforts, as when one is engaged in "hearing someone out." Hearing has further connotations that involve not only attention, audience, reception, understanding, and learning but also judgement (as in a judicial hearing), obedience, and compliance.[3] Despite these overlaps with listening, hearing is perhaps most colloquially understood as a physiological, involuntary function, a sensation. Listening is perhaps more voluntary, considered, and practiced. Yet we also conflate hearing with understanding any time we reassure with the phrase "I hear you" or ask, "Do you hear what I'm saying?" Nancy indicates that there is a "slight, keen indecision that grates, rings out, or shouts between 'listening' and 'understanding' [or] between two kinds of hearing, between two paces of the same ... between a tension and a balance, or else, if you prefer, between a sense (that one listens to) and a truth (that one understands)" (1–2). He goes on to suggest that, due to their overlapping reverberations, hearing and listening cannot be hygienically disentangled. Both faculties are fundamentally bound up with overlapping questions of sensation, sense-making, knowledge, understanding, memory, truth, and desire.

Bringing Nancy into proximity with Burke, we propose that listening may operate not only as an interpretive form of symbolic action but also as part of one's own attitude and framework for hearing. Despite the etymological overlaps between listening and hearing, we could return to the "list" as a cloth filter for an especially apt metaphor for listening as active, voluntary, and interpretive in contradistinction to hearing as

passive, involuntary, and physiological. One must always call into question one's own "listening filter." As Burke says of terministic screens,
theoretical filters sieve and direct our listening capacities. The filters can
reveal "notable distinctions in texture, and even in form depending on
which ... filter [is] used" (*LSA* 45). Nevertheless, every listening praxis
will have its limitations. What is it that we do not hear while we are
actively and desirously filtering? When the analysand bends the analyst's
ear, we propose that the analyst must receive such speech as an injunc-
tion to cultivate an elasticity of listening, as in the French phrase *tendre
l'oreille* (literally to stretch the ear), or even go so far as to change the
filter altogether.

Unconscious Transmissions: Listening
as Free-Floating Attention

Freud instructed analysts to practice what English translators have rendered
as "evenly suspended attention," "free floating attention," or "evenly hov-
ering attention."[4] In 1912, Freud wrote that, in contrast to the analysand's
imperative to speak freely, "[t]he rule for the doctor may be expressed:
'He should withhold all conscious influences from his capacity to attend,
and give himself over completely to his unconscious memory.' Or, to put
it purely in terms of technique: 'He should simply listen, and not bother
about whether he is keeping anything in mind'" ("Recommendations"
112). In light of his forebears' emphases on appearance and neurophysiol-
ogy, his advice that analysts attend to the patient's discourse and hear what
the person has to say remains a radically open approach to listening. "This
way of listening," writes Bollas, "is revolutionary" and "Freud's method
was so disturbing that even his followers could not adhere to his explicit
instructions and their implications" (12–13). For many analysands, there
is also an affectively liberating aspect to the experience of psychoanalytic
free association in that the practice of speaking "freely," hearing oneself,
and being heard by a judicious listener can be a uniquely intimate and
cathartic experience.

Freud's insistence on the value of close listening necessitates that the analyst maintain an attitude that suspends personal inclinations and theoretical
assumptions. The analyst must try "to avoid so far as possible reflection and
the construction of conscious expectations, not to try to fix anything that
he heard particularly in his memory, and by these means to catch the drift of
the patient's unconscious with his own unconscious" ("Two" 239). The free
speech of the analysand meets the free listening of the analyst, who seeks to
gather information without assigning special significance to any aspect of
the analysand's associations:

> Just as the patient must relate everything that his self-observation can
> detect, and keep back all the logical and affective objections that seek

to induce him to make a selection from among them, so the doctor must put himself in a position to make use of everything he is told for the purposes of interpretation and of recognizing the concealed unconscious material without substituting a censorship of his own for the selection that the patient has forgone.

("Recommendations" 115)

Free listening is an attempt to suspend the motives that typically govern our everyday attention. This rule enables the analyst to listen for unconscious connections in what the analysand is saying and has said, but not necessarily for what the analysand means or intends. Bruce Fink has described it as *"an attentiveness that grasps at least one level of meaning and yet hears all the words and the way they are pronounced as well*, including speed, volume, tone, affect, stumbling, hesitation, and so on" (*Fundamentals* 11; Fink's emphasis). As a *techne*, or system of techniques, psychoanalytic listening attunes itself to the analysand's associative logic, including what is absent, present, emphasized, or deflected from in their discourse.

Freud likens the task of psychoanalytic listening to a telephone call with the patient's unconscious. After the Austrian Post and Telegraph Administration nationalized telecommunications in 1895, Freud had a phone installed in his Vienna consulting room and often characterized his work in telephonic terms.[5] He writes,

> To put it in a formula: he must turn his own unconscious like a receptive organ towards the transmitting unconscious of the patient. He must adjust himself to the patient as a telephone receiver is adjusted to the transmitting microphone. Just as the receiver converts back into sound waves the electric oscillations in the telephone line which were set up by sound waves, so the doctor's unconscious is able, from the derivatives of the unconscious which are communicated to him, to reconstruct that unconscious, which has determined the patient's free associations.

("Recommendations" 115)

Freud's practical conceptualization of psychoanalysis in telephonic terms, which, in the words of Burke, "makes a new machine from some old process ... carried over into some set of facts to which no one had previously felt that it belonged" (*PC* 96). Freud figured free association and free listening as a telephone-like transmission between the unconscious of the analysand and the receptive unconscious of the analyst.[6] The attentive analyst must know how to receive the analysand's call and respond appropriately.

Freud's metaphorical economy of the telephone conversation is a stark shift from Charcot's metaphorical economy of the forensic photograph.[7] Media theorist Friedrich Kittler (1943–2011) notes that psychoanalysis has a history of theorizing "partial objects," such as the gaze and the voice, that can be separated from the supposed unity of the body and excite desire. "This is psychoanalysis in the media age," writes Kittler, "for only cinema can restore the disembodied gaze, and only the telephone was able to transmit a disembodied voice" (57). In free association, the analysand disembodies their own speech and hears their own voice from the outside as they transmit to the analyst. This transferential telephone exchange undoubtedly involves both a range of feedback process and what media scholars refer to as asignifying background "noise" (whether it be psychological, physiological, semantic, or environmental distortion).[8]

Listening Awry: The Psychoanalytic Hearing Cap

Freud advises that the analyst avoid the illusion of clarity or comprehension and remain open to surprise. Free-floating attention retroactively considers the meaning of speech in relation to what has already been said. It is a matter of the analysand's own retrospection and the analyst being there to hear it:

> For as soon as anyone deliberately concentrates his attention to a certain degree, he begins to select from the material before him; one point will be fixed in his mind with particular clearness and some other will be correspondingly disregarded, and in making this selection he will be following his expectations or inclinations. This, however, is precisely what must not be done. In making the selection, if he follows his expectations he is in danger of never finding anything but what he already knows; and if he follows his inclinations he will certainly falsify what he may perceive. It must not be forgotten that the things one hears are for the most part things whose meaning is only recognized later on.
>
> ("Recommendations" 112)

Free-floating listening allows realizations to appear in what Freud called *Nachträglichkeit* or what Lacan called *après coup*, that is, an "afterwardness" or belated understanding of critical events. Freud believed that the analyst must listen carefully while keeping in mind innumerable inconsequential details whose links may gradually be made apparent over the course of treatment."[W]e often do not recognize the psychological significance of the things that we were told until afterward," writes Reik, "even when we recognize a certain meaning immediately, our reaction is restricted to the acknowledgement of the recognition; and we have to wait until new insight leads to its full understanding" (*Listening* 160). For Freud and Reik, reflection on what has been said during free association allows for the analysand and analyst to notice the sudden importance of material that may have previously been heard only on the periphery of attention. Since the unconscious manifests itself in overdetermined distortions and displacements of the analysand's speech, evenly suspended attention requires that the analyst's attention float patiently alongside the analysand's stream of memories, ideas, and affects. The analyst must have the composure to resist the urge to interrupt the flow with their own judgements or narrative summaries.

Some observers contend that Freud's theoretical framework is an unattainable ideal that actually presents impediments to attentive listening. If we take seriously the notion that every interpretation is contingent on and shaped through what we have been calling a listening filter, we can understand why Serge Leclaire wrote that Freud's rules of analytic attention are ultimately "impossible to uphold" and that notion of the "analyst's neutrality" or what is often called a "non-judgemental approach" (Leclaire 14) in the contemporary clinic is questionable.[9] A formulation of free listening that precludes making selections, offering constructions, or providing interpretations may be unachievable. Laplanche and Pontalis have outlined the paradox in the form of a question: "How is it conceivable ... that the transition from interpretation to construction could be made without the analyst, at some point, giving special attention to particular material, without his comparing it, schematising it and so on?" (44).

Furthermore, the analyst rarely provides direct answers when questioned and perhaps aims for a rhetorical position that is never found where one might expect. For Leclaire, this also constitutes a particular filter or attitude towards listening:

> In fact, this neutrality of the analyst aims only to describe a certain affective or libidinal position, since, as everyone knows who has ever been around a psychoanalyst, your average Freudian is anything but the totally unprejudiced scholar. One could even say that by becoming an analyst he agreed to take on new prejudices and that he very often presents himself as someone who has taken a position, who never wants to listen to the reasoning that supports his interlocutor's discourse, and who seems very adept at the sidestepping game, which he plays with a remarkable flair for the systemic .... [E]veryone knows that there is...one place where one is more or less certain to run into a psychoanalyst: at the crossroads ... there where any discourse whatsoever can be interpreted in terms of sexual value. (14)

Floating alongside the analysand's stream of consciousness, the analyst struggles against interference from their own emotional and cognitive currents.

In keeping with Burke's notion of "occupational psychosis," we suggest that each analyst's capacity for listening remains shaped through a personal "mental set" grounded in theoretical or philosophical preconceptions.

The analyst will inevitably select and recognize aspects of the analysand's discourse for interpretation or construction but endeavours to recognize their own preconceptions and listen openly beyond such limitations. "A stance of evenly suspended attention," writes Richard D. Chessick, "is a necessary, deliberately conscious effort to reduce the influence of this mental set" (4). Some contemporary psychoanalysts suggest that the clinician adopt an eclectic approach to listening from various psychoanalytic standpoints. Nancy McWilliams has suggested, for instance, that the analyst listens for Freudian themes of drive motivation, dynamic conflicts, and defence mechanisms, Kleinian themes of greed, envy, hatred, and the paranoid-schizoid position, self-psychological themes of cohesion and fragmentation, or object relations themes of attachment, separation, and individuation (138). But if these paradigms impose themselves on the task of close listening, they can readily flip over into a form of trained incapacity to meaningfully hear the analysand through a distorting network of prefabricated filters.

Leclaire underscores the paradox of Freud's rule for listening. Every clinician must attempt to work in reference to a theoretical system that allows for the gathering of information without prejudice while at the same time suspending reference to this very theoretical system. This practice necessarily foregrounds certain elements over others and tests out pre-existing assumptions. Evenly suspended attention, then, figures as a productive but unattainable ideal for listening amidst the chatter of the analyst's own unconscious motives, character, attitudes, and countertransference. A cacophonous rhetorical scene necessarily reverberates through the analyst's psyche, and this is why Freud recommends, not unproblematically, that analysts listen to themselves in their own analytic sessions and even diligently practice self-analysis. Evenly suspended attention is, according to Leclaire, an endeavour to question and renounce one's own prejudices "so as to keep [an] ear absolutely open." But sustaining this potentially precarious form of attention is also "a matter of holding on just as firmly, not to the privilege of some obscure origin, but to the very principle of an open logic that...takes account of the facts of sex and *jouissance*" (15).[10] In the right hands, psychoanalysis is a *techne* of open listening that also orients the analysand towards the subtle relationships between repetition compulsion, the body, and discourse.

The analyst also listens for digressions and other detours that may lead to unexpected associations. Lacan's own training analyst Rudolph Loewenstein, for instance, once described the analyst's task of listening in a schematic way. "The analyst," he writes, listens "to what is being said; to how it is being said, when and in what context it is being said; to what is not said, but deliberately or unwittingly omitted; and ... to the absence of communication – listening to silence" (179–180). The psychoanalyst listens to these different layers of speech from a multitude of angles, any one

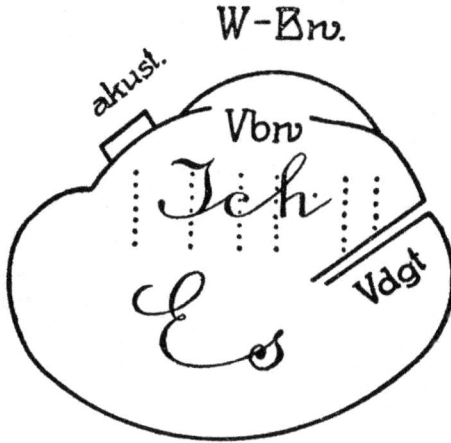

Figure 6.1 Freud's drawing of his second topography in German from 1923, which includes the *Ich* [Ego], *Es* [Id], W-Brv [*Wahrnehmung-Bewusstein* or Perception-Consciousness], Vbrv [*Vorbewusstein* or Preconscious], Vdgt [*Verdrängte* or Repression], and *akust.* [hearing cap].

of which might open onto a breakthrough for the patient. But, of course, such breakthroughs can never be predicted or forced.

When Freud presented his second topography of the psyche in his famous 1923 diagram in *The Ego and the Id*, he mapped the relations between the ego, id, and superego along with the levels of conscious, preconscious, and unconscious activity. In an odd twist without further elaboration, he also drew what he calls a "cap of hearing" on the left side of the diagram resting above the ego (see Figure 6.1). Few scholars ever address this anomaly in the diagram. It is unclear if this cap denotes an aperture or a protective covering. It appears to be the prosthetic ear of an uncanny creature, not unlike the primordial vesicle that Freud imagines in *Beyond the Pleasure Principle*. Curiously, Freud notes that the ego in the diagram not only wears this "cap of hearing" but "might be said to wear it awry" (25). Perhaps he meant to imply that one's capacity for hearing is always skewed, filtered as it is by the dramatism of the ego in dynamic tension with the superego and id.

Digging into Archaeological Listening

In his early work on hysteria, Freud provides yet another metaphorical framework, comparing the analyst's task of psychoanalytic listening to that of an explorer studying the ruins and hieroglyphics of an ancient society. With help from the locals, the archaeological explorer "may start upon the ruins, clear away the rubbish, and, beginning from the visible remains, uncover what is buried" ("The Aetiology" 192). With any luck, Freud adds, they may discover a mysterious temple's remains along with "numerous inscriptions" that "reveal an alphabet and a language" (293). When this script is "deciphered and translated," it may "yield undreamed-of information about the events of the remote past, to commemorate which the monuments were built" (192). Here, the analyst perhaps attends to the ways in which the analysand has been mining a hole, has dug in their heels, or has been digging an early grave, only to proceed with treatment as another modality of hole-digging exercise. Freud envisioned a process of listening and asking questions that would allow for information-gathering as a reconstruction of the analysand's past experiences. He thought such a reconstruction of personal history could lead them towards a new archaeological relationship with the past that would potentially facilitate unearthing and working through difficult thoughts, emotions, and behaviours.[11]

Psychologist Lawrence Josephs described the trajectory of archaeological listening as a method:

> Archaeological analysis involves two steps. Firstly, the analyst must undo the formal regression by decoding the condensation, displacements, symbolizations, and secondary elaborations inherent in the patient's communications. Secondly, the analyst must undo the temporal regression by discerning the past experiences which have been represented in terms of a current reality. Presumably, once these two steps have been successfully accomplished the topographic regression will have been undone, that is, the unconscious will have been made conscious.
>
> (Josephs 283)

Josephs seems to suggest that the analyst's task is to help the analysand reconstruct their own history from the traces of the past that manifest through speech. The analyst merely aids the analysand in drawing out germane inferences from their own speech. Freud wrote that the analyst/ archaeologist listens in hope to liberate "the fragment of historical truth from its distortions and its attachments to the actual present day and in leading it back to the point in the past to which it belongs" ("Constructions" 268). Archaeological listening is a practice, a *techne*, that makes temporal links through a process of retrospective reconstruction during free association.

Extending Freud's archaeological metaphor to thinking about the traumatic experience, Wilfred Bion later suggests, in "Attacks on Linking," that the analyst listens not so much to a ruin but rather to a "primitive disaster" since "we are confronted not so much with a static situation that permits leisurely study, but with a catastrophe that remains at one and the same moment actively vital and yet incapable of resolution into quiescence" (311). Bion emphasizes the immediacy of the patient's traumatic experience of the exceptional catastrophes of their past as an ongoing dynamic phenomenon in the unfolding present. He suggests that these experiential disasters often continue in compulsive repetition, disrupting the patient's capacity to stabilize thought, emotion, and behaviour.

Synaesthetic Listening

In his classic book, *Listening with the Third Ear*, Theodor Reik (1888–1969) offers "poised attention" as another way to conceptualize Freud's free listening. Poised attention entails wielding one's "particular attitude of mind" while also suspending understanding in order to maintain an open mind about the patient's symptoms and history (159–160). In keeping with Freud's recommendations, Reik advocates for a form of attention that relies on patience; analysts must refrain from forcing any immediate connections based on the analysand's reportage:

> Poised attention generally involves the renunciation of the immediate recognition of links of association. It apprehends the several details of the psychical data equally and prepares the way for us to work our way among them later. Free-floating attention provides, so to speak, a storeroom of impressions, from which later knowledge will suddenly emerge. It also creates the prerequisite conditions for those surprising results that appear in analysis as the product of a prolonged unconscious condensation and disassociation of impressions. (172)

Reik reconceptualized Freud's archaeological approach to listening in terms that echo Enlightenment metaphors and reassert the priority of the visual register. "We rarely realize that there is a pre-knowledge within us while we wait for illumination," writes Reik. "Sudden clarity is preceded by increasing darkness" (172). Reik's visual metaphor likely emerged out of his military experience as an officer in the Austrian cavalry from 1915 to 1918 and his interest in the traumatic neuroses of combat veterans suffering from "shell shock." He often compares psychoanalytic listening to the observational methods one might employ with a searchlight. Listening becomes a matter of bumbling through a dark fog and quietly shining a vital light on flittering shadows rather than cleverly interrogating the patient for forensic details about their inner life.

Reik fled the Nazis to Holland in 1934 only to flee again in 1938 to the United States. Searchlights were employed during both world wars to provide "artificial moonlight" for defence against night attacks and bombings. Soldiers could also aim searchlights into the sky so as to bounce light off of cloud cover to expose tactical opportunities on the ground. Perhaps with this context in mind, Reik contributed the searchlight as a metaphor for psychoanalytic listening:

> Voluntary attention, which is restricted to a narrow sector of our field of experience, may be compared in its effect to the turning of the searchlight upon a particular piece of ground. If we know beforehand that the enemy is coming from that direction, or that something is going to happen upon that field, then we have anticipated the event, as

it were. It is advantageous to illuminate that particular sector brightly. Let us assume a different case, that something, for instance a noise, has turned our attention to a particular zone. Only then do we turn the search light upon it. Our attention did not rush on in advance of the perception, but followed it. This is the case of involuntary attention. If we drive at night along the road near New York, we may notice that a searchlight in the middle of the road is scouring the surrounding country uninterruptedly. It illuminates the road, is then directed to the fields, turns toward the town, and swings in a wide curve back to the road, and so repeats its circuit. This kind of activity, which is not confined to one point but is constantly scouring a wide radius, provides the best comparison with the function of free-floating attention.

(Reik 163)[12]

Reik frames attention as a beam of light that can be aimed and moved. What his visual metaphor shares with Freud's archaeological explorer is the drive to uncover what is buried, hidden, or merely left unsaid in discourse. The analyst digs and sheds light through listening. It is an approach that sometimes listens against the grain, underlines contradictions and omissions, and evades obvious meanings in order to unearth or highlight (depending on the operative trope) connections that are not immediately visible to the patient. But neither the light nor the archaeological dig purports to capture and immobilize the patient's flux of experience.

Expanding on Freud's description of free listening, Reik suggests that the analyst listen as an observer with two apprehensions:

One perception in which [the analyst] clearly recognizes what the words and movements of the person observed mean: just what they say; and a second which sets small value upon the conscious meaning in contrast with another which [the analyst] does not know and which has still to be discovered.

("Noticing" 35)

Archaeological listening and Reik's searchlight curiously intermingle listening and looking. In Reik's own words, the searchlight as a form of listening "casts a brilliant light upon a small area" and "makes us realize in what profound darkness the greater part of the field is plunged" (41). He nevertheless advises that when our attention is intensely focused on one area, we will also be distracted from other possibilities. As Burke says of our hard-wired occupational dispositions, every "way of seeing is also a way of not seeing—a focus on object A involves a neglect of object B" (*PC* 49).

Extending Nietzsche's employment of the phrase in *Beyond Good and Evil*, Reik proposes that it is not sufficient for the analyst to listen with just two ears: They need to grow a "third ear" so as to "develop a special kind of perceptiveness for ... undertones" ("Theodor" 17). Operating in the interzone between bodily organ and media technology, the third ear receives, records, and decodes the "asides" that are "whispered between sentences and without sentences" in the clinic (145). Reik describes a kind of listening filter that would attend to what eludes our grasp since "[t]he small fish that escapes through the mesh is often the most precious" (*Listening* 145). He writes,

> The voice that speaks in him, speaks low, but he who listens with a third ear hears also what is expressed almost noiselessly .... There are instances in which things a person has said in psychoanalysis are consciously not even heard by the analyst, but none the less understood or interpreted. There are others about which one can say: in one ear, out the other, and in the third .... One of the peculiarities of this third ear is that it works two ways. It can catch what other people do not say, but only feel and think; and it can also be turned inward. It can hear voices from within the self that are otherwise not audible because they are drowned out by the noise of our conscious thought-processes. (145–146)

Reik's third ear amounts to the analyst engaging in two orders of listening. If they can direct the third ear inward, they will be able to listen to their own "inner voice," to their own intuition, and to their own counter-transference (i.e. their largely unproductive overidentifications and feelings for the patient). The wager is that this will better equip them to listen between the lines, as it were, and attend to undulations in the unconscious of the patient as communicated through subtle traces in their speech and behaviour.

Empathetic Listening

"Archaeological listening" should be contrasted with what is commonly referred as "empathetic listening" in contemporary clinical counselling discourse. In keeping with its Greek roots, "empathy" literally means "in sense" or "in feeling" and denotes an overpowering identification with the emotions, thoughts, state of mind, or point of view of another person in an effort to comprehend their experience. We often distinguish "empathy" from "sympathy," which also comes from the Greek for "having a fellow feeling" or "with feeling." In popular parlance, sympathy often implies an understanding of and kinship with another person's (usually negative) experience, which remains distinct from one's own, while empathy refers to a shared affective experience whereby one almost preternaturally experiences another's feelings. This mystical experience of the other's experience explains why empathy has become such a hot concept in new age spiritual circles.

We might further distinguish empathy from pity or compassion, which Aristotle defined as "a feeling of pain at an apparent evil, destructive or painful, which befalls one who does not deserve it, and which we might expect to befall ourselves or some friend of ours, and more over to befall us soon" ("Rhetoric" 2207). "Pity" (in Latin, "piety" or "clemency") includes paternalistic overidentification with another person's feelings or sensing the injustice of their suffering. Pity should arguably be distinguished from "compassion" (in Latin, "suffer with"), which speaks to not only the capacity to feel for another but also the desire to help or act on behalf of the suffering person.

In psychoanalytic and psychotherapeutic literature, the distinctions between sympathy and empathy often collapse and become rather messy. Perhaps this confusion has something to do with the fact that, in the English language, "empathy" did not even exist as a word until 1909, when British psychologist Edward Bradford Titchener (1867–1927) translated the German *Einfühlung* ("feeling into") as "empathy." Titchener was introducing the work of German philosopher Theodor Lipps (1851–1914), who wrote about the manner in which a person might project their own experience onto artistic objects through contemplation and introspection. The spectator empathetically projects himself into and feels the artistic image. He described empathy as an upsurge of emotional introspection engendered by memory or aesthetic experience:

> In this particular instance, the picture is combined with an empathic attitude; and all such 'feelings' – feelings of if, and why, and nevertheless, and therefore – normally take the form, in my experience, of motor empathy. I act the feeling out, though as a rule in imaginal and not in sensational terms. It may be fleeting, or it may be relatively stable; whatever it is, I have not the slightest doubt of its kinaesthetic character. Sometimes it has a strong effective colouring – this statement holds of all my attitudinal feels – and sometimes it is wholly indifferent.
>
> (Titchener 185–186)

Titchener describes motor empathy as a "kinaesthetic" emotional reaction that may take place between the spectator and an object, and later psychological theorists of empathy applied the term to interpersonal communication. In popular discourse, empathy now refers to one's capacity to read, appreciate, or understand another person's emotions. But, paradoxically, this form of so-called "emotional intelligence" or "emotional literacy" always involves the projection of oneself into another person. Popular depictions suggest that empathy is an exercise in imagining the world of another person so faithfully that one can expect to not only *comprehend* but also somehow *experience* the other's experience as they do. In the context of psychoanalytic technique, the analyst's well-meaning aspiration to engage in empathetic listening is often a two-fold error because it bespeaks the therapist's capacity to hear the presenting problems from the analysand's perspective and assumes that such a connection conduces to productive therapy.

Freud understood empathy as a form of identification. He describes a path "that leads from identification by way of imitation to empathy, that is, to the comprehension of the mechanism by means of which we are enabled to take up any attitude at all towards another mental life" ("Group" 110). So understood, empathy mediates how a listener will be shaped by their own identifications and attitudes towards others. Although he recommends the analyst maintain a "sympathetic understanding" of the analysand, especially at the beginning of treatment, he does not often refer to empathy as a technique per se and has good reason to be wary of the cult of shared sentiment.[13]

Sandor Ferenczi also discussed empathy in his correspondence with Freud. He expressed a fear that the employment of empathy as a technique allowed the clinician to rationalize a break with the practice of "analytic neutrality." Although Reik did not speak much of empathy in his work, many scholars have transposed and recontextualized the notion of the third ear as a sort of "sixth sense" for empathy. An analyst who possesses this mystical "six sense" becomes emotionally contemplative by identifying with the analysand's experience, incorporating and feeling it in order to "reduce the perceived distance between their respective perspectives." The analyst then experiences the world from the perspective of the analysand, only to detach from this form of listening to later provide an impassive analysis of the situation (Clark 100–101). "In order to comprehend the unconscious of another person," writes Reik, "we must, at least for a moment, change ourselves into and become that person" (361). If empathy has its roots in an unconscious identification with the other, Reik adapted this identification as a method for listening in the clinic.

In "The Metapsychology of the Analyst," Robert Fliess (1895–1970), the son of Freud's interlocuter Wilhelm Fliess (1858–1928), engaged in one of the earliest concerted efforts to conceptualize empathy in psychoanalytic terms. Fliess called the analyst's expression of empathy a "trial identification" that relied on the analyst's ability to step into the analysand's shoes and "obtain in this way an inside knowledge" (212). Fliess describes empathy in the language of object relations theory and, in yet another sensory shift, equated empathic listening to systematic tasting:

> a person who uses empathy on an object introjects this object transiently, and projects the introject again onto the object. This alone enables him in the end to square a perception from without with one from within; it is a trick that one can see operated by anyone who attempts anywhere a psychological evaluation. Any practical

psychologist, analytic or nonanalytic, has to be able to perform this particular test just as quickly and reliably and as undisturbedly as, for example, the tea taster, who introjects materially a small sample only long enough to be able to taste it. (214)

Fliess understood empathy as a paradoxically indifferent analytic technique that necessitates a stoic detachment from the object and the impulsive demands of one's digestive system.

Against the grain of Fliess' disinterested tea taster, many proponents of contemporary modes of empathic listening describe empathy as though it were possible to take in the other's experience and gain an understanding by imagining how the other must think or feel. Psychoanalyst Sarah Usher has compared empathetic listening to the way one might listen to both the words and music of a song in that we might "hear the content of what the patient is saying and try to hear the underlying feelings, or affect, that is attached to the content, as well as what the patient is not saying" (33). Usher's version of the empathetic ear is oriented towards listening for the intention of the analysand's speech along with the emotion being expressed. The maxim of empathetic therapeutic attention is most commonly expressed in a statement so often encouraged in psychotherapy textbooks: the analyst must "follow the affect" of the analysand.

Following the Affect

Ideas surrounding empathy in communications and psychoanalytic treatment have been shaped through various theoretical models. Throughout the 1950s and 1960s, empathy became a popular concept in the areas of self-psychology and ego-psychology. There are numerous discussions on the importance of empathy as a listening technique in the works of Donald Winnicott (1896–1971), Margaret Mahler (1897–1985), Charles Brenner (1913–2008), and Jacob Arlow (1912–2004). An influential discussion of empathetic attention as a psychoanalytic technique was Heinz Kohut's (1913–1981) conceptualization of "vicarious introspection" in the field of "self-psychology," the antecedent to relational approaches to psychotherapy. Kohut posited that the analyst ought to listen for the analysand's state of mind or feeling in the moment. In his paper of 1959, "Introspection, Empathy, and Psychoanalysis," he provided a somewhat strange example of how the clinician might approach being empathetic towards the patient:

We see a person who is unusually tall. It is not to be disputed that this person's unusual size is an important fact for our psychological assessment – without introspection and empathy, however, his size remains simply a physical attribute. Only when we think ourselves into his place, only when we, by vicarious introspection, begin to

feel his unusual size as if it were our own and thus revive inner experiences in which we had been unusual or conspicuous, only then
begins there for us an appreciation of the meaning that the unusual
size may have for this person and only then have we observed a psychological fact. (461)

Strangely, Kohut's example does not actually involve listening but,
rather, resorts to a kind of clinical observation. He also seems to suggest that the introspection of the analyst could aid them in uncovering
"psychological fact[s]" about the analysand. Whereas the archaeological
model for listening aims to hear links between the analysand's present
and their past, Kohut's vicarious introspection suggests that the analyst
ought to observe or listen while comparing their own thoughts and feelings to those of the analysand so as to more fully appreciate their experience. This practice of listening requires that the clinician reflect on
their own countertransference, imagination, and emotions as part of the
information used to create a shared understanding. The analyst's empathy and emotional attunement then presumably create the conditions for
reparative care.

Humanist psychologist Carl Rogers also advocates for an interpersonal approach that incorporates empathetic listening. At face value,
his approach resembles Freud's. He advises the clinician to maintain an
"unconditional positive regard" and a general willingness to attentively
listen without giving advice or expressing judgement. The empathetic
listener's task becomes a process of drawing inferences regarding the
intentions and affective state of the speaker. In contemporary relational psychoanalysis, for instance, listening is a practice of tuning in
to what the patient is feeling. Much like Kohut, Rogers suggests that
the clinician imaginatively insert herself into the patient's subjective
world:

It means entering the private perceptual world of the other and
becoming thoroughly at home in it. It involves being sensitive,
moment by moment, to the changing felt meanings which flow in
this other person, to the fear or rage or tenderness or confusion or
whatever that he or she is experiencing. It means temporarily living in the other's life, moving about in it delicately without making
judgments; it means sensing meanings of which he or she is scarcely
aware, but not trying to uncover totally unconscious feelings, since
this would be too threatening. It includes communicating your sense
of the person's world as you look with fresh and unfriend frightened
eyes at elements of which he or she is fearful. It means frequently
checking with the person as to the accuracy if you're sensing, and
being guided by the responses you receive. (142)

In *Active Listening*, Farson and Rogers emphasize the importance of the listener's "presentness" to the speaker. They advocate for a form of "active listening" whereby the practitioner "does not passively absorb the words which are spoken to him" but rather "actively tries to grasp the facts and the feelings in what he hears, and he tries, by his listening, to help the speaker work out his own problems" (Rogers and Farson 1). This empathy-centric approach encourages clinicians to drink in the emotional states of their patients. Through the mobilization of a kind of pseudo-telepathy, the therapist attempts to imagine, reconstruct, and then occupy their patient's subjective experience. This interpersonal or intersubjective approach (which has been popularized in recent theories of attachment) ultimately presumes to build a "therapeutic alliance" or "working relationship" with the analysand by listening to emotional experience in the "here and now."

Against Empathy

In *Inessential Solidarity*, Diane Davis brings Freud's concept of identification into reverberation with new-rhetorical accounts of persuasion. She proffers the concept of affectability as a rhetorical-psychoanalytic disposition that precedes and subtends distinctions between self and other in matters of identification:

> Identification could not operate among self-enclosed organisms; it would have to belong to the realm of affectable beings, infinitely open to the other's affection, inspiration, alteration; it would have to belong to the realm of a radically generalized rhetoricity, then, an affectability or persuadability that is at work prior to an in excess of any shared meaning.
>
> (*Inessential* 26)

Following Freud, Burke, and Nancy, Davis attempts to underscore the asymbolic libidinal susceptibility that must exist for identification to occur. This organismic affectability is a fundamental condition of connection and symbolic action. This primordial rhetorical disposition, our infinite openness to each other, serves as a compelling explanation for the illusion that we can feel vicariously. Still, no matter how comforting it might be to believe that, with the right kind of "emotional intelligence," we can properly empathize, it is not the task of psychoanalysis to paint over the opacity of others, or even ourselves, in order to consolidate illusions of understanding.

In their critique of empathetic listening, communications theorists Ronald Arnett and Gordon Nakagawa suggest that the literature of humanistic psychology has created "a normative emphasis on a subject's *unmediated, personal and direct experience* of others' internal states, which transcends social constraints in the form of façades, rules, conventions, artifices, etc." (370; emphasis in original). Empathy-focused listening practices tend to aim at facilitating the growth of the patient by reflecting back and paraphrasing their accounts of experiences. The "unconditional positive regard" of such a listening filter operates on "an assumption of the innate goodness of the human being" and *"confirmation* of the other, but not necessarily as *agreement"* (Arnett and Nakagawa 370; emphasis in original). The putative benefit of empathetic listening is that the clinician, for instance, does not present a threat to the "self-picture" of the patient who then does not have to defend their own perspective or experience.[14] Rogers advocates for a "client-centred approach" that would attempt to avoid dynamics of power, but also suggests that the practitioner take a non-evaluative stance insofar as the person in treatment should not be subjected to the listener's value judgements. This listening hinges on the imaginary relation between one ego and the ego of another; the analyst and analysand would interact as if a common consensus surrounding meaning could be reached.

There are significant problems with a theory of empathetic listening that calls for the analyst's introspection so that they can better understand the patient's self. "[T]he communicator, who sees empathy as a universal approach to listening," write Arnett and Nakagawa, "fails to recognize the uniqueness or non-interchangeability of people" (373). It is in this regard that empathetic listening appears to stray far from Freud's recommendations for free floating attention, which the analyst "cultivate[s] ... as part of an attempt to recognize the otherness of the other, the other's differences from ourselves" (Fink 10). Most often, empathetic listening appears to culminate in a rhetoric organized around paraphrasing and consolidating the speaker's thoughts and feelings rather than attending to their discourse. One troubling assumption of this approach to empathetic identification is the assumption that the patient's internal feelings are what is most important to treatment, almost as though feelings could be communicated telepathically between patient and therapist.

If empathetic listening involves "putting oneself in the other's shoes," philosopher Martha Nussbaum has also raised important questions about why one would even try on this footwear in the first place: "Does one actually think, for the time being, that one is oneself the sufferer, putting oneself in his or her own place? Does one imagine one's own responses as *fused* in some mysterious way with those of the sufferer?" (327). Nussbaum's critique is that the empathetic approach risks the assumption of shared experience. This might entail an imaginary connection between two people that conjures fantasies of mutual understanding and a tendency to insinuate that clinicians can actually deeply comprehend an analysand's experience as if it were their own. It is a style of listening that can flip over into a debilitating trained incapacity to attend to divergence and difference in favour of a presumed universal emotional experience. In other words, the danger is that the clinician risks confusing and conflating their own experience with that of the patient. For Nussbaum, it is crucial that the person who practices sympathy for others be able to acknowledge their own separate existence: "For if it is to be for *another*, and not for oneself, that one feels compassion, one must be aware both of the bad lot of the sufferer and of the fact that it is, right now, not one's own" (327). If the analyst, for instance, begins to identify with the analysand's suffering as though there could be an experiential fusion between the two parties, they dangerously and deludedly fail to comprehend the suffering of another as *an other*.

Lacan viewed empathy and the pretence of understanding as lures that mislead the clinician into a labyrinth of misrecognition. Analysts stop listening attentively when they succumb to countertransference or provide self-satisfied, clever interpretations. Building on Freud's approach to free-floating attention, Lacan advocates for a radically open listening practice that attends to the symbolic dimensions of language during the analysand's free association:

> But what need can an analyst have for an extra ear, when it sometimes seems that two are already too many, since he runs headlong into the fundamental misunderstanding brought on by the relationship of understanding? I repeatedly tell my students: 'Don't try to understand!' and leave this nauseating category to Karl Jaspers and his consorts. May one of your ears become as deaf as the other one must be acute. And that is the one that you should lend to listen for sounds and phonemes, words, locutions, and sentences, not forgetting pauses, scansions, cuts, periods, and parallelisms, for it is in these that the word-for-word transcription can be prepared, without which analytic intuition has no basis or object.
>
> ("The Situation" 394)

Opposing the popular empathic mode of listening organized around restoring meaning to the analysand and linking thoughts with feelings, Lacan insists that analysis cannot be taken as a transparent or reciprocal exchange. For Lacan, the analyst ought to let the ear of the Imaginary become hard of hearing and listen to the analysand with the ear of the Symbolic instead. This is a practice of listening that attends closely to the speech of the analysand rather than empathetically imagining their experience. The analysand expresses transference (their redirection of emotional investments towards the analyst) in the form of identifications, demands, and projections. The analyst qua "listener is thus situated in it as an *interlocutor*"; Lacan nevertheless insists that the analyst remain silent and "patiently refuses to play this role" so as to facilitate the process of free association ("Beyond" 67).

Lacan describes the psychoanalytic scenario in the context of transference and its relation to the discourse of free association:

> It is simply because the analyst is there listening that the man who speaks addresses him, and since he forces his discourse not to want to say anything, he becomes what this man *wants to tell him*. What the man says may, in fact, 'have no meaning,' but what he says *to the analyst* conceals one anyway. It is in the impulse to respond that the listener senses this; and it is by suspending this impulse to respond that the analyst understands the meaning of the discourse.
>
> ("Beyond" 66)

If the analyst's aim is to help the analysand make new associations and locate repressed content, they must suppress the urge to play an overly conversational interpretive role in analysis. Instead, they spend much of the session quietly poised as a would-be interlocutor who could reply at any moment, but, for the most part, refrains from doing so. "In the name of this patient," asserts Lacan, "our listening too will be patient" ("On the Subject" 191).

Instead of making empathetic connections with the patient, Lacan encouraged psychoanalysts to pay attention to "the signifier" while listening to the Symbolic aspects of language. This close listening psychoanalytic method has nothing to do with shared understandings. "Hearing," wrote Lacan, "does not force me to understand" and cautioned that "if I do understand something I am sure to be mistaken" ("The Direction" 515). Not to be confused with symbolism or symbolic action, Lacan's notion of the Symbolic refers to the grammatical, rhetorical, and sonorous aspects of the analysand's speech that could be understood in multiple ways. He even went so far as to suggest that reading poetry could help the analyst sharpen the ear towards the Symbolic "for a polyphony to be heard" and "for it to become clear that all discourse is aligned along the several staves of a musical score" ("The Instance" 419).

Following Lacan, Leclaire maintains that free listening should not be conceptualized as mystical attunement to the psychic experience of the analysand but rather as holding an ear towards the unconscious aspects of language in all of their overdetermination (15). It would seem that empathetic listening troublingly posits the analyst as the one who can inhabit and traverse the analysand's inner world through the gift of psychic intuition. In stark contrast to the projects of self-psychology or relational analysis, Lacanian psychoanalysis avoids the imaginary traps of empathy, which is always already a form of unreliable projection and misrecognition. Instead of focusing on understanding patients, the analyst's job is often to help what Kenneth Burke refers to as "the symbol-using, symbol-misusing animal" experience the hiccups and internal inconsistencies of the symbolic order that operates with, against, and through all of us.

An empathetic listening practice of the sort proffered by Rogers or Kohut tends to slip into compassionate listening or a listening of over-identification whereby the practitioner presumes to know how the patient might be feeling. Nussbaum is dismissive of the pretence that an empathetic analyst can cultivate a "twofold attention," imaginatively projecting themselves into the position of the suffering analysand while steadily maintaining the capacity to acknowledge that they are not in that position. We might attempt to listen empathetically in an attempt to think or feel from the perspective of another person, but we must still acknowledge that this perspective is always already mediated by our own "mental set" of assumptions, prejudices, and attitudes. We can certainly endeavour to imagine what it would be like to walk down the street in another person's shoes, but it takes a great deal of sensitivity to interpersonal nuance to recognize that they will never quite fit – no matter how similar we might appear to each other as we stare into the mirror.

Notes

1 The joke is an obvious allusion to the plight of Dutch artist Vincent Van Gogh, who cut off his own ear during a crisis of psychosis and asked a cleaner at a brothel to keep it safe for him. See Murphy, Bernadette. *Van Gogh's Ear.* Toronto: Random House Canada, 2016.

2 In *Listening*, Nancy claims that each sensory register has both a simple (or natural) sense and an elevated subjective one (often connoting tension, attention, or anxiety). These couplings include seeing and looking, smelling and sniffing, tasting and savouring, touching and feeling, and hearing and listening.

3 There is an ambivalence at play in the British expression "to pin back one's ears," which suggests not only harsh admonitions, including the act of beating or striking a person (especially in the head), but also a demand for someone to listen carefully.

4 Freud's German term for how the analyst ought to freely listen is *gleichschwebende Aufmerksamkeit*. American psychoanalyst A.A. Brill first translated Freud's term in English as "mobile attention" to emphasize thought in motion, attention that moves freely and easily. Reik took issue with Brill's translation in *Listening with the Third Ear*, which is why he offered his own term "poised attention" (157) as a superior encapsulation of the notion.

5 In *Gramophone, Film, Typewriter*, Friedrich Kittler notes the influence of multimedia technology like the telegraph and telephone on Freud's theorization of psychoanalysis.

6 Despite having a phone installed in his office, Freud's nephew, Harry, recalled that his uncle actually "did not like the telephone and refused to use it" (313). In *A Lover's Discourse*, Roland Barthes reflects on Freud's hostility towards the telephone and draws attention to its uncanny, anxiety-provoking aspects in his work: "Freud, apparently, did not like the telephone, however much he may have liked *listening*. Perhaps he felt, perhaps he foresaw that the telephone is always a *cacophony*, and that what it transmits is the *wrong voice*, the false communication. . . No doubt I try to deny separation by the telephone – as the child fearing to lose its mother keeps pulling on a string; but the telephone wire is not a good transitional object, it is not an inert string; it is charged with a meaning, which is not that of junction but that of distance: the loved, exhausted voice heard over the telephone is the fade-out in all its anxiety. First of all, this voice,

when it reaches me, when it is here, while it (with great difficulty) survives, is a voice I never entirely recognize; as if it emerged from under a mask (thus we are told that the masks used in Greek tragedy had a magical function: to give the voice a chthonic origin, to distort, to alienate the voice, to make it come from somewhere under the earth). Then, too, on the telephone the other is always in a situation of departure; the other departs twice over, by voice and by silence: whose turn is it to speak? We fall silent in unison: crowding of two voids. *I'm going to leave you*, the voice on the telephone says with each second" (114–115). Barthes characterizes listening on the telephone as a precarious connection conducted through an alienating distorter of the voice that produces a sense of distance in spite of its immediacy.

7 "A rough but not inadequate analogy to this supposed relation of conscious to unconscious activity," writes Freud, "might be drawn from the field of ordinary photography. The first stage of the photograph is the 'negative'; every photographic picture has to pass through the 'negative process,' and some of these negatives which have held good in the examination are admitted to the 'positive process' ending in the picture" (Freud, "A Note on the Unconscious," *SE* XII, 264). In Freud's view, the development of a negative into a positive print serves as a useful metaphor for the return of the repressed.

8 In a comparable vein, Lacan suggests that "the analytic interpretation is not meant to be understood; it is made to produce waves" ("Yale" 35).

9 Leclaire underscores the pitfalls of reductive or deterministic listening methods: "Thus, if you arrive for your appointment on time, early, or late, and if in trying to respond to his questioning insinuations you say that it was, respectively, just out of politeness, out of prudence, or by accident, [the analyst] will nevertheless think silently or even out loud that you are obsessive if you are on time, anxious if you are early, and deceitfully aggressive if you were held up by a breakdown of the subway" (14).

10 Lacan puns on *jouissance* with the French phrase "*j'ouïr sens*," which could be translated as "I hear sense" or "I enjoy sense."

11 The "classical" attitude towards listening situates the analyst in the position of detached observer and encourages what philosopher Paul Ricoeur has called a "hermeneutics of suspicion" in relation to the patient's discourse. Ricoeur noted that Nietzsche, Marx, and Freud share a modern style of interpretation that views seemingly obvious lines of interpretation with scepticism. See Ricoeur's *Freud and Philosophy* of 1970.

12 This analogy of the searchlight appears almost verbatim, with only minor changes, in Reik's *Surprise and the Psychoanalyst* of 1936 in a chapter called "Noticing, Attention, and Taking Note" (38). In this text, Reik compares listening to the task of learning words in a new language or the process of translating one language into another.

13 Freud first explored empathy as a concept in *Jokes and their Relation to the Unconscious* of 1905. See pages 196–197 of this text for Freud's discussion on the importance of empathy in the context of jokes and humour.

14 The work of Rogers and Farson exemplifies an approach to listening that aims towards understanding the "total meaning" of the patient's feeling or attitude underlying a given utterance. With this goal in mind, they advocate for an analytic environment that facilitates the patient's adaptation: "If I want to help a man reduce his defensiveness and become more adaptive, I must try to remove the threat of myself as his potential changer. As long as the atmosphere is threatening, there can be no effective communication. So I must create a climate which is neither critical, evaluative, nor moralizing. It must be an atmosphere of equality and freedom, permissiveness and understanding, acceptance and warmth. It is in this climate and this climate only that the individual feels safe enough to incorporate new experiences and new values into his concept of himself" (9).

7 Lacan's Psychoanalytic Rhetoric

The Power of Non-Understanding

Lacan Parle

During the early 1950s, Jacques Lacan gave private seminars on Wednesdays at lunchtime in Sylvia Bataille's living room at 3 Rue de Lille in Paris.[1] In front of a small gathering of psychoanalytic trainees, he lectured on the canonical case histories, including Dora, the Rat Man, and the Wolf Man. He also engaged the group in close readings of Freud's books on dreams, parapraxes, and jokes. Lacan eventually relocated his private seminars to the Saint-Anne Hospital, where they evolved into the much more public Seminar in 1953. Élisabeth Roudinesco recounts that the early years at "the amphitheatre at Sainte-Anne acted as a kind of research laboratory for everyone who attended the lectures .... The atmosphere resembled that of a Socratic symposium" (260). In his seminars, Lacan reinvented psychoanalysis as a modern quasi-Socratic dialectical process that evolved into "a technique which substitutes the strange detours of free association for the sequence of the Dialogue" ("Some" 12).

Rather than focusing on its Socratic dialectical dimension, the rhetorician Kenneth Burke would likely have characterized the scene as an expansive parlour. For Burke, the parlour represents a charged, open-ended rhetorical crucible, where speakers and listeners, operating as both orators and audiences, discuss matters of great importance. While the Socratic philosopher, who supposedly distinguishes the Truth from fiction, ironically feigns ignorance in order to win over his dialectical interlocutors, the scene of Burkean rhetoric admits of no such hard-and-fast distinctions. The philosophical dialogue, according to Burke, is merely one of many possible varieties of rhetorical gatherings: "Bring several *rhetoricians* together," writes Burke, and "let their speeches contribute to the maturing of one another by the give and take of question and answer, and you have the *dialectic* of Platonic dialogue" (*A Rhetoric* 53; Burke's emphases). While those in attendance may seek out "a higher order of truth," (*A Rhetoric* 53), the endeavour may never transcend the realm of mere "opinion," which the rationalist philosopher too readily dismisses as inconsequential.

DOI: 10.4324/9781003214069-8

Viewed from this angle, Lacan's rhetorical method and the ongoing parlour that it has engendered (which far transcends the space of the rooms in which he spoke) figures not as a knowing philosopher's dissemination of his proper understanding of the objective Truth (as viewed from an imagined God's-eye-view) but as an ingenious act of rhetorical choreography. In Lacan's galvanic parlour, interlocutors' "opinions" (the signifiers they produce and the attitudes they betoken) come into relief, and the psychoanalyst's hallowed status as the "subject supposed to know" the truth of their patients' and acolytes' desires is productively undermined.

In order to present a more rhetorically-informed perspective on the style and import of Lacan's pedagogical method, we will begin by presenting the context, coordinates, and mise-en-scène of Lacan's parlour. We will then zero-in on pivotal aspects of his rhetorical method, including his unprecedented integration of rhetorical theory into his ideas about psychoanalysis, in order to make the case that Lacan's unique pedagogical rhetoric was engineered to perform, through its suasive effects, the very same revelatory transformation of subjectivity that it theorized. His migration away from a moribund philosophical investment in the idea of Truth, and its proper arbiters, was undertaken to create a space for subjects to carve out their own interpretations of their utterances. And this rhetorical manoeuvre, Lacan's *unheimlich* manoeuvre on the seductive figure of the Socratic Truth, is germane not only to the practice of psychoanalysis and clinical counselling but also, more broadly, to the entire spectrum of humanistic inquiry concerning the circulation of opinions, attitudes, subjectivity, and pedagogy.

Setting the Scene

Following the schisms within the French psychoanalytic schools and his "excommunication" from the International Psychoanalytic Association in 1963 (for refusing to adhere to the standard 50-minute therapeutic session), Lacan continued his Seminar at the École Normale Supérieure from 1964 through 1968. Philosophers, psychoanalysts, psychiatrists, anthropologists, sociologists, mathematicians, literary theorists, and students across the humanities and social sciences were in attendance. The popularity of the Seminar snowballed both despite and because of Lacan's peculiar style and manner of address. By the same token, when the *Écrits* was published in 1966, it sold five thousand copies in its first two weeks, even before reviews appeared in the press. The release of the 900-page tome broke numerous sales records when reprints were issued as mass-market paperbacks in two volumes (Roudinesco, *Jacques Lacan* 328). The works collected in the *Écrits* were delivered predominantly as oral presentations to psychoanalytic trainees, as conference presentations, and as public lectures; they persist as palpable remainders of a discourse that was transmitted through an evanescent voice.

After his expulsion from the École Normale Supérieure, Lacan was able to continue at the Paris Law Faculty for another decade.[2] At this point, the Seminar became an overcrowded spectacle and charged dramatic scene. The audience poured in from all over Europe. One would have to arrive hours beforehand and wait in a long line in hopes to get a seat. People clambered on top of each other to see the great orator in the flesh. Packed crowds of cigarette smokers generated a floating miasma in the grand lecture hall. At the front of the room, a pitcher of water and several glasses were placed upside down on a tray. People chattered excitedly until he entered alongside his entourage. Known for his unique sense of style, he appeared to many as a dandy: "Lacan, looking very majestic with his mane of white hair, would often arrive in a checked purple suit and a gray astrakhan overcoat; he always wore a light-colored shirt with a mandarin collar" (Roudinesco, *Jacques Lacan* 344). He would draw deeply on a twisted cigar, the ember flaring and then fading. He would eye the audience and exhale, adding a plume to the fog. Gradually, the crowd would settle into murmurs. Then, an assistant would bring him the microphone. Maria Pierrakos, the stenographer of the Seminar's last 12 years, recalls the moment: "the Master ... ascends the podium and begins to speak. Mystical silence falls; the only noise is the tense scratching of pens and agitated switching on of tape recorders: how could one bear to lose even a single word?" (8–9).[3] It is a question worth taking seriously. The frenzy of notetaking, stenography, transcription, and translation seemed to bespeak a pervasive anxiety that the vapours of Lacan's discourse might slip through the cracks and vanish from the archive.

Lacan fascinated his audience, occasionally shocking them, as he held their attention with an animated performance almost every other Wednesday afternoon throughout the Seminar's 27-year run. The Seminar became a para-academic gathering pond, where people of every stripe hoped to achieve some measure of clarity about the operations of the unconscious. Half a century later, his author function continues to attract readers, incite curiosity, and provoke intense transferences (ranging from adoration and respect to confusion and contempt). In this chapter, we probe the rhetorical dimensions of the Lacanian phenomenon as Lacan's oratory persuaded and entertained his audience, hailing it into being as a cultural force that persists to this day. Yet so few scholars have probed the enduring import of the rhetorical dimensions of Lacan's discourse.

In this chapter, we take up Lacan's admixture of eccentric style and enigmatic expositions on psychoanalysis, which has been characterized as seductive, psychotic, sadistic, non-sensical, masterful, dreamlike, and poetic.[4] Reflecting on its amalgam of style and substance, Barbara A. Biesecker has compared Burke's "new rhetoric" to what she calls Lacan's "new psychoanalysis" (222). She suggests one way of understanding Lacan's rhetorical practice during his Seminar is that, in true Burkean form, he conducted his discourse through a supple union of form, content, and purpose. As a result of his erudite approach, his presentations elicited powerful identification – or, as Burke would put it, "consubstantiality" (i.e. a sense of shared substance) – from his audience. His listeners were vigorously called into being as active participants as he enlisted them to work through a dense fog of interpretations, images, and attitudes (Biesecker 229–231). According to Biesecker's rhetorically informed view, Lacan's oratory not only addressed and analysed psychoanalysis but enacted it. Even to this day, Lacan's written discourse sends out complex rhetorical effects into his readership. When we encounter Lacan's work, we engage with a rhetoric that not only describes the unconscious processes of clinical psychoanalysis but also *engenderes* a variation of these very processes through his singular manner of expression.

The history of rhetoric also constituted some of Lacan's explicit subject matter. In *Lacan in Public*, Christian Lundberg explores Lacan's expositions on the work of Aristotle, Augustine, and Quintilian. He was keenly aware that, for Quintilian, rhetoric is less about persuasion and more about the systemic education of young people whose training in virtue and eloquence aids them in becoming good citizens who speak well on a broad range of subjects.

Moreover, in the *Écrits*, Lacan points to Quintilian's *Institutio Oratoria* [*Institutes of Oratory*] as a handbook of rhetorical strategies that double as defence mechanisms. Because analysis is conducted through speech, defence mechanisms must be understood as largely rhetorical.[5] Although Freud, with his emphases on condensation and displacement, gets remarkably close to this insight, Lacan formalizes it by routing psychoanalysis through not just philosophy, anthropology, and linguistics but also, importantly, rhetoric. In his paper on "The Situation of Psychoanalysis and the Training of Psychoanalysts in 1956," he emphasizes the importance of rhetoric and suggests that the analysand's defence mechanisms would be "hard to conceptualize without resorting to the tropes and figures, those of speech or words that are as true as in Quintilian, and which run the gamut from accismus and metonymy to catachresis and antiphrasis, and on to hypallage and even understatement" ("The Situation" 390). If unconscious desire is structured like a language, as Lacan famously suggested, we might go a step further and claim that, in both the Seminar and analysis, this desire is transmitted in rhetoric that addresses an "other" or group of others (i.e. what rhetoricians call an audience) through the vehicle of speech.

But decades after his death, most of Lacan's audience consists of readers who encounter him primarily through his writing (and the writing of those who take it up). In a "Postface" to *Seminar XI*, not included in Alan Sheridan's English translation, Lacan addresses the question of reading directly: "This seminar will be read – I bet this book on it.

It will not be like my *Écrits*, which is purchased but not read. It is no accident that the *Écrits* are difficult …. My writing … is made not to be read" (251; our translation). Of course, a great deal of Lacan's speech was perhaps not meant to be read. It was designed to be heard and directly encountered from within the theatre of the Seminar. But, in the postface, Lacan implies that his discourse alters our reading practice altogether and, by extension, transforms our listening practice as well.

During an interview with Italian journalists in Rome at the French Cultural Centre in 1974, Lacan once responded to a question about the difficulty a layperson may experience when reading his *Écrits*: "I did not write them in order for people to understand them, I wrote them in order for people to read them. Which is not even remotely the same thin …. What I have noticed, however, is that, even if people don't understand my *Écrits*, the latter do something to people" (*Triumph* 70–71). Part of Lacan's inimitable rhetorical style entailed providing stumbling blocks to understanding so that enthusiasts would be empowered to become psychoanalytic readers, that is, interpreters of the work itself. Following Burke and Lacan, we highlight the importance of this claim that rhetoric *does something*.[6] We are interested in the status of Lacan's discourse as a speech-act that enacts psychoanalytic pedagogy by inviting his audiences to engage in the rhetorically fraught act of interpretation.

Readers often struggle to make sense of an opaque and obscure discourse that is apparently intended to be heard or read but not understood. Even so, Lacan's influence spread primarily through the dissemination of his oft-polemical writings on psychoanalytic training and treatment. Gilbert Chaitin asserts that Lacan reinterpreted Freud with a deep attention to language and "assimilated virtually every key psychoanalytic concept to a rhetorical function" (688). While the seminars and the *Écrits* are often criticized for not satisfying the demand for perspicuous communication, we seek to highlight the rhetorical function of Lacan's own discourse and its pivotal role in the constitution of "Lacanese."

Given the vast number of seminars, many of which remain untranslated, we focus primarily on three lectures recently translated and collected under the English title, *Talking to Brick Walls*. Lacan presented these lectures in the chapel at Sainte-Anne Hospital as a supplement to Seminar XIX for junior psychiatrists in 1971–1972.[7] The lectures provide a survey of some of Lacan's major theoretical contributions, with particular emphasis on the relationship between psychoanalytic knowledge, truth, and *jouissance*. We suggest that one framework for conceptualizing the elusive (difficult to catch), allusive (suggestive), and illusive (deceptive or misleading) style of Lacan's discourse is to read it as exemplifying the very notion of the *objet petit a*. The object-cause of desire, as formulated by Lacan, can never be obtained but sets one's desire in motion in relation to the Other. By operating through a style that antagonizes the audience's faculty of understanding and even our conception of what it means to understand discourse, Lacan's discourse both activates readerly desire and renders it reflective. In this way, the rhetorical form of Lacan's discourse is just as instructive about psychoanalytic practice as it is about psychoanalytic theory (and their interwovenness). The sophisticated interoperation of this form and content, the manner in which they are co-implicated, conveys the tension between understanding and non-understanding on the part of the analyst, who listens to the analysand's free associations but never, in spite of appearances, exercises interpretive mastery over their significance.

Symbolic Action and the Voice

Lacan's Seminars can be understood as a form of symbolic action, the embodied effects that discourse sends out into the world. A follower and audience member of Lacan's Seminar, Philippe Sollers observes,

> The most important thing is Lacan's body speaking....[Lacan's] Seminar makes it clear that it is the body that comes out of the voice and not the other way round. The great importance of his physical posture sheds light on the way he could listen, or intervene during the sessions. (3; our translation)

Sollers understands the Seminar as something like improvisatory performance art showcasing Lacan's poetic acts of association. "Lacan would allow his audience to *watch him think*," writes Sergio Benvenuto, "Lacan always improvised; he would twist his discourse around, wrestle with it. In short, he allowed us to watch the labour of the word, at once loose and troublesome" (2). Each session of Lacan's Seminar was prepared in several pages of notes, but it ultimately took on the trappings of a spontaneous speech that allowed audiences to feel like witnesses to the grammar of Lacan's own unfolding thoughts on psychoanalytic theory and praxis. He worked through unique conceptualizations of the psyche and simultaneously enacted this conceptualization through his performances, which often drew attention to the body's entanglement in the voice. We may have the writings, transcriptions, and translations, but we must not forget that the Seminar was a live event organized around the bodily presence of an orator oriented towards an immediate audience.

Benvenuto writes that the most important features of Lacan's Seminar were "the rhythm of his discourse, the changes in tone and timber of his voice, and his pauses and falsettos" (2). This aspect of the real of the Seminar is lost, and what we have are only traces or copies of the original event. In *Twenty-First Century Psychoanalysis*, Thomas Svolos notes the significance of Lacan's dramatic presence:

> I never met Lacan, never saw him, never heard him speak. When we talk about Lacan's Legacy ... there is a gulf between the notion of a legacy among those who knew Lacan, who heard him, who went into analysis with him; and those without that personal connection. If, like me, you have no personal experience of the man, I think you will have missed something important about him, something associated with his corporeal existence. (13)

When we read Lacan's Seminar, we reckon with the presence of an absence. If we can no longer immerse ourselves in an immediate experience of the Seminar, we must still acknowledge Lacan's body of work as a distinctive act of oration. Even though this corporeal dimension is absent from any present-day reading of Lacan's *corpus*, we can still endeavour to conjure the traces of this voice in order to appreciate the singular rhetorical effects of the Seminar.

During those Wednesday afternoons, Lacan's vocal folds came together, vibrating as his breath passed through the smooth muscle tissue of his larynx. His voice reverberated in the hall as it entered the ears of the audience. Sometimes it erupted through a groan or came as a whisper that was barely discernable to those assembled in the front row. Part of his rhetorical allure emerged out of his deployment of inflection and intonation, along with his facial expressions, bodily movements, and postures. Roudinesco describes Lacan's oratorial style:

> He spoke in fits and starts, with now and then a sigh or a roar. He always brought with him a few sheets of paper covered with notes in sketches; these served to maintain the suspense created by his intermittent delivery. Sometimes he muttered, like Oedipus at Colonus trying by ominous silence to suspend the course of time; sometimes he raised his voice like Hamlet facing death, as if to contradict the slowness of impending thought. At once sombre and tumultuous, he could bring forth from broken speech or imperfect memory the rigorous logic of an unconscious whose ebb and flow he seemed to echo.
>
> (*Jacques Lacan* 260)

He communicated through dramatic gestures, sounds, and punctuating moments of silence. Rather than interpreting or teaching in the ponderous, imperious style of what he called "the master's discourse," Lacan delivered a performance that insidiously inserted his audience within "the analytic discourse," the rhetorical microcosm of psychoanalysis. An important implication of this change of discursive register is that he purloined his audience from the position of passive recipients of wisdom and placed them, perhaps even in spite of their intentions, in the difficult position of engaged interpreters.

Roudinesco provides an illustration of how Lacan free associated within the bounds of his own defences and resistances while speaking to an audience that would have to endure an analytic position of non-understanding through an encounter with the alterity of Lacan's body:

> Lacan yelled and made noises, some of them scarcely human. Lacan cajoled, caressed, seduced, shouted. Lacan imitated the cries and whistles of animals, as if to remind himself of the Darwinian origin of the totemic meal: '*père Orang*,' he said. Guttural noises, chuckles, ruminations: he let his body speak as much in its silences as in a gasp accompanying some histrionic gesticulation. Lacan was theatrical, ludic, similar to Charcot's hysterics, always inclined to invent the most exuberant figures of discourse.
>
> (*Lacan: In Spite* 60)

Roudinesco's account conjures a portrait of a speaker engaged in a mysterious glossolalia that seemed to invite bewildered interpretation. The fluctuations of his voice, posture, energy, and breath brought the vibratory presence of his embodied *jouissance* into the play of his cryptic discourse. Lacan echoes the Aristotelian perspective on rhetoric as a "substance" or "body of persuasion" (Walker 48). In *Counter-Statement*, Burke refers to a "natural dogmatism of the body," the fact that body's appetites (its needs) can become "a generator of belief" (*CS* 105). We posit that Lacan's Seminar aimed at a demonstrative embodiment of psychoanalytic understandings of the dogmatic body as inextricably interwoven with symptomatic speech. This revelation, in turn, reinforces the premise of the talking cure, the revolutionary idea that just as the body has a subterranean impact on one's speech, language exercises an uncanny effect on the life of the body. The parlour audience was placed in the unsettling position of taking all of this embodied semiotic distortion in through Lacan's speech and processing it through their interpretive mill wheels.

Drawing on Lacanian theory, Mladen Dolar writes that what the subject's body and language share is the invocatory object of the voice; this object remains separate in its emanation of the ephemeral *objet petit a*, which can only emerge in the speaker's link to an audience or listener:

> The voice stems from the body, but is not its part, and it upholds language without belonging to it, yet, in this paradoxical topology, this is the only point they share – and this is the topology of the *objet petit a* .... In order to conceive the voice as the object of the drive, we must divorce it from the empirical voices that can be heard.

> Inside the heard voices is an unheard voice, an aphonic voice, as it were. For what Lacan called *objet petit a* … does not coincide with any existing thing, although it is always evoked only by bits of materiality, attached to them as an invisible, inaudible appendage, yet not amalgamated with them: it is both evoked and covered, enveloped by them. (73–74)

When the subject releases a hitherto unrevealed utterance, the exposure of this cluster of signifiers to the light of day may give rise to a fleeting experience of a particular subjective truth (for patient and analyst alike). In the context of the Seminar, Lacan's voice became a vector of rhetorical persuasion, holding the audience's attention and commingling with his utterances to create a dialectical tension between non-understanding and understanding. His oratory created the impression that somewhere in the midst of this oracular discourse, some kind of truth might spring forth from the fog. This esoteric pedagogical process allowed, even compelled, his audience members to undergo a role reversal by assuming the uncanny position of Lacan's analysts.

Style and Sub-Stances

To say that Lacan's style challenges audiences is an understatement. He openly resisted speaking or writing in a more colloquial or understandable manner: "I absolutely refuse," he once told his audience, "to give you my teaching in the form of a little pill" (*My Teaching* 4). Two early commentators on the *Écrits* in English, John P. Muller and William Richardson, have likened Lacan's discourse to Freud's description of the dream as a rebus, a puzzle composed of words and pictures, which appears non-sensical but requires association and lateral thinking to solve:

> The encrustation with rhetorical tropes, the kaleidoscope erudition, the deliberate ambiguity, the auditory echoes, the oblique irony, the disdain of logical sequence, the prankish playfulness and sardonic (sometimes scathing) humor – all of these forms of preciousness that Lacan affects are essentially a concrete demonstration in verbal locution of the perverse ways of the unconscious as he experiences it. (3)

Lacan's style defied a typical audience's expectations that a therapeutic interlocutor be relatively comprehensible. His discourse refused typical reasoning and aimed at a dimension beyond human consciousness that might be glimpsed through the diffusion and diffraction of free association.[8] Philosopher Alain Badiou characterizes the thoughts carried in Lacan's discourse as "made up of layers and strata whose arrangements have nothing systematic to them. Lacan puts into circulation and makes available ... a whole series of notions that are at the same time complex and singular, which are sometimes dispersed, sometimes connected. It is up to the reader to take them one by one or link them up" (Badiou and Roudinesco 64). The complexity of his discourse manifests itself as a challenge to reading strategies and rereading tactics, which, in turn, engender a mobile army of interpretations and associations.

Most readers admit that their initial encounters with Lacan's discourse provoked some affective mixture of bewilderment, indignation, vulnerability, and awe in response to his strange and elevated command of language. Ellie Ragland's first confrontation with Lacan's enigmatic style resonates with these sentiments:

> My colleague threw these volumes on my desk and said, 'this man is unreadable and he's a mean person....You like this sort of thing, so, here, take it!' I went home that day and I started reading the "Discourse of Rome" from 1953. This paper would be called "The Function and Field of Speech and Language in Psychoanalysis" in the *Écrits*. It was terrible. I couldn't stop. I was getting a headache, a stomach-ache. I was getting hungry, but I couldn't stop reading. I was completely mesmerized.
>
> (qtd. in Vanderwees, *Speaking*)

Ragland's description expresses the potential for ambivalence, situated between repulsion and attraction, to Lacan's discourse. Lacan virtuosic oratory draws attention to language as a medium that operates through wordplay, overdetermined statements, polysemantic maxims, allusions to obscure texts, abstruse philosophical notions, refusals of logical arrangement of thoughts, and purposeful equivocations.

Lacan communicated to his audience in a disorienting but seductive mode. In *Psychoanalytic Thinking*, Donald Carveth elaborates on his own experience of reading Lacan, but from the position of transference:

> The Lacanian text not only frustrates by its obscurity, frequently having led me at least to the point of giving up in exasperation and angrily dismissing the man, but to make matters simultaneously better and worse, every so often it seemed to offer a comprehensible insight of sufficient importance to make it impossible to overcome the transference attachment to this object. Perhaps, one felt, if only one read on, tried harder, consulted yet another secondary source promising to elucidate the Lacanian mysteries, sources, which themselves, I found, were increasingly more obscure than the object they promised to illumine – perhaps then all would become clear and one would find oneself in possession of a rare and valuable type of

psychoanalytic wisdom of which Lacan and the Lacanians appeared to hold a monopoly. (134)

Carveth highlights the often maddening experience of trying to understand Lacan's discourse while attempting to follow his numerous allusions and intertextual references. At the same time, this very mode of incomprehension paradoxically fosters in Carveth a desire to know more. Readers may follow one subordinate clause after another in the edited transcriptions, seeking the main idea that might illuminate or give meaning to the rest. This rhetorical situation seems to set the stage for the figure of Lacan to emerge as a subject-supposed-to-know, an arbiter of truth whose auratic wisdom catalyses his audience's transferential desires.

In *Seminar VIII*, Lacan investigates the analyst's aura as the subject-supposed-to-know through the Ancient Greek concept of the *âgalma*, the term that Alcibiades employs, in Plato's *Symposium*, to describe the concealed but enticing mystical object that he believes resides inside Socrates' body. The *âgalma* is a hidden gem, an ornament, but one that cannot be directly accessed. Lacan notes that the word connotes admiration, envy, jealousy, bearing pain, and indignancy (*Seminar VIII*, 141). Seemingly speaking to all of these resonances, Alcibiades describes his experience of an *âgalma*, the mystical substance that accounts for his mentor's preternatural charisma. The *âgalma* is, according to Lacan, a metaphor for the hallucinatory experience of *objet petit a*, the mythical object-cause that seems to reside in the subject's object of desire, subtending and generating that desire while evading direct scrutiny.

Because of Lacan's polysemic, polyphonic discourse, the reader's or listener's encounter with his work may bring out a transferential relation to him as the *sujet supposé savoir*, the one who possesses the *âgalma*, the hidden object-cause of desire. In order to stave off countertransference or counterproductive "empathy" with the patient, the ethical analyst must set aside their own desire in order to help the analysand find and clarify their own. By the same token, the impossibility of reducing Lacan's discourse to a cohesive message produces a lack that brings out the reader's desire to engage in the simultaneously psychoanalytic and rhetorical practices of deciphering and free association. By constantly performing a metonymic discourse that never arrives at a definitive meaning or says exactly what it means, Lacan demonstrates that no signifying chain is ever complete or internally consistent, which is why new interpretive frames on his discourse are constantly being generated to this day. This is why contemporary readers may undergo what they experience as a form of poetic therapy as their own interpretive desires come into relief through their encounters with Lacan's semantically slippery texts.

For Lacan, the "symptom is a truth-value" (*Talking* 45) and "[s]peech defines the place of what is called truth" (*Talking* 19). Therefore, psychoanalytic treatment aims at translating the truth-value of the analysand's bodily symptoms into speech. Lacan does not refer here to any sort of universalization or institutionalization of truth but rather to the singular truth of each subject, a form of knowledge that emerges in the subject's relation to the Symbolic. The psychoanalyst must situate his or her discourse in the space between truth and knowledge (occupying the place of the subject supposed to know in the transference) in order to allow the analysand's know-how (*savoir*) of their symptoms to surface. Nevertheless, the subject remains divided, as there can be no totalization or pure form of knowledge since access to the unconscious is always indirect.[9] According to Lacan, it is through speech that the subject engages with *savoir*, symbolic knowledge, and takes up a relation to his or her own unconscious desire. This truth, however, can never be fully articulated and can only ever be, as Lacan maintains, "half-said." This is why the patient keeps speaking during analysis, in the hope that casting out all these lines might lead to a big catch; all the while, the competent analyst must, above all else, keep quiet and listen attentively so as not to overturn the boat.

Passion for Ignorance

Those who approach Lacan's text with the transactional intention of accumulating knowledge and arriving at a more optimal plateau of self-awareness along a trajectory to achieving happiness may have another thing coming. Jason Glynos and Yannis Stavrakakis have written that Lacan's theoretical poetry sends out productively unsettling rhetorical effects:

> No one likes to feel stupid. A very rare person indeed is she who, having struggled to make sense of Lacan's *Écrits,* has not entertained such thoughts of vulnerability. This vulnerability is only exacerbated if a Lacanian seminar or essay has been recommended as reading material by a friend or professor whom we respect. It is a vulnerability that can very quickly turn to frustration, intimidation, and even anger. (208)

Still, Lacan provided no apology for his manner of speaking. He exclaimed, "There's nothing I can do about it – my style is what it is" (*Seminar V* 23). The reader is left alone to find their way within a dense cloud of signifiers.

The opacity of Lacanian discourse is likely to have a distressing effect on readers placed in the unnerving position of grappling with these signifiers' simultaneous suggestiveness and intractability. Muller and Richardson suggest that Lacan's rebus-like work presents a deliberate "hermetic obscurity" that can become "infuriating" and this partially explains the process of interpellation at stake: "The reader feels that something significant is being said if only he could find out what it is" (3). During *Seminar II*, Lacan remarked on the pedagogical logic of his psychoanalytic–rhetorical strategy:

> The attention you're willing to give to quite straightforward things is somewhat wavering. We are confronted by this singular contradiction ... that the less you understand the better you listen. For I often say very difficult things to you, and I see you hanging on every word, and I learn later that some of you didn't understand. On the other hand, when you're told things that are very simple, that are almost too well known, you are less attentive. (141)

Against the grain of popular philosophical and psychological doctrines of clear communication, Lacan employed his polysemic, intertextual rhetoric in order to wield his audience's attention and impel them to reflect on their habitual interpretive strategies.

Lacan's discourse is directed towards a particular audience, the psychoanalytic community: "Do not ... get the idea that I address everyone at large," says Lacan in "Television" (which is, ironically, a transcript of his oration that was broadcast on French television). "I am speaking to those who are savvy, to the nonidiots, to the supposed analysts" ("Television" 3). He stated throughout his work that he was speaking primarily to psychoanalysts and the broader psychoanalytic community, which he addressed as his Other:

> I may reasonably suppose there to be analysts listening now also .... I expect of the supposed analysts nothing more than their being this object thanks to which what I teach is not a self-analysis. On this point, they alone, among those who are listening, are sure to understand [*entendre*] me. But even in understanding nothing an analyst plays this role I have just defined .... I would add that these analysts who are such only insofar as they are object – the object of the analysand – it happens that I do address them, not that I am speaking to them, but that I speak about them: if only to disturb them. Who knows? This could have some effects of suggestion. (4)

His rhetoric does not lend itself easily to the listener's understanding but rather puts the audience in the position of the analyst who must not presume to know, must, at all costs, maintain a stance of ignorance. This unusual interpretive practice necessitates listening without any pretence of understanding. Unlike Socrates, whose ironic disavowal of his own wisdom functioned as a rhetorical trap, the savvy analyst recognizes that they *genuinely* do not understand the truth of the patient's desire; and, more importantly, even if they could somehow fully comprehend its motivational structure, disrupting the flow of their speech to impose an interpretive frame is often counterproductive to treatment.

"Attentive listening is of the utmost importance in psychoanalysis," writes Bruce Fink. "[I]f we are focused solely on understanding (listening in the imaginary register instead of the symbolic), we will let an awful lot slip by" (268). Lacan's refusal to speak in a fashion that consolidates "common sense" about the rules of discourse puts the reader in the agonizing position of enduring and working through confusion. Reading and puzzling over Lacan's writing can, as a result, be an exceptional exercise for analysts who seek to enhance their clinical listening techniques by attending to the myriad ways that language always already exceeds our capacity to understand it. As Kenneth Burke writes of the word "understanding," the very concept of "standing under" something in order to "get to the bottom" of it suggests that we are separated from its essence from the outset (*GM* 23). And yet the symbolic order is structured in such a way that we are constantly deluded into believing that we can arrive at a stable plateau of comprehension, that we can "get it" once and for all.[10]

Against Understanding

In *Critique and Conviction*, Paul Ricoeur recalls his experience of confusion at the semiotic spectacle of Lacan's Seminar:

> I remember going home one afternoon and saying to my wife, 'I've just come from the seminar; I didn't understand a thing!' At that moment the phone rang; it was Lacan who asked me, 'What did you think of my talk?' I told him, 'I didn't understand a thing.' He hung up on me.
> (Ricoeur 70)

The anecdote highlights Ricoeur's frustration with the experience of non-understanding and Lacan's refusal to clarify his discourse. Lacan's perplexing actions impress on us that the aim to understand actually closes down free association and limits the potential for interpretation to do its work.

In many cases, Lacan's rhetoric suggested that in psychoanalysis, it is probably better that analysts do not understand; that is to say that an analyst who assumes to have a clear comprehension of a case or empathizes profoundly with the analysand may already be delusional. Instead of presuming to understand the subject's experience, he encouraged analysts to listen without understanding so as to evade sliding into assumptions and countertransference. The dangers of projection involved in any so-called understanding of the analysand's description of their own experience are outlined by Bruce Fink:

> It is the job of analysts to listen in the symbolic register, in other words, to pay careful free-floating attention so that we hear what the analysand actually says, not just what he intended to say or what we believe he meant to convey. For what we believe he meant to convey is, after all, always a projection on our part, and projection is part and parcel of the imaginary register. Just as the analysand may believe he knows precisely what we meant despite our deliberately having made a polyvalent interpretation (one that syntactically and/or contextually allows for several different readings), projecting onto us and our speech a single intended meaning, we too are projecting whenever we imagine we know what he meant. We form images of ourselves as the kind of people who are capable of performing the difficult task of understanding others. But, strictly speaking, all we can know is what was actually said and that likely there were competing intentionalities that led to the words actually uttered, all speech essentially constituting a compromise formation of sorts.
>
> (Fink 269–270)

When the analyst interprets from a *topos* of understanding, this may simply expose their own countertransference (i.e. their own charged interpretive desire) and jeopardize the treatment. In this respect, the presumption to understand might be considered a part of the analyst's own resistance to the treatment and an abandonment of "the discourse of the analyst." This analytic station dictates that the analysand's own associations (not the analyst's frames) produce vital knowledge about their symptoms. To deign to understand the analysand could disastrously fortify their defences and stem the flow of their speech. The analyst must instead occupy something like the Socratic rhetorical position of claiming to know nothing (or, rather, not claiming to know anything), but the psychoanalyst has to actually *mean it* in order to precipitate the very unusual form of unperipatetic dialogue that is the psychoanalytic session.

By subverting his audience's wishes to derive clear meanings from his discourse, Lacan sought to disrupt identifications with his own thinking and to challenge listeners to hear the symbolic aspects of language. He insisted that what is most important in listening to the analysand's account of a dream, for instance, is not that the analyst distil meaning or make sense of the content, but rather that they pay close attention to the rhetorical tropes:

> Ellipsis and pleonasm, hyperbaton or syllepsis, regression, repetition, apposition – these are the syntactical displacements; metaphor, catachresis, antonomasia, allegory, metonymy, and synecdoche – these are all semantic condensations; Freud teaches us to read in them the intentions – whether ostentatious or demonstrative, dissimulating or persuasive, retaliatory or seductive – with which the subject modulates his oneiric discourse.
>
> (Lacan, "The Function" 221–222)

Celebrating these syntactical displacements and semantic condensations, Lacan encourages analysts to attune themselves to the particularities of the analysand's discourse. This task necessarily involves asking questions and making occasional interpretations, but the interpretations are best made from a place of non-understanding, whereby the analyst may simply repeat a word or phrase or offer a polyvalent statement so as to allow the analysand to continue to associate and to interpret further for themselves. The Seminar itself obliquely reflects this clinical scenario as Lacan situates his audience in the position of non-understanding, which is, counter-intuitively to most, the position of the analyst.

In a lecture presented to students at Yale University in 1975, Lacan claimed that analytic interpretation operates according to a different logic: "In no case should a psychoanalytical intervention be theoretical, suggestive, that is to say imperative; it must be ambiguous. Analytic interpretation is not meant to be understood; it is made to produce waves" ("Yale" 35). This brand of interpretation is meant to send out rhetorical effects that rock the listener's boat. This mandate calls for a soft touch, which Lacan contended is exponentially more valuable than overflowing empathy or a pretence of definitive understanding within a narrow interpretive frame.

Lacan proposed that the analyst deliver "oracular speech," which could allow for a multiplicity of different understandings when it is heard. One example of such an interpretive oracular act might be a polyvalent question regarding what the analysand has said, perhaps a particular repetition they have uttered; the question would then be overdetermined and the analysand would take it up along a particular line of interpretation that becomes activated. This activation of associations is catalysed not by the analyst's understanding but by their attentive "close listening" practice. Lacan was, not incidentally, fond of American writer Edgar Allan Poe's mysteries and conceived of the analyst's task as akin to that of detective work. The analyst, like the classical detective, is trained to ask trenchant questions and "to remember everything having to do with the signifier even if he does not always know what to do with it" ("Seminar on 'The Purloined Letter'" 8). No clue can ever be neglected because it might be linked to other clues required to help the analysand find the underlying pattern. The analyst does not know the truth of the matter, but they can certainly guide the analysand in attending to pathways that were hiding in plain sight.

Bumping into Brick Walls

Lacan provides a few insights into the motivations underlying his own discourse in a supplement to his seminars, which has been published under the title *Talking to Brick Walls*. He opened these talks with the promise of edifying his audience, but he admits that this education may only arrive in dialectical tension with ignorance. When we presume to understand, we foreclose opportunities to pursue another association, angle, memory, trace, or approach to the given material. "[T]he most dangerous situation for a psychoanalyst," writes Jacques André, "is to think he or she is speaking the same language as the patient" (557). In this regard, the analyst's drive to understand has nothing to do with the discourse of the analysand but rather involves the imposition of constructions. These constructs are not necessarily always fatuous, but as André continues, they often run "the risk of adding another screen to the screens that are already there, screens that contribute to the situation of nothing being heard—and thus of nothing changing" (563). Lacan is very clear that if anyone is to understand, construct, or interpret anything in psychoanalysis, it ought to be the analysand rather than an "empathetic" analyst. "Most therapy," one analysand said of the empathetic listening approach, "is like rent a friend – the therapist just tells you what they think you want to hear" (Anonymous). This astute indictment of the pitfalls of contemporary therapeutic approaches is why we are wary of ego psychology and relational approaches to therapy. In spite of some therapists' best intentions, "understanding" and "empathy" all-too-often amount to a failure to listen attentively to the patient's discourse. This pervasive misrecognition of the proper role of the therapist impelled Lacan to alert us to the importance of the Symbolic register (wherein the meanings of our utterances always exceed anyone's grasp, including that of the analyst) while cautioning us against the imaginary lures of understanding, empathy, and identity.

Perhaps this is why Lacan insisted that ignorance as a "passion" and gestured towards the word's meaning in both Buddhism and Christian theology, as a strong emotion or suffering that was once thought to be "the highest form of knowledge" (*Talking* 5). Apropos of the Buddha, Lacan designated truth as a form of non-knowledge and reiterated the point that "analytic discourse lies precisely on the palpable frontier between truth and knowledge" (10). His readers experience this limit when they endeavour to grasp the relationship between his style and the meaning of his discourse. If psychoanalysis is a discipline designed to aid the analysand in their search for subjective truth, analysts must listen to this speech as aiming at something beyond commonplace understandable knowledge. "Namely, the one who knows that he knows is the ego," says Lacan. "If the unconscious is something surprising it's because this kind of knowledge is something else" (16). Lacan's rhetoric obliquely encourages psychoanalysts to sustain an openness to the pursuit of unknown knowledge alongside their analysands. In this way, he reaffirms the significance of *savoir*, a knowledge which the subject does not know he or she knows. This is the knowledge of which psychoanalysis seeks to progressively uncover as the subject speaks, as much as possible, everything that comes to mind.

In *Seminar II*, Lacan introduces the metaphor of the *le mur du langage*, "the wall of language" (*Seminar II* 244). We encounter the virtual wall of language when we experience intractable linguistic impasses as barriers to clear communication and mutual understanding. In the original French, Lacan crafts puns out of the wordplay of wall [*mur*], mirror [*miroir*], and love [*amour*] so as to bring out connotations of the Imaginary (i.e. the register of bounded identity and comprehensible discourse) at stake with the wall of language. Lacan remarks that, even for the most studied communicators, this wall seems to disrupt, block, or invert discourse. Therefore, "The entire development of the analysis consists in the progressive displacement of this relation, which the subject can grasp at any moment, beyond the wall of language, as being the transference, which is his and in which he doesn't recognize himself" (*Seminar II* 246). The analyst must interpret the analysand's discourse but remains "up against the wall—up against the wall of language .... on the same side of the wall as the patient." Nevertheless, "it is off this wall—which is the same for him as for us—that we shall try to respond to the echo of his speech" ("Function" 260). Without any "immediate" access to the patient's desire, the analyst is there to listen for the echo and provide a rhetorically informed reply to the cascade of signifiers; and none of this esoteric dialectical choreography hinges on a proper "understanding" of the patient's subjectivity.

Highlighting the experience of incomprehension that some listeners or readers discover in the encounter with his discourse, Lacan wonders if he has not been speaking to anyone in particular all this time, but perhaps only to the brick walls [*murs*] within the Chapel of the Sainte-Anne:

> How is one to know to whom I am speaking? .... I'm speaking to the chapel, that is, to the brick walls. This bungled action is becoming increasingly successful. Now I know to whom I've come to talk, to the very same I've always talked to at Sainte-Anne – to the brick walls .... I've always been talking to the brick walls here.
>
> (*Talking to Brick Walls* 80)

Figuring the unresponsive interlocutor as a brick wall conveys the position of the analyst as a "blank screen," whose role is to help the analysand hear their own discourse as it echoes from the walls of the consulting room. In psychoanalytic treatment, "one has to tune one's voice to the reverberation off the walls" (*Talking to Brick Walls* 86). For the analysand, it is largely a matter of listening together with the analyst so as to hear what was not previously available through their speech.

Not unlike the words of the analysand in treatment, Lacan's speech reverberates back to him from these walls but also resonates as something else for those in the audience (who occupy the position of ersatz analysts). He told his chapel audience, "It cannot be said that my speech, which does nonetheless bear a particular relationship to my discourse, has absolutely not been understood." He continued, "More to the point, one can say that the number of you here is proof of that. If my speech were incomprehensible, I don't really see what you would be doing here in such large numbers, especially given how these numbers are made up of people who come back" (*Talking to Brick Walls* 38).

Against the cult of proper understanding, Lacan suggests that the listener or reader may never completely understand him per se, but they may nonetheless cultivate a method for navigating their own way within the dense symbolic fog of his teachings as it commingles with their interpretive desires.

In *Seminar V*, Lacan asks his audience to make an effort to follow his style as illustrative of the importance of listening in psychoanalysis:

> Since the point ... is to speak in a valid way about the creative functions that signifiers exercise over signifieds[,] ... not simply to speak about speech but to speak wholly in keeping with speech ... so as to evoke its very functions, perhaps there are internal necessities of style that are required – such as conciseness, illusion, and even a few barbs, which are elements needed for entering the field where they dominate not only its avenues but its entire texture. (23)

With a style that draws attention to the innovative symbolic action of his own discourse, Lacan postulates that no member of the audience hears him in the same way as any other. He therefore "endeavor[s] to make it so that access to this meaning is not easy" (*Talking* 86). This call for interpretation requires that they "put something of [their] own into it, which is a salubrious secretion, and even a therapeutic one" (*Talking* 87).[11] The paradoxical sub-stance of Lacan's rhetoric situates the audience as analysts who listen without understanding. In so doing, his inscrutable discourse calls for an interpretive response, which arises from the recipients' attempts to contend with their own network of associations and make some kind of "sense" of them amidst all of the nonsense.

"[I]nterpretation neglects and destroys in search for hidden meanings," writes Jean Baudrillard. "This is why interpretation is what, *par excellence*, is opposed to seduction, and why it is the least seductive of discourses" (Baudrillard 53). The seductive quality of Lacan's discourse derives from its short-circuiting of immediate comprehension and definitive interpretations while providing pedagogical apertures to its somewhat alien, somewhat familiar symbolic logic. With the supportive aid of an analyst who is attuned to this symbolic logic, the analysand may also begin to gain a measure of traction with their own rhetorical economy. Perhaps they even begin to recognize their own desires lurking around the edges of their speech patterns.[12]

For Lacan, the psychoanalyst is a teacher of rhetoric but not a teacher who relies on the university discourse: "The psychoanalyst is a rhetor (*rhêteur*): to continue equivocating, I would say that he 'rhetifies' (*rhêtifie*), which implies that he rectifies. The analyst is a rhetor, namely, that '*rectus*', a Latin word, equivocates with '*rhêtification*'" (Lacan *Seminar XXV*, Trans. Gallagher).[13] Here, he invokes the etymology of the word "rectify," which suggests not only setting aright but producing something new (*facere*). The cumulative semiotic effect is a remarkably Burkean understanding of rhetoric as a power for good rather than deceptive "sophistry." Returning to this motif in *Seminar XX*, Lacan encouraged analysts to acknowledge that the "universe is a flower of rhetoric." This "literary echo may perhaps help us understand that the ego (*moi*) can also be a flower of rhetoric" (56). Rather than providing empathy, advice, or answers, the Lacanian analyst plays a modest role, merely planting the seeds for the analysand to reconstruct their history through "chains of speech" ("Variations" 277). This fecund rhetorical manoeuvre may even aid them in integrating their barbed history into their present and give root to a new array of perspectives about what it means to be a speaking being entangled in a densely networked world.

Michel de Certeau writes that Lacan engages in a "rhetoric of withdrawal" that "grounds speech just as he theorizes about it and just as he upholds its act" (21).[14] Lacan's rhetoric of withdrawal is bound up with a radical ethics of speech that opens up a space for his extended audience to, as Burke put it, "interpret our interpretations" (*A Rhetoric* 6). Operating from this ethical *topos*, Lacan advises his audience to exercise caution. As analysands listen for the echoes of their words (as they are transmitted from their mouths to the analyst's ears and back through his mouth in slightly modified form), they must come to recognize that even the most skilled clinician "is bound to the walls by a definition of discourse" (100). After all, any discourse or theoretical scaffolding, including Lacan's, is saddled with its own oversights and obstructions; thus, recognizing and integrating the limits of the analyst's authority is, for Lacan, of paramount importance to the therapeutic process.

Just when Lacan uttered his claim that he had been speaking to brick walls, a woman from the audience called out: "We should all leave if you're talking to brick walls" (80). Lacan replied to the call, "Who is speaking to me?" and then admitted that "talking to brick walls does indeed concern a few people" after all (80–81). It was a momentary exchange that seemed to radiate out of the frustrated murmur of the flesh-and-blood others lurking just outside the confines of the prisonhouse of language. The incident evokes one of Simone Weil's aphorisms about a paradox of speech that seems to bespeak a ground-swell of common ground between rhetoric and psychoanalysis, two kindred disciplines that probe the unknowable limits of connection and eloquence: "Two prisoners whose cells adjoin communicate with each other by knocking on the wall. The wall is the thing which sepa-rates them but it is also their means of communication .... Every sepa-ration is a link" (145). The order of symbols simultaneously divides and connects us. It is, paradoxically, both our most powerful instrument and our most alienating milieu. No philosophy or self-help move-ment offers the hope of preventing us from ever bumping into walls or succumbing to mirages. But the echoes of Lacan's refulgent rhetoric from within the symbolic fog might just galvanize us to embark on an uncertain journey out of the house of mirrors organized around "understanding" towards newly-configured plateaus of eloquence, insight, and transformation.

Notes

1 Lacan turned 50 years old in 1951. His early private seminars took place on Wednesdays from 1951 to 1953. For more on these early years of the seminar, see Roudinesco (1990).
2 "In March 1969 [Lacan] received a letter from Robert Flacelière, the director of the ENS, telling him that the Salle Dussane would not be available to him for his seminar the following year. No serious reason was given for the expul-sion, but it was common knowledge that Flacelière had complained of hearing too much talk about 'phalluses' at the school, and had been annoyed to see the sidewalk in the rue d'Ulm blocked by smart automobiles at Wednesday lunchtimes" (Roudinesco, 1997, 341–342).
3 Pierrakos was Lacan's stenographer from 1967 to 1979. She later became a psychoanalyst.
4 See Sigler, David. "The Rhetoric of Anti-Pedagogical Sadism in Jacques Lacan's 'Seminar VII.'" *Interdisciplinary Literary Studies*. 9.2 (2008): 71–86.
5 Lacan mentions Quintilian's rhetorical theories several times in "The Situation of Psychoanalysis and the Training of Psychoanalysts in 1956" as well as in "The Instance of the Letter in the Unconscious, or Reason Since Freud," which was delivered as a talk in 1957.
6 In this respect, Lacan's discourse and its motives could be read through Burke's dramatistic hexad for analysing language as a medium for communication: act (what it does), scene (when or where it was done), agent (who did it), agency (how was it done), purpose (why it was done), and attitude. In many ways, this

dramatistic frame for understanding the mediality of language comports with the theatricality of the Seminar, aligning rhetoric, theatre, psychoanalysis, and even philosophy within a Burkean choreographic frame.

7 Lacan held these three sessions in the Chapel at the Sainte-Anne Hospital on 4 November 1971, 2 December 1971, and 6 January 1972. Concurrent with his delivery of Seminar XIX, ... *or Worse*, from 8 December 1971 to 14 June 1972 at the Paris Law Faculty, Jacques Lacan also gave a series of seven talks under the title, *The Psychoanalyst's Knowledge*, for an audience of junior psychiatrists in the Chapel at the Sainte-Anne Hospital. *Talking to Brick Walls* features the first three of these seven talks. Since the last four sessions at the Sainte-Anne engage the themes of Lacan's main seminar at the Law Faculty, Jacques-Alain Miller, editor of Lacan's *oeuvre*, has decided to include these sessions chronologically within the publication of Seminar XIX. *Talking to Brick Walls* (*Je Parle Aux Murs*) and Seminar XIX, ... *Or Worse* (... *Ou Pire*) were published in original French by Éditions du Seuil (Paris) in 2011, respectively, but there have been few efforts at translating *The Psychoanalyst's Knowledge* to English until this new rendition from A.R. Price. Thus, Price's lucid and highly readable rendition of *Talking to Brick Walls* (including the translation of Seminar XIX from Polity Press) marks the first time that *The Psychoanalyst's Knowledge* has been available in English under the official editorship of Miller. In 1981, Denise Green translated the 3 March 1972 talk under the title "Ste Anne," which appeared in the *Semiotext(e)* special issue, *Polysexuality*. Apart from this, Cormac Gallagher's adequate but rough translation of all seven Sainte-Anne presentations (as Seminar XIXa, *The Knowledge of the Psychoanalyst*) was the only version of this work available to those who study Lacan in English until the arrival of Price's fresh rendition of *Talking to Brick Walls*. For a longer overview of *Talking to Brick Walls*, see Vanderwees, Chris. "*Talking to Brick Walls: A Series of Presentations in the Chapel at the Sainte-Anne Hospital, Jacques Lacan* (Trans. A. R. Price)." *Psychoanalytic Discourse*. 4.1 (2019): 104–108.

8 Lacan's rhetoric is far from apolitical. He was not only portraying the resemblance of the split subject under free association but speaking in a fashion that would defend and protect his main ideas from hostilities towards psychoanalysis or his own theories. In an interview, Raul Moncayo reminds us that there is also a political edge to Lacan's rhetoric that one could construe as protective or defensive: "I also understood something else about Lacan. People will say 'Why can he not write clearly or just in regular prose? Why do you have to make it so complicated?' And then I understood something political. If it's too simple and you can clearly extract some kind of meaning out of it, it can be accepted, but it can also be rejected. If it's not so clear, then it is not easily reduced to a stereotype that can be rejected" (Vanderwees 16–17).

9 In Seminar XXIII, Lacan returns to the importance of *savoir* through the subject's identification with the symptom, reformulated as the *sinthome*.

10 It is important to note that several commentators have observed that the difficulty of Lacan's discourse resembles the language of psychosis as it persistently unfurls in tangentiality, derailment, circumstantiality, incoherence, intellectualization, and grandiosity, all while reveling in Joycean word play. Jon Mills, for instance, writes that "[i]f you were to randomly open any texts of Lacan's and begin to read, you might immediately think that the man is mad. In a word, his writing is psychotic: it is fragmentary, chaotic, and at times incoherent" (11). Lacan spent his early years as a psychiatric intern listening to patients struggling with psychosis and schizophrenia at the Sainte-Anne Hospital. Psychosis was the subject of his doctoral thesis, in which he presented the now famous case of "Aimee," whose paranoia, hallucinations, and delusional speech were not, he believed, nonsensical at all. He posited that such manifestations were

actually important and meaningful to the patient. Unlike many psychiatrists of his time, Lacan understood psychotic speech as the patient's unconscious offering itself openly to the clinician, and he proposed that this opaque rhetoric actually "says some things very clearly" (*Seminar III* 122). If Lacan's style comes across as something like psychotic speech, Juliet Mitchell has suggested that it also resembles its subject matter, that is, what Lacan calls the split subject or the subject of the unconscious: "The matter and manner of all Lacan's work challenges this notion of the human subject: there is none such. In the sentence structure of his most public addresses and of his written style, the grammatical subject is either absent or shifting or, at most, only passively constructed. At this level, the difficulty of Lacan's style could be said to mirror his theory" (Mitchell 4). Lacan provided his listeners and readers with an opportunity to practise interpretation in relation to the symbolic action of a rhetor who might initially present as incomprehensible. But, over time, his discourse becomes more intelligible as a form of symbolic action that does what it describes and performs the operations of the unconscious.

11 Bruce Fink (2004) has also translated this passage nicely: "I strive to ensure that access to the meaning [of what I say] not be too easy, such that you must contribute some elbow grease of your own (or work hard at it)" (178). Lacan concludes his introduction to *Écrits*, "Overture to this Collection," with a very similar statement.

12 Analysts do have to intervene with symbolic action in many circumstances. Lacan suggested, for instance, that analysts must become readers of discourse and, in spite of appearances to the contrary, have a "duty to interpret" [*devoir d'interpréte*] as analysts (Le séminaire 252). However, analysts must not presume to understand but must, rather, remain attuned to the many potential openings at stake in language. While attempting to occupy a position of non-understanding, the analyst maintains a supportive listening presence while helping the analysand to speak about the symptom. The analyst's listening presence may help the analysand become reflexively acquainted with personal demand and desire through attention to the repetition of subjective signifiers.

13 For numerous practical examples of methods for undertaking interpretations that are not based in the traps of understanding, see Fink, Bruce. *Fundamentals of Psychoanalytic Technique: A Lacanian Approach for Practitioners*. New York: W.W. Norton & Company, 2007.

14 Michel de Certeau suggested that Lacan's *Seminar* embodied an ethics of speech that "could not be reduced to a descriptive catalogue of 'manners' (or tropes) of ornamenting the discourse." Instead, it operated according to "the logic of 'displacements' (*Verschiebungen*) and. . . 'distortions' (*Entstellungen*) which the relationship to the other produces in language" (26).

References

Adleman, Daniel. "The Late Oedipal Genre, Thantagonists, and Secondary Televisuality." *Canadian Review of American Studies*, vol. 51, no. 3, 2021 pp. 290–307.

Adleman, Daniel. "'Where We Go One, We Go All': QAnon and the Mediology of Witnessing." *communication +1*, vol. 8, no. 1, 2021, pp. 1–27.

Akhtar, Salman. *Psychoanalytic Listening: Methods, Limits, and Innovations*. Karnac, 2013.

André, Jacques. "The Misunderstanding." 2005. Translated by Richard B. Simpson. *Psychoanalytic Quarterly*, vol. 75, no. 2, 2006, pp. 557–581.

Angus, Ian. "Media, expression and a new politics: Eight theses." *International Journal of Media & Cultural Politics* 1.1, 2005, 89–92.

Anonymous. Interview by Chris Vanderwees. January 2022.

Aristotle. *Rhetoric*. Translated by W. Rhys Roberts. Dover, 2004.

_____. "Rhetoric." *The Complete Works of Aristotle*. Ed. Jonathan Barnes. Princeton University Press, 1984, pp. 2152–2269.

Arnett, Ronald C., and Gordon Nakagawa. "The Assumptive Roots of Empathic Listening: A Critique." *Communication Education*, vol. 32, no. 4, 1983, pp. 368–378.

Atkinson, Paul. *Henri Bergson and Visual Culture: A Philosophy for a New Aesthetic.* Bloomsbury, 2021.

Austin, J. L. *How to Do Things with Words*. Clarendon Press, 1962.

Badiou, Alain, and Élisabeth Roudinesco. *Jacques Lacan, Past and Present: A Dialogue.* Translated by Jason E. Smith. Columbia University Press, 2014.

Bain, Alexander. *The Senses and the Intellect*. London: John W. Parker and Son, 1855.

Barnett, Lauren Jane. "The Living and Dead Body in Foucault's Clinical Gaze." *The Body in Theory: Essays after Lacan and Foucault*. Eds. Becky R. McLaughlin and Eric Daffron. McFarland & Company, 2021, pp. 34–41.

Barry, Peter. *Beginning Theory*. Manchester University Press, 2002.

Barthes, Roland. *A Lover's Discourse: Fragments*. 1977. Translated by Richard Howard. Hill and Wang, 1978.

Baudrillard, Jean. *Seduction*. 1979. Translated by Brian Singer. New World Perspectives, 1990.

Biesecker, Barbara A. "Rhetorical Studies and the 'New' Psychoanalysis: What's the Real Problem? Or Framing the Problem of the Real." *Quarterly Journal of Speech*, vol. 84, 1998, pp. 222–259.

Bender, John, and David Wellbery. *The Ends of Rhetoric: History, Theory, Practice.* Stanford University Press, 1990.

Berlo, David R. *The Process of Communication*. Holt, Reinhart and Winston, 1960.

Bergson, Henri. *Creative Evolution*. 1911. Translated by Arthur Mitchell. Random House, 1944.

Bergson, Henri. *Matter and Memory.* 1896. Translated by Nancy Margaret Paul and W. Scott Palmer. Zone Books, 2005.

Bessner, Daniel, and Amber A'Lee Frost. "How the QAnon Cult Stormed the Capital." *Jacobin*, January 2021.

Bigi, Sarah S. "The Persuasive Role of *Ethos* in Doctor-Patient Interactions." *Communication & Medicine*, vol. 8, no. 1, pp. 67–75.

Bion, Wilfred R. "Attacks on Linking." *International Journal of Psychoanalysis*, vol. 40, 1959, pp. 308–315.

Bion, Wilfred R. *Attention and Interpretation.* 1970. Karnac, 1984.

Bollas, Christopher. *Free Association.* Icon Books, 2002.

Booth, Wayne. "Kenneth Burke's Way of Knowing." *Critical Inquiry*, vol. 1, no. 1, 1974, pp. 1–22.

_____. *Modern Dogma and the Rhetoric of Assent.* University of Chicago Press, 1974.

_____. *The Rhetoric of Rhetoric: The Quest for Effective Communication.* Blackwell, 2004.

Bratton, Benjamin. *Revenge of the Real: Politics for a Post-pandemic World.* Verso, 2021.

Burke, Kenneth. *A Rhetoric of Motives.* G. Braziller, 1950.

_____. "Symbol and Association." *The Hudson Review*, vol. 9, no. 2, 1956, pp. 212–225, https://doi.org/10.2307/3847364.

_____. *Language as Symbolic Action: Essays on Life, Literature, and Method.* University of California Press, 1966.

_____. "Dramatism." *Communication: Concepts and Concepts and Perspectives.* Ed. Lee Thayer, Spartan Books, 1967, pp. 12–40.

_____. *Counter-Statement.* 1931. University of California Press, 1968.

_____. *A Grammar of Motives.* University of California Press, 1969.

_____. *Permanence and Change: An Anatomy of Purpose.* University of California Press, 1935.

_____. *The Philosophy of Literary Form.* 1941. University of California Press, 1973.

_____. "Words as Deeds." *Centrum*, vol. 3, no. 2, 1975, pp. 147–168.

_____. "Postscript." *Criticism and Social Change.* Ed. Frank Lentricchia, University of Chicago Press, 1983.

_____. *Attitudes Toward History.* 1937. University of California Press, 1985.

Carveth, Donald. *Psychoanalytic Thinking: A Dialectical Critique of Psychoanalytic Theory and Practice.* New York: Routledge, 2018.

Chaitin, Gilbert. "Rhetoric and Psychoanalysis." *Oxford Handbook of Rhetorical Studies.* Ed. Michael J. MacDonald. Oxford University Press, 2017. pp. 683–694.

Chase, Cynthia. "'Transference' as Trope of Persuasion." *Discourse in Psychoanalysis and Literature.* Ed. Shlomith Rommon-Kenan. Routledge, 1987, pp. 211–232.

Chessick, Richard D. *The Technique and Practice of Listening in Intensive Psychotherapy.* Jason Aronson, 1992.

Cicero. *De Oratore.* Translated by H. Rackha. Harvard University Press, 1959.

Clark, Arthur J. *Empathy in Counselling and Psychotherapy: Perspectives and Practices.* Routledge, 2013.

Critchley, Simon. "The Dangers of Certainty: A Lesson from Auschwitz." The Stone, Opinionator Blogs, *New York Times*, February 2014.

_____. *Tragedy, the Greeks, and Us.* New York: Pantheon, 2019.

Critchley, Simon, and Jamieson Webster. *Stay Illusion! The Hamlet Doctrine.* Vintage Books, 2014.

Cubitt, Geoff T. "Conspiracy Myths and Conspiracy Theories." *Journal of the Anthropological Society of Oxford*, vol. 20, no. 1, 1989, pp. 12–26.

Daley, James W. "Psychoanalysis, Science, and Philosophy." *The Centennial Review*, vol. 12, no.1, 1968, pp. 23–39.

Davis, Diane. "Identification: Burke and Freud on Who You Are." *Rhetoric Society Quarterly*, vol. 38, no. 2, 2008, pp. 123–147.

Davis, Diane. *Inessential Solidarity: Rhetoric and Foreigner Relations*. University of Pittsburgh Press, 2010.

De Certeau, Michel. "Lacan: An Ethics of Speech." Translated by Marie-Rose Logan. *Representations*. Vol. 3, 1983, pp. 21–39.

De Man, Paul. *Blindness & Insight: Essays in the Rhetoric of Contemporary Criticism*. Oxford UP, 1971.

Dean, Jodi. "Theorizing Conspiracy Theory." *Theory & Event* 4, no. 3, 2000. muse.jhu.edu/article/32599.

_____. *Democracy and Other Neoliberal Fantasies: Communicative Capitalism and Left Politics*. Duke University Press, 2009.

Decker, Hannah S. "The Reception of Psychoanalysis in Germany." *Comparative Studies in Society and History*, vol. 24, no. 4, 1982, pp. 589–602.

Deleuze, Gilles, and Felix Guattari. *Anti-Oedipus: Capitalism and Schizophrenia*. Translated by Robert Hurley, Mark Seem, and Helen R. Lane. Continuum, 2003.

Derrida, Jacques. *Dissemination*. Translated by Barbara Johnson. University of Chicago Press, 1981.

Didi-Huberman, Georges. *Invention of Hysteria: Charcot and the Photographic Iconography of the Salpêtrière*. 1982. Translated by Alisa Hartz. MIT Press, 2003.

Dolar, Mladen. *A Voice and Nothing More*. Cambridge: MIT Press, 2006.

Douglas, Karen M., et al. "The Psychology of Conspiracy Theories." *Current Directions in Psychological Science*, vol. 26, no. 6, 2017, pp. 538–542, doi:10.1177/0963721417718261.

Earlie, Paul. "Psychoanalysis and the Rhetorical Tradition: Theory and Technique." *Psychology and the Classics: A Dialogue of Disciplines*. Eds. Jeroen Lauwers, Hedwig Schwall and Jan Opsomer. De Gruyter, 2018. pp. 223–238.

Ellis, Havelock. "Freud's Influence on the Changed Attitude Toward Sex." *American Journal of Sociology*, vol. 45, no. 3, 1939, pp. 309–317.

"empathy, n." *OED Online*. Oxford University Press, September 2021. Web. 13 February 2022.

Eysenck, Hans J. *Decline & Fall of the Freudian Empire*. 1985. Routledge, 2017.

Felski, Rita. *The Uses of Literature*. Blackwell, 2008.

Fenichel, Otto. *The Psychoanalytic Theory of Neurosis*. 1945. Norton, 1996.

Fergusson, Francis. "Kenneth Burke's Grammar of Motives." *The Sewanee Review*, vol. 54, no. 2, 1946, pp. 325–33, http://www.jstor.org/stable/27507651.

Fink, Bruce. *A Clinical Introduction to Lacanian Psychoanalysis: Theory and Technique*. Harvard University Press, 1997.

_____. "The Master Signifier and the Four Discourses." *Key Concepts of Lacanian Psychoanalysis*. Ed. Dany Nobus. Other Press, 1999, pp. 29–47.

_____. *Lacan to the Letter: Reading Écrits Closely*. University of Minnesota Press, 2004.

_____. "Against Understanding: Why Understanding Should Not Be Viewed as the Essential Aim of Psychoanalytic Treatment." *Journal of the American Psychoanalytic Association*, vol. 58, no. 2, 2010, pp. 259–285.

_____. *Fundamentals of Psychoanalytic Technique: A Lacanian Approach for Practitioners*. W. W. Norton & Company, 2011.

———. *A Clinical Introduction to Freud: Techniques for Everyday Practice*. W. W. Norton & Company, 2017.

Fonagy, Peter. "The Effectiveness of Psychodynamic Psychotherapies: An Update." *World Psychiatry*, vol. 14, no. 2, 2014, pp. 137–150.

Forrester, John. "On Kuhn's Case: Psychoanalysis and the Paradigm." *Critical Inquiry*, vol. 33, no. 4, 2007, pp. 782–819.

Foucault, Michel. *The History of Sexuality: Volume 1, An Introduction*. 1978. Vintage, 1990.

———. *The Birth of the Clinic: An Archaeology of Medical Perception*. 1963. Translated by A.M. Sheridan Smith. Vintage, 1994.

———. *Psychiatric Power: Lectures at the College de France, 1973–1974*. 2003. Ed. Jacques Lagrande. Translated by Graham Burchell. Picador, 2006.

Freud, Harry. "My Uncle Sigmund." *Freud: As We Knew Him*. Ed. Hendrik M. Ruitenbeek. Wayne State University Press, 1973, pp. 312–313.

Freud, Sigmund. *On Aphasia*. 1891. Translated by E. Stengel. International Universities Press, 1953.

———. "Mourning and Melancholia." *The Standard Edition of the Complete Psychological Works of Sigmund Freud, Volume XIV (1914–1916): On the History of the Psycho-Analytic Movement, Papers on Metapsychology and Other Works*. Translated by James Strachey. Hogarth Press, 1957, pp. 237–302.

———. "The Question of Lay Analysis." *1926. The Standard Edition of the Complete Psychological Works of Sigmund Freud, Volume XX (1925–1926): An Autobiographical Study, Inhibitions, Symptoms and Anxiety, The Question of Lay Analysis and Other Works*. Vintage & Hogarth Press, 1957, pp. 177–258.

———. *The Psychopathology of Everyday Life*. 1901. Translated by James Strachey. Hogarth Press, 1960.

———. "February 1, 1900." *The Complete Letters of Sigmund Freud to Wilhelm Fliess: 1887–1904*. Edited and Translated by Jeffrey Moussaieff Masson. Cambridge: Belknap Press of Harvard University Press, 1985, pp. 397–398.

———. "July 17." *The Letters of Sigmund Freud to Eduard Silberstein, 1871–1881*. Ed. Walter Boehlich. Translated by Arnold J. Pomerans. Harvard University Press, 1990, pp. 23–24.

———. "The Aetiology of Hysteria." *1896. The Standard Edition of the Complete Psychological Works of Sigmund Freud: Vol. III (1893–1899)*. Edited and Translated by James Strachey. Vintage and Hogarth Press, 2001, pp. 187–221.

———. "Charcot." *1893. The Standard Edition of the Complete Psychological Works of Sigmund Freud, Volume III*. Edited and Translated by James Strachey. Vintage and Hogarth Press, 2001, pp. 7–23.

———. "Constructions in Analysis." *1937. The Standard Edition of the Complete Psychological Works of Sigmund Freud: Vol. XXIII*. Edited and Translated by James Strachey. Vintage and Hogarth Press, 2001, pp. 25–270.

———. "The Ego and the Id." *The Standard Edition of the Complete Psychological Works of Sigmund Freud, Volume XIX (1923–25): The Ego and the Id and Other Works*. Edited and Translated by James Strachey. Vintage & Hogarth, 2001, pp. 1–68.

———. "Group Psychology and the Analysis of the Ego." *1921. The Standard Edition of the Complete Psychological Works of Sigmund Freud: Vol. XVIII*. Edited and Translated by James Strachey. Vintage and Hogarth Press, 2001, pp. 65–144.

———. *The Interpretation of Dreams. The Standard Edition of the Complete Psychological Works of Sigmund Freud, Volume IV (1900): The Interpretation of Dreams (First Part)*. 1900. Edited and Translated by James Strachey. Vintage and Hogarth Press, 2001.

_____. "Instincts and Their Vicissitudes." 1915. *The Standard Edition of the Complete Psychological Works of Sigmund Freud, Volume XIV (1914–1916): On the History of the Psycho-Analytic Movement, Papers on Metapsychology and Other Works.* Edited and Translated by James Strachey. Vintage & Hogarth, 2001, pp. 109–140.

_____. "Jokes and Their Relation to the Unconscious." 1905. *The Standard Edition of the Complete Psychological Works of Sigmund Freud: Vol. VIII.* Edited and Translated by James Strachey. Vintage and Hogarth Press, 2001.

_____. "A Note on the Unconscious." 1958. *The Standard Edition of the Complete Psychological Works of Sigmund Freud, Volume XII.* Translated and Edited by James Strachey. Vintage and Hogarth Press, 2001, pp. 260–266.

_____. "On Beginning the Treatment (Further Recommendations on the Technique of Psycho-Analysis I)." 1913. *The Standard Edition of the Complete Psychological Works of Sigmund Freud: Vol. XII (1911–1913).* Edited and Translated by James Strachey. Vintage and Hogarth Press, 2001, pp. 121–144.

_____. "On the History of the Psycho-Analytic Movement." 1914. *The Standard Edition of the Complete Psychological Works of Sigmund Freud, Volume XIV (1914–1916): On the History of the Psycho-Analytic Movement, Papers on Metapsychology and Other Works.* Edited and Translated by James Strachey. Hogarth Press, Vintage & 2001, pp. 7–67.

_____. "The Psychotherapy of Hysteria from Studies on Hysteria." 1893. *The Standard Edition of the Complete Psychological Works of Sigmund Freud, Vol. II.* Vintage and Hogarth, 2001, pp. 253–305.

_____. "Recommendations to Physicians Practising Psycho-Analysis." 1912. *The Standard Edition of the Complete Psychological Works of Sigmund Freud, Volume XII.* Edited and Translated by James Strachey. Vintage and Hogarth Press, 2001, pp. 109–120.

_____. "Two Encyclopaedia Articles." 1923. *The Standard Edition of the Complete Psychological Works of Sigmund Freud, Volume XVIII.* Edited and Translated by James Strachey. Vintage and Hogarth Press, 2001, pp. 233–260.

Freud, Sigmund, and Josef Breuer. "Frälein Elisabeth von R. (Freud)." 1893. *The Standard Edition of the Complete Psychological Works of Sigmund Freud, Volume II (1893–1895): Studies on Hysteria.* Edited and Translated by James Strachey (2001). Vintage & Hogarth Press, pp. 135–181.

Gammelgaard, Judy. "Metaphors of Listening." *Scandinavian Psychoanalytic Review,* vol. 21, no. 2, 1998, pp. 151–167.

Girard, René. "Interview: René Girard." *Diacritics,* vol. 8, no. 1, 1978, pp. 31–54, https://doi.org/10.2307/464818.

Glynos, Jason. "Psychoanalysis Operates upon the Subject of Science: Lacan between Science and Ethics." *Lacan and Science.* Eds. Jason Glynos and Yannis Stavrakakis. Karnac, 2002, pp. 51–88.

Glynos, Jason, and Yannis Stavrakakis. "Postures and Impostures: On Lacan's Style and Use of Mathematical Science." *Lacan & Science.* Eds. Jason Glynos and Yannis Stavrakakis. Karnac, 2002, pp. 207–231.

Goetz, Christopher G., Michel Bonduelle, and Toby Gelfand. *Charcot: Constructing Neurology.* New York: Oxford University Press, 1995.

Gorgias. *Encomium of Helen.* Translated by D.M. Macdowell. Bloomsbury Academic, 1982.

Gusfield, Joseph R. "Introduction." *On Symbols and Society.* University of Chicago Press, 1989, pp. 1–35.

Haggbloom S.J., Warnick R., Warnick J.E., et al. "The 100 Most Eminent Psychologists of the 20th Century." *Review of General Psychology,* vol. 6, no. 2, 2002, pp. 139–152.

Hamilton, Sir William. *Lectures on Logic, Volume II.* Sheldon and Company, 1883.

Harrington, Anne. *Mind Fixers: Psychiatry's Troubled Search for the Biology of Mental Illness.* New York: W. W. Norton & Company, 2019.

Harris, Tristan. Interview with Travis View. "Your Undivided Attention." Podcast audio. 8 July 2020. https://www.humanetech.com/podcast/21-the-worldaccording-to-q.

"hear, v." *OED Online.* Oxford University Press, September 2021. Web. 6 November 2021.

Herzovich, Yael Peri, and Aner Govrin. "Psychoanalysis and Interdisciplinarity with Non-Analytic Psychotherapeutic Approaches Through the Lens of Dialectics." *Frontiers in Psychology*, vol. 1, no. 12, 2021, pp. 1–13.

James, William. *The Principles of Psychology.* 1890. Harvard University Press, 1983.

Jameson, Fredric. "The Symbolic Inference; Or, Kenneth Burke and Ideological Analysis." *Critical Inquiry*, vol. 4, no. 3, 1978, pp. 507–523, http://www.jstor.org/stable/1343072.

Johnston, Adrian, "Jacques Lacan." *The Stanford Encyclopedia of Philosophy* (Fall 2018 Edition). Ed. Edward N. Zalta, https://plato.stanford.edu/archives/fall2018/entries/lacan.

Jones, Ernest. *Sigmund Freud Life and Work, Volume Three: The Last Phase 1919–1939.* The Hogarth Press, 1957.

Josephs, Lawrence. "A Comparison of Archaeological and Empathic Modes of Listening." *Contemporary Psychoanalysis*, vol. 24, 1988, pp. 282–300.

Kittler, Freidrich A. *Gramophone, Film, Typewriter.* 1986. Translated by Geoffrey Winthrop-Young and Michael Wutz. Stanford University Press, 1999.

Kohut, Heinz. "Introspection, Empathy, and Psychoanalysis – An Examination of the Relationship Between Mode of Observation and Theory." *Journal of the American Psychoanalytic Association*, vol. 7, 1959, pp. 459–483.

Kumar, David R., et al. "Jean-Martin Charcot: The Father of Neurology." *Clinical Medicine & Research*, vol. 9, no. 1, 2011, pp. 46–49.

Lacan, Jacques. "Some Reflections on the Ego." *International Journal of Psycho-Analysis*, vol. 34, 1953, pp. 11–17.

_____. *Le séminaire de Jacques Lacan: Livre XI, Les quatre concepts fondamentaux de la psychanalyse.* 1964. Paris: Éditions du Seuil, 1973.

_____. "The Neurotic's Individual Myth." 1953. Translated by Martha Noel Evans. *Psychoanalytic Quarterly*, vol. 1, no. 48, 1979, pp. 405–425.

_____. "Conférences Et Entretiens Dans Des Universités Nord-Américaines." [Lectures and Interviews at North American Universities]. *Scilicet*, vol. 6/7, 1976, pp. 5–67.

_____. "Yale University, 24 Novembre 1975, Entretien Avec Les étudiants, Réponses à Leurs Questions." *Scilicet*, vol. 6/7, 1976, pp. 32–37.

_____. *The Seminar of Jacques Lacan: Book I, Freud's Papers on Technique 1953–1954.* 1975. Translated by John Forrester. W. W. Norton & Company, 1988.

_____. "Television." *Television/A Challenge to the Psychoanalytic Establishment.* 1974. Ed. Joan Copjec. Translated by Denis Hollier, Rosalind Krauss, and Annette Michelson. W. W. Norton & Company, 1990, pp. 3–46.

_____. *The Seminar of Jacques Lacan, Book II: The Ego in Freud's Theory and in the Technique of Psychoanalysis, 1954–1955.* 1978. Ed. Jacques-Alain Miller. Translated by Sylvana Tomaselli. W. W. Norton & Company, 1991.

_____. *The Seminar of Jacques Lacan, Book III: The Psychoses, 1955–1956.* 1981. Ed. Jacques-Alain Miller. Translated by Russell Grigg. W. W. Norton & Company, 1993.

_____. *The Seminar of Jacques Lacan Book XI: The Four Fundamental Concepts of Psycho-Analysis*. Ed. Jacques-Alain Miller. Translated by Alan Sheridan. W. W. Norton & Company, 1998.

_____. *The Seminar of Jacques Lacan Book XX: On Feminine Sexuality, The Limits of Love and Knowledge, 1972–1973. 1975*. Ed. Jacques-Alain Miller. Translated by Bruce Fink. W. W. Norton & Company, 1998.

_____. "Appendix II: Metaphor of the Subject." *Écrits*. Translated by Bruce Fink with Heloise Fink and Russell Grigg. New York: W. W. Norton & Company, 2006, pp. 755–758.

_____. "Beyond the 'Reality Principle.'" *Écrits*. Translated by Bruce Fink with Heloise Fink and Russell Grigg. New York: W. W. Norton & Company, 2006, pp. 58–74.

_____. "The Direction of the Treatment and the Principles of Its Power." 1958. *Écrits*. 1966. Edited and Translated Bruce Fink. W. W. Norton & Company, 2006, pp. 489–542.

_____. *Écrits*. 1966. Edited and Translated by Bruce Fink with Heloise Fink and Russell Grigg. W. W. Norton & Company, 2006.

_____. "The Freudian Thing or the Meaning of the Return to Freud in Psychoanalysis." *Écrits*. Translated by Bruce Fink with Heloise Fink and Russell Grigg. New York: W. W. Norton & Company, 2006, pp. 334–363.

_____. "The Function and Field of Speech and Language in Psychoanalysis." *Écrits*. Translated by Bruce Fink with Heloise Fink and Russell Grigg. New York: W. W. Norton & Company, 2006, pp. 197–268.

_____. "The Instance of the Letter in the Unconscious, or Reason Since Freud." 1957. *Écrits*. 1966. Edited and Translated by Bruce Fink with Heloise Fink and Russell Grigg. W. W. Norton & Company, 2006, pp. 412–445.

_____. "The Mirror Stage as Formative Function of the *I* as Revealed in Psychoanalytic Experience." 1966. *Écrits*. Translated by Bruce Fink with Heloise Fink and Russell Grigg. W. W. Norton & Company, 2006, pp. 75–81.

_____. "On the Subject Who Is Finally in Question." *Écrits*. Translated by Bruce Fink with Heloise Fink and Russell Grigg. W. W. Norton & Company, 2006, pp. 189–196.

_____. "Science and Truth." *Écrits*. Translated by Bruce Fink with Heloise Fink and Russell Grigg. New York: W. W. Norton & Company, 2006, pp. 726–745.

_____. "Seminar on 'The Purloined Letter.'" 1956. *Écrits*. Translated by Bruce Fink. W. W. Norton & Company, 2006. pp. 6–50.

_____. "The Situation of Psychoanalysis and the Training of Psychoanalysts in 1956." 1956. *Écrits*. 1966. Edited and Translated by Bruce Fink with Heloise Fink and Russell Grigg. New York: W. W. Norton & Company, 2006, pp. 384–411.

_____. "Variations on the Standard Treatment." 1955. *Écrits*. 1966. Translated by Bruce Fink with Heloise Fink and Russell Grigg. W. W. Norton & Company, 2006, pp. 269–303.

_____. *My Teaching*. 2005. Translated by David Macey. Verso, 2008.

_____. *Je Parle aux Murs: Entretien de la Chapelle de Sainte-Anne*. Éditions du Seuil, 2011.

_____. *The Triumph of Religion Preceded by The Discourse to the Catholics*. 2005. Translated by Bruce Fink. Polity Press, 2013.

_____. *The Seminar of Jacques Lacan, Book VIII: Transference (1960–1961)*. 1991. Ed. Jacques-Alain Miller. Translated by Bruce Fink. Polity Press, 2015.

_____. *The Seminar of Jacques Lacan, Book V: Formations of the Unconscious (1957–1958)*. 1998. Ed. Jacques-Alain Miller. Translated by Russell Grigg. Polity Press, 2017.

_____. *Talking to Brick Walls: A Series of Presentations in the Chapel at the Sainte-Anne Hospital*. 1971–1972. Translated by A.R. Price. Polity Press, 2017.

_____. *The Seminar of Jacques Lacan, Book XXV: The Moment to Conclude*. Translated by Cormac Gallagher. Unpublished.

Laing, R.D. *The Voice of Experience: Experience, Science, and Psychiatry*. Allen Lane, 1982.

Laplanche, Jean, and J.-B. Pontalis. *The Language of Psycho-Analysis*. W. W. Norton & Company, 1974.

Leclaire, Serge. *Psychoanalyzing: On the Order of the Unconscious and the Practice of the Letter*. 1968. Translated by Peggy Kamuf. Stanford University Press, 1998.

"list, n.1." *OED Online*. Oxford University Press, September 2021. Web. 6 November 2021.

Loewenstein, Rudolph. *Practice and Precept in Psychoanalytic Technique*. Yale University Press, 1982.

Lundberg, Christian O. *Lacan in Public: Psychoanalysis and the Science of Rhetoric*. University of Alabama Press, 2012.

M. Joe. "The Power of Memes." *An Invitation to the Great Awakening*. Eds. Captain Roy D. and Dustin Nemos. Relentlessly Creative Books, 2019, pp. 3–10.

Makari, George. *Revolution in Mind: The Creation of Psychoanalysis*. New York: Harper Perennial, 2009.

Markari, George, and Theodore Shapiro. "On Psychoanalytic Listening: Language and Unconscious Communication." *Journal of the American Psychoanalytic Association*, vol. 41, 1993, pp. 991–1020.

Markel, Howard. *An Anatomy of Addiction: Sigmund Freud, William Halsted, and the Miracle Drug Cocaine*. Pantheon Books, 2011.

Marneffe, Daphne. "Looking and Listening: The Construction of Clinical Knowledge in Charcot and Freud." *Signs*, vol. 17, no. 1, 1991, pp. 71–111.

Matlock, Jann. *Scenes of Seduction: Prostitution, Hysteria, and Reading Difference in Nineteenth-Century France*. Columbia University Press, 1994.

McLuhan, Marshall. "Catholic Humanism and Modern Letters." *The Medium and the Light: Reflections on Religion*. Eds. Eric McLuhan and Jacek Czklarek. Wipf and Stock, 1999, pp. 153–174.

McQuillan, Martin. *The Political Archive of Paul De Man: Property, Sovereignty, and the Theotropic*. Edinburgh UP, 2012.

McWilliams, Nancy. *Psychoanalytic Psychotherapy: A Practitioner's Guide*. New York: Guilford Press, 2004.

Meynert, Theodor. *Psychiatry: A Clinical Treatise on the Fore-Brain Based upon Its Structure, Functions, and Nutrition*. Translated by B. Sachs. G.P. Putnam's Sons, 1885.

Miller, Carolyn. "Genre as Social Action." *Quarterly Journal of Speech*, vol. 70, no. 2, 1984, pp. 151–167.

Miller, Laurence. "*On Aphasia* at 100: The Neuropsychodynamic Legacy of Sigmund Freud." *Psychoanalytic Review*, vol. 78, no. 3, 1991, pp. 365–378.

Miller, Michael E. "Pizzagate's Violent Legacy." *Washington Post*, 16 February 2021, http://thewashingtonpost.newspaperdirect.com/epaper/viewer.aspx.

Mills, Jon. "Lacan on Paranoiac Knowledge." *Lacan on Psychosis: From Theory to Praxis*. Eds. Jon Mills and David L. Downing. Routledge, 2019, pp. 10–47.

Mitchell, Juliet. "Introduction." *Feminine Sexuality: Jacques Lacan and the Ecole Freudienne*. Eds. Juliet Mitchell and Jacqueline Rose. W. W. Norton & Company, 1982.

Misra, Pushpa. *The Scientific Status of Psychoanalysis: Evidence and Confirmation*. 2016. New York: Routledge, 2018.

Morawski, Jill. "The Replication Crisis: How Might Philosophy and Theory of Psychology Be of Use?" *Journal of Theoretical and Philosophical Psychology*, vol. 39, no. 4, 2019, pp. 218–238.

Morton, Timothy. *Realist Magic: Objects, Ontology, Causality*. Open Humanities Press, 2013.

Muller, John P., and William Richardson. *Lacan and Language: A Readers Guide to Écrits*. Universities Press, 1982.

Nancy, Jean-Luc. *Listening*. 2002. Translated by Charlotte Mandell. Fordham University Press, 2007.

Nietzsche, Friedrich. "Nietzsche's 'Lecture Notes on Rhetoric': A Translation." Translated by Carole Blair. *Philosophy & Rhetoric*, vol. 16, no. 2, Penn State University Press, 1983, pp. 94–129, http://www.jstor.org/stable/40237356.

Nunberg, Herman. *Principles of Psychoanalysis: Their Application to the Neuroses*. International Universities Press, 1955.

Ogden, Thomas. "Some Thoughts on the Use of Language in Psychoanalysis." *Psychoanalytic Dialogues*, vol. 7, no. 1, 1997, 1–21.

Paris, Joel. "Is Psychoanalysis Still Relevant to Psychiatry?" *The Canadian Journal of Psychiatry*, vol. 62, no. 5, 2017, pp. 308–312.

Petermann, W. "Attitudes as Equipment for Living," *KB Journal*, vol. 11, no. 1, 2015, https://kbjournal.org/petermann_attitudes.

Pierrakos, Maria. *Transcribing Lacan's Seminars: Memoirs of a Disgruntled Keybasher Turned Psychoanalyst*. Translated by Angela M. Brewer. Free Association Books, 2006.

Plato, *Phaedrus*. Translated by Benjamin Jowett. Dover, 1956, pp. 274–275.

Popper, Karl. *Unended Quest: An Intellectual Autobiography*. 1974. New York: Routledge, 1992.

_____. *Conjectures and Refutations: The Growth of Scientific Knowledge*. 1963. Routledge, 2002.

Porter, Roy. *Madness: A Brief History*. Oxford: Oxford University Press, 2002.

Quandahl, Ellen. "'More Than Lessons in How to Read': Burke, Freud, and the Resources of Symbolic Transformation." *College English*, vol. 63, no. 5, 2001, pp. 633–654, https://doi.org/10.2307/379048.

Quintilian. *Institutio Oratoria Vol III*. Translated by Harold Edgeworth Butler. Loeb Classical Library Edition, 1920.

Reik, Theodor. "Theodor Reik Speaks of His Psychoanalytic Technique." *American Imago*, vol. 25, no. 1, 1968, pp. 16–20.

_____. *Listening with the Third Ear: The Inner Experience of a Psychoanalyst*. 1948. Farrar, Straus and Giroux, 1998.

_____. "Noticing, Attention, and Taking Note." 1936. *Surprise and the Psychoanalyst*. Routledge, 1999, pp. 31–50.

Richards, I.A. *Principles of Literary Criticism*. 1924. Routledge, 2017.

Ricoeur, Paul. *Critique and Conviction: Conversations with Francois Azouvi and Marc de Launay*. 1995. Translated by Kathleen Blamey. Columbia University Press, 1998.

Ricoeur, Paul. *Freud and Philosophy: An Essay on Interpretation*. Yale University Press, 1970.

Rockmore, Tom. "Freud's Dream Theory and Social Constructivism." *Rereading Freud: Psychoanalysis through Philosophy*. Ed. Jon Mills. State University of New York Press, 2004, pp. 17–34.

Rogers, Carl. *A Way of Being*. Houghton Mifflin Company, 1980.

Rogers, Carl, and Richard E. Farson. *Active Listening*. 1957. Martino Publishing, 2015.

Roudinesco, Élisabeth. *Jacques Lacan and Co: A History of Psychoanalysis in France, 1925–1985.* 1986. Translated by Jeffrey Mehlman. University of Chicago Press, 1990.

_____. *Jacques Lacan.* 1993. Translated by Barbara Bray. Columbia University Press, 1997.

_____. "Lacan, the Plague." Translated by John Forrester. *Psychoanalysis and History*, vol. 10, no. 2, 2008, pp. 225–235.

_____. *Lacan: In Spite of Everything.* Translated by Gregory Elliott. Verso, 2014.

_____. *Freud: In His Time and Ours.* Translated by Catherine Porter. Harvard University Press, 2016.

Rycroft, Charles. *A Critical Dictionary of Psychoanalysis.* New York: Basic Books, 1968.

Santner, Eric L. *My Own Private Germany: Daniel Paul Schreber's Secret History of Modernity.* Princeton University Press, 1996.

Schafer, Roy. "Listening in Psychoanalysis." *Narrative*, vol. 13, no. 3, 2005, pp. 271–280.

Segal, Judy. *Health and the Rhetoric of Medicine.* Southern Illinois University Press, 2008.

Selzer, Jack. *Kenneth Burke in Greenwich Village: Conversing with the Moderns, 1915–1931.* University of Wisconsin Press, 1996.

Shedler, Jonathan. "The Efficacy of Psychodynamic Psychotherapy." *American Psychologist*, vol. 65, no. 2, 2010, pp. 98–109.

Slochower, Harry. "Applied Psychoanalysis as a Science and as an Art." *American Imago*, vol. 21, no. 1–2, 1964, pp. 165–174.

Sloterdijk, Peter. *What Happened in the 20th Century?* Translated by Christopher Turner. Polity, 2018.

Sollers, Philippe. "Le Corps Sort de la Voix: Propos recueillis par Adrian Price et Guillaume Roy." ["The Body Comes Out of the Voice: Interview by Adrian Price and Guillaume Roy."] *Lacan Quotidien*, vol. 8, 2011, pp. 1–8, http://www.philippesollers.net/PDF/lacan-quotidien08-sollers.pdf.

Solms, Mark. "The Scientific Standing of Psychoanalysis." *British Journal of Psychiatry*, vol. 15, no. 1, 2018, pp. 5–8.

Spence, Donald P. "Listening for Rhetorical Truth." *Psychoanalytic Quarterly*, vol. 72, no. 4, 2003, 875–903.

Starbird, Kate. "Examining the Alternative Media Ecosystem Through the Production of Alternative Narratives of Mass Shooting Events on Twitter," Proceedings of the Eleventh International AAAI Conference on Web and Social Media (Montreal, 2017), pp. 230–239.

"Stream of consciousness, n." *OED Online.* Oxford University Press, January 2022. Web. 4 January 2022.

Sulloway, Frank J. *Freud, Biologist of the Mind.* Burnett Books, 1979.

Svolos, Thomas. *Twenty-First Century Psychoanalysis.* Karnac, 2017.

"sympathy, n." *OED Online.* Oxford University Press, September 2021. Web. 13 February 2022.

Teslenko, Tatiana. *Feminist Utopian Novels of the 1970s: Joanna Russ & Dorothy Bryant.* Routledge, 2003.

Thayer, L. "On the Limits of Western Communication Theory." *Communication*, vol. 4, no. 1, 1979, pp. 9–14.

Thompson, Jason. "Magic for a People Trained in Pragmatism: Kenneth Burke, 'Mein Kampf', and the Early 9/11 Oratory of George W. Bush." *Rhetoric Review*, vol. 30, no. 4, 2011, pp. 350–371, http://www.jstor.org/stable/23064014.

Titchener, Edward Bradford. *Lectures on the Experimental Thought-Processes*. Macmillan, 1909.

Tolentino, Gia. "The Age of Instagram Face." *The New Yorker*, 12 December 2019.

Usher, Sarah. *Introduction to Psychodynamic Psychotherapy Technique*. International Universities Press, 1993.

Valdés, Alicia. *Toward a Feminist Lacanian Left: Psychoanalytic Theory and Intersectional Politics*. Routledge, 2022.

Vanderwees, Chris. "Reflections on Training Institutions and the San Francisco Bay Area Lacanian School of Psychoanalysis, An Interview With Raul Moncayo." *Lacunae: APPI International Journal for Lacanian Psychoanalysis*, vol. 19, 2019, pp. 8–37.

———. "Topology, Knots, and Ordinary Psychosis: Interview with Ellie Ragland." *Speaking of Lacan: Conversations on the History and Transmission of Psychoanalysis*. 4 February 2020. Routledge, 2023.

Verhaeghe, Paul. *On Being Normal and Other Disorders: Manual for Clinical Psychodiagnostics*. Translated by Sigi Jottkandt. Other Press, 2004.

von Unwerth, Matthew. *Freud's Requiem: Mourning, Memory, and the Invisible History of a Summer Walk*. Continuum, 2006.

Walker, Jeffrey. "The Body of Persuasion: A Theory of the Enthymeme." *College English*, vol. 56, no. 1, 1994, pp. 46–65.

Weil, Simone. *Gravity and Grace*. 1947. Translated by Emma Crawford and Mario von der Ruhr. Routledge, 2002.

Weiser, Elizabeth. *Burke, War, Words: Rhetoricizing Dramatism*. University of South Carolina Press, 2008.

Wess, Robert. *Kenneth Burke: Rhetoric, Subjectivity, Postmodernism*. Cambridge University Press, 1996.

Wiggins, Bradford J., and Cody D. Christopherson. "The Replication Crisis in Psychology: An Overview for Theoretical and Philosophical Psychology." *Journal of Theoretical and Philosophical Psychology*, vol. 39, no. 4, 2019, pp. 202–217.

Yakeley, Jessica. "Psychoanalysis in Modern Mental Health Practice." *The Lancet Psychiatry*, vol. 5, no. 5, 2018, pp. 443–450.

Žižek, Slavoj. "Invisible Ideology: Political Violence Between Fiction and Fantasy." *Journal of Political Ideologies*, vol. 1, no. 1, 1996, pp. 15–32.

———. *Disparities*. Bloomsbury, 2016.

Index

For Product Safety Concerns and Information please contact our EU
representative GPSR@taylorandfrancis.com
Taylor & Francis Verlag GmbH, Kaufingerstraße 24, 80331 München, Germany